EASTER ISLAND

ALFRED METRAUX

Easter Island

A STONE-AGE CIVILIZATION OF
THE PACIFIC

Translated from the French by
MICHAEL BULLOCK

ANDRE DEUTSCH

FIRST PUBLISHED APRIL 1957 BY
ANDRE DEUTSCH LIMITED
105 GREAT RUSSELL STREET
LONDON WC1
SECOND IMPRESSION AUGUST 1957
THIRD IMPRESSION OCTOBER 1974
© COPYRIGHT ALFRED METRAUX 1957
ALL RIGHTS RESERVED
PHOTOSET, PRINTED AND BOUND
IN GREAT BRITAIN BY
REDWOOD BURN LIMITED
TROWBRIDGE & ESHER

ISBN 0 233 96616 1

CONTENTS

Foreword   *Page* 9

Introduction   15

I   Easter Island and the Lost Continent   29

II   Easter Island—Polynesian Soil   33

III   The Tragic Story of Easter Island   38

IV   How the Easter Islanders Live   61

V   A Cannibal Society   83

VI   From Birth to the Tomb   105

VII   Religion and Magic   121

VIII   Ancestor Images   146

IX   The Great Statues   151

X   Feasts   173

XI   Poetry, Music and Dancing   180

XII   The Mystery of the Tablets   185

XIII   Easter Island Myths and Legends   211

XIV   The Origins of Easter Island Civilization   224

       Bibliography   243

       Index   247

ILLUSTRATIONS

View of the Rano-raraku volcano

An Easter Island native selling curios

Beating tapa cloth

Viriamo, who was born about 1845

Juan Tepano, our informant, carving a wooden image

A girl on her way to church

Playing cat's cradle

Victoria Rapahango, descendant of kings

Petroglyphs of the bird-man

A petroglyph of a shark

A *tupa*, probably a shelter for fishermen

Stone houses at Orongo

Ancestor image, back view

The head of an ancestor image

Portion of the tablet Aruku-kurenga

Two views of a female ancestor image

Stone statues on the slopes of Rano-raraku

Recumbent statue in the quarry where it was
sculpted

ILLUSTRATIONS

Unfinished statue

Head of fallen statue, crowning the Ahu Tonga-riki

Stone 'hat', lying near statue on which it once stood

Seaward façade of Ahu Tepen

Fallen statues on an *ahu* of the south coast

Seaward façade of Ahu Vinapu, built of dressed slabs

Another view of the façade of Ahu Vinapu

Statues on the slopes of Rano-raraku

Statue on the slopes of Rano-raraku

ILLUSTRATIONS IN THE TEXT

1. Easter Island canoe with outrigger   *Page* 70
2. Images made of bulrushes covered with tapa cloth painted to show patterns of body painting and tattooing   *Page* 78
3. Types of obsidian spear-heads (*mataa*)   *Page* 101
4. Similar symbols in the Indus script: (a) on the Easter Island tablets; (b) in the most ancient forms of Chinese writing   *Page* 205
5. Sequences of identical signs in Row 1 of tablet Aruku-kurenga   *Page* 206
6. Easter Island *ahu* compared with religious stone structures from eastern Polynesia   *Page* 239

FOREWORD

EVER SINCE the day it was discovered by the Dutch, Easter Island, that tiny patch of land standing solitary amidst the 'immense wastes' of the South Pacific Ocean, has been surrounded by a halo of mystery and strangeness. The ideas about Easter Island that have gained currency, even in educated circles, deserve a place in the annals of folklore. It is held to be the last vestige of a submerged continent, once the seat of a brilliant civilization. Reference is even made to 'triumphal ways', which are said to run across the island and lose themselves in the sea. The inhabitants found there by Europeans were looked upon as 'savages' or 'degenerates', incapable of having erected the monuments in the midst of which they eked out a miserable existence. It has often been claimed that a link exists between the island and the ancient civilizations of Central and South America, and its statues are said to hold the secret of migrations that took place thousands of years ago. In the United States, Easter Island has been associated by one writer with a certain continent of Mu, whose vanished glories he has described.

Works of a more scientific character speak of a megalithic civilization said to have spread to Easter Island from Asia, impressive relics of which are distributed at intervals across Indonesia and Micronesia. The gigantic trilith of Tonga, a distant replica of the Cornish dolmens, is identified as one of the mute testimonies to the passage of this people of builders over the Polynesian islands. To these men, enamoured of the colossal, Easter Island was no more than a stepping-stone: it is claimed that they also landed on the American continent, where the monolithic Tiahuanaco Gate and the palaces of Cuzco are held to be their handiwork.

These interpretations of the Easter Island monuments imply a kind of mystic faith in a golden age of humanity and betray the desire to ascribe to the distant past an aureole of grandeur and mystery; but they show little respect for the precise data of archaeology and ethnography. Since the statues and other ruins on the island belong not to the domain of mythology, but to that of reality, the problems they raise demand to be studied on the spot and according to the methods of science. In point of fact, the work

9

of the British expedition led by Mrs C. Routledge in 1914 served to
dissipate more than one legend and more than one error.

Despite the important results obtained by Mrs Routledge, one
enigma remains, infinitely more disturbing than the weight or the
height of the giant statues with their disdainful scowl. A few years
after the catastrophe that wiped out the island's civilization,
missionaries found a number of wooden tablets covered with odd
signs. At first sight these rows of complicated symbols looked like a
system of hieroglyphics. Now, no Polynesian island appeared to
have possessed a script. If, alone in Polynesia, the inhabitants of
this Ultima Thule knew the art of writing, and if they alone had
been able to carve and erect great statues, they had a right to pro-
claim themselves the survivors of a glorious past and the scions of a
privileged race. Perhaps the visions of grandeur and splendour attached to their island were not all fantasies of over-imaginative
minds.

This hypothesis of an Easter Island whose civilization was
linked with that of the ancient peoples of Asia seemed to be confirmed a few years ago, when a Hungarian, Guillaume de Hévesy,
pointed out some remarkable parallels between the symbols
engraved on the Easter Island tablets and elements of the script
just then discovered in the Indus Valley and undoubtedly going
back some 3,000 years before the Christian era. These analogies
appeared to cast an entirely new light on the origin of Oceanian
culture and the migrations that contributed to its diffusion.

The theory made great strides. It was not merely India that was
joined to Polynesia by a common script, but also prehistoric
China. Dr Heine-Geldern drew attention to the apparently very
close resemblance between certain archaic Chinese characters of
the Shang epoch and the Easter Island 'glyphs'. These comparisons, together with other factors of a similar nature, seemed to
indicate a common centre, situated in Asia, from which various
cultural elements—if not whole peoples—had detached themselves and swarmed towards the Pacific. These reconstructions of
hypothetical migrations extended to pre-Columbian America,
which was also brought within the orbit of the ancient Asiatic
civilization.

The audacious solutions to the problems of Easter Island that have been proposed give some idea of the importance the latter has assumed in the history of civilization. It was in the hope of bringing to light fresh facts which might solve this two-centuries-old riddle that a scientific mission was organized on the initiative of Dr Paul Rivet, Director of the Musée de l'Homme, Paris, and with the support of the French and Belgian Governments. Supervision of archaeological research was entrusted to M. Charles Watelin and Dr Henry Lavachery. I was in charge of the ethnographic and linguistic enquiries.

M. Watelin nursed hopes I did not share. Indifferent to the modern Easter Islanders and the traditions that might still survive in the island, he expected to see the walls of ancient cities—similar to Mohenjo-daro—emerge beneath his pick. He was certain that the trenches he was going to open at the foot of the volcanoes would lay bare an unknown civilization. For my part, I must confess, I was attracted by these few hundred Polynesians who have survived so many disasters and continue to speak their ancient language and hand down the legends and stories of their distant ancestors. I was not unaware of their state of decadence, their ignorance of the old religion and past customs, but I hoped, in spite of everything, that in the rare techniques which might have survived and in the traditions still known to a few old people I should perhaps be able to catch a faint murmur from the old times which would give me fresh insight into the 'mysteries' of this island.

The French Navy assisted the expedition by providing the members of the mission with passage on board the colonial despatch vessel 'Rigault-de-Genouilly', which had only recently left the naval dockyards and was going out on its first cruise.

Our voyage took five months and was made in several stages. It began with the departure from Lorient on a rainy day, to the sound of fanfares and bells and an accompaniment of salvoes. A priest blessed our cruise from the top of a belfry standing on the tip of a promontory. We received a farewell according to the old traditions of the Royal French Navy still honoured in this Breton port. Not unnaturally, I recalled M. de La Pérouse who, like ourselves, once set sail for Easter Island on a warship whose pennants flapped as they were caught by the wind of the open sea.

First we visited the West African ports, then those of South

America. In four months we sailed from Gabun to the glaciers of Tierra del Fuego. There we lost Charles Watelin. In spite of his advanced age, he had preserved an alert and youthful mind that had made of our voyage a glorious adventure. He wanted to see everything and know everything. He contracted pneumonia during a hunting-party in Patagonia and passed away in sight of the Chilean coast, after we had crossed the Gulf of Peñas.

My colleague, Dr Henry Lavachery, formerly Chief Conservator of the Brussels Royal Museums of Art and History, joined us at Lima. From that moment forward our work became a joint enterprise, pursued in a spirit of comradeship that remains for me the most pleasant memory of this expedition.

We reached Easter Island on July 27, 1934, and we left it on January 2, 1935, aboard the Belgian training-ship 'Mercator', which took us to Pitcairn, Tahiti, the Tuamotus, the Marquesas and the Hawaiian Islands.

The aim of this book is to give a picture of the old Easter Island culture based on the material gathered by our expedition. It would have been impossible to reconstruct this past without the comparative elements furnished by the ethnology and archaeology of the neighbouring archipelagos, which are inhabited by peoples of the same language and the same race.

In calling to life this civilization which had been dead for almost a century I had only its wreckage to help me. In the interpretation of this collection of disconnected and second-rate evidences I was assisted by two eminent specialists on Polynesia—Dr Peter Buck (Te Rangi Hiroa) and Dr Kenneth Emory. During my stay at the Bishop Museum, Honolulu, both these ethnologists were devoting themselves to the resurrection of the civilization of Mangareva (the Gambier Islands), whose traditions and history are much better known to us than those of Easter Island.

The names of two natives who were among our principal informants, Juan Tepano and Victoria Rapahango, will occur frequently in the course of this book. Tepano knew the civilization of his fathers only through a few childhood memories and old men's stories. Victoria Rapahango, a woman of about thirty-six, introduced us into the closed gossipy little world which is the modern village of Hanga-roa.

This book is not addressed either to archaeologists or anthropologists. Detailed information of interest to them is given in a voluminous monograph published in 1940 by the Bernice P. Bishop Museum under the title *Ethnology of Easter Island*.[1] The conclusions are presented here without the scientific paraphernalia that might repel the reader who is not a specialist in Polynesian ethnology. Several chapters of this English edition have been revised in the light of studies of Easter Island published during the last ten years. There have not been as many of these as one might have wished, and they have not produced many new facts or interpretations. The literature of the island's ethnography has, however, been enriched by one valuable work—the Rev. Father Sebastian Englert's *La Tierra de Hotu-Matu'a*.[2] Englert spent more than twelve years as a missionary on Easter Island, where he settled in 1936, a year after our expedition. His excellent knowledge of the Easter language—of which he has given us a dictionary and a grammar—enabled him to become acquainted with details of native folklore and the ancient culture of the island that had escaped his predecessors; but they do not alter, in any significant way, the facts already established. I fear that it has now become almost impossible to obtain any fresh information concerning the island's past. This is growing dim in the memories of the new generations, who reinterpret it in their own way. The voyage of the 'Kon-Tiki' and Thor Heyerdahl's theories on the peopling of the Pacific islands have given the problem of Easter Island fresh topicality. It would have been difficult to ignore them in this edition. That is why, in response to my publisher's request, I have added a few pages in which I have tried to summarize the views of this intrepid seafarer and my objections to them. I have also felt it necessary to present, in the chapter on the Easter script, the opinions of Professor R. von Heine-Geldern and the more recent views of Professor J. Imbelloni. Although I do not share the conclusions of these two scholars, I did not wish to diminish the scope of the problem by neglecting the important studies they have devoted to

[1] A. Métraux, *Ethnology of Easter Island*, Bernice P. Bishop Museum, Bulletin 160, Honolulu, 1940.

[2] *La Tierra de Hotu-matu'a. Historia, Etnologia y Lengua de la Isla de Pascua.* ed. 'San Francisco', Padre Las Casas, 1948.

it. In the final chapter I have likewise noted recently published monographs in the field of Polynesian research having a direct bearing on the interpretation of the origin and development of Easter Island civilization.

If I had resigned myself to regarding the problems of Easter Island as insoluble, I should have been justly accused of following the line of least resistance. The solutions of numerous 'mysteries' put forward here may displease those who prefer the attraction of enigmas to the rational explanations that can be offered. But it must also be frankly admitted that certain riddles of Easter Island remain only half-solved and will perhaps never be fully elucidated.

I have occasionally had recourse to psychological arguments to explain the energy demonstrated by the Easter Islanders. The miracle of Easter Island is the audacity that impelled the inhabitants of a small island, destitute of resources, to raise on the horizon of the Pacific monuments worthy of a great nation.

NOTE: In transcribing native words I have used the spelling adopted in most recent works dealing with Polynesia. The sound transcribed by *ng* is a nasalized *g*. An inverted comma (') between vowels represents the glottal stop. All other letters are pronounced as in Italian.

INTRODUCTION

EASTER ISLAND appeared to us one rainy day during the southern winter, at the end of July 1934. I can still see the tall cliffs of Poike peninsula looming through the mist, the rounded mass of the volcanoes, and the black, twisted reef bristling with sharp ridges and needles on which the waves are torn to pieces. There is something profoundly peaceful and rural about the meadows that stretch far back into the interior, and the regular and gentle contours of the hills. In places, their soft pastel green recalls the coast of Scania. The resemblance to Sweden would be complete, if it were not for the strange, forbidding, diabolical rocks in the foreground.

The commander of the despatch-vessel had called us together on the poop-deck and given us a piece of bad news: there was a high sea running on the side of the island where Hanga-roa lay, and he could not guarantee to get our ninety packing-cases, which were cluttering up his hold, safely ashore there. As his instructions did not specify the part of the island on which he was to land us, he had decided to set us down, together with our supplies, at any convenient spot he could find.

Meanwhile, the 'Rigault-de-Genouilly' anchored outside the bay of Hanga-roa, the only village on the island still inhabited by the surviving Easter Islanders. A few moments earlier, looking at the rugged coastline of the northern shore, I had been reminded of faraway Sweden. Now this first impression was intensified by the native dwellings we could distinguish through our binoculars, dotted about close to the shore and imperfectly concealed behind fig-trees. If we had cherished the dream of seeing the classical silhouette of the Polynesian beach rise before us here, we should have been sadly disillusioned. The capital of the legendary Easter Island looked for all the world like a humble European hamlet on a rainy autumn day.

That first day on Easter Island will remain forever engraved in our memories. The wind, which was blowing in gusts, was driving great rollers towards the land, and as we drew nearer the reef the surf assumed increasingly alarming proportions. The natives massed on the sea-front did not, at first, seem inclined to come out

15

and meet us. News of our arrival had spread through the village, and along all the paths leading to the sea, riders were galloping as fast as their mounts would carry them. A palaver was in progress on the beach beside the boathouses, and we watched impatiently as opinion seemed to sway now this way, now that. We were worried by the natives' failure to reach a decision: if they refused to row out to our ship we should be faced with the disagreeable necessity of sailing back to the north of the island and landing on a lee shore, but far from any centre of habitation. It was therefore with great relief that we saw first one, then two, then three native vessels heading towards us. In the first, steered by the Governor of the island, a crew of Easter Islanders in Chilean naval uniform was rowing in perfect unison. The occupants of the other vessels showed more imagination. These two boats were filled almost to sinking point with natives sporting rags and tatters of European clothing. The only exotic note was struck by a few feather head-dresses, which—far from being relics of a bygone age—were cheapjack goods intended to arouse the interest of the sailors and stimulate the sale of the 'curios' with which these boats were crammed.

Every time I use the word 'natives' to describe the present inhabitants of Easter Island, I experience the same hesitation I felt when I first saw them, as I leaned on the bulwarks. This term, which conjures up dark skins and unfamiliar features, seemed hardly appropriate to these faces that looked so European. How many nations have mingled their blood with that of the ancient Maoris? The same story that is repeated at many ports of call could be read in the faces turned up towards us. What glimpses could we catch of old Polynesia, of the ancient race of seafarers and learned priests? There was certainly a hint in the aquiline nose of one of the helmsmen, in the little pointed beard of a young man with an emaciated face, and in the bulging forehead of a vendor of statuettes. The Polynesian heritage was also evident in the softness of their language, the mischievous sparkle of their eyes, and in their vivacity and easy gaiety. They addressed us in English, French and Spanish. 'Soap, soap, Captain, Lieutenant, soap.' 'Two cakes of soap for my statuette, and throw in a loaf of bread.' 'Your soap is too small, Chilean soap is bigger. Give me another piece. You are *rakerake*, mean. Remember me when you come ashore; I've got a good horse to take you to the volcano.'

In the midst of all this turmoil a great melancholy took possession of me. Were these shady hucksters the legitimate descendants of the sculptors of the giant statues and the priests who had peopled earth and sky with divinities invested with subtle symbols?

The deck was piled high with grotesque statuettes, walking-sticks and wooden swords. I found all these 'curios' equally repulsive. They had replaced the splendid images of former times, carved with patience and skill from wretched scraps of wood. All that was left were ridiculous puppets, bartered for a pair of trousers or a few cakes of soap to the accompaniment of mocking laughter.

A rather handsome lad, Pedro Atam, who had learnt that we intended to stay on the island, asked us the reason for our visit. We explained to him that we were archaeologists in search of ancient objects. He had no difficulty in understanding what we meant, and declared in a detached tone: 'There aren't many ancient objects about nowadays and it will take time to find them. But don't worry, we'll make you as many as you want. We'll give you whatever you ask for. When you get home, nobody will know the difference.' Pedro, with his moustache and his fine presence, appeared to us on the threshold of this new world like Satan come to lead us into temptation. We declined his offer, at the same time ardently hoping that the specimens his compatriots would offer us might prove to be *genuinely* old.

Leaving the Easter Islanders to sort things out with the sailors, we went to introduce ourselves to the Governor—or Subdelegado, to give him his correct title. He was in full-dress uniform and seemed thoroughly dumbfounded by our visit. In a few words, we told him of our troubles and of the refusal of the Commander of the 'Rigault-de-Genouilly' to land our cases at Hanga-roa. He promised to arrange everything for us with the assistance of the natives, and invited us to enter his boat.

Once aboard the latter, we became fully aware of the state of the sea. We were thrown this way and that and deluged with spray from the waves that assailed us from every side. True, the calm and confidence of the oarsmen dispelled all sense of danger, but things deteriorated when we reached the harbour-bar. We had a sudden sensation of being lifted up above the water, then of a struggle between the muscles of our oarsmen and the waves that were pulling us backwards, and finally of hurtling down a toboggan run. A few minutes later we were in calm water alongside a stone jetty. Since our anxiety had been brief, we felt disposed to examine the masonry of the breakwater, which was constructed of rubble from ancient mausoleums. It is all that remains of the monuments described by Cook and La Pérouse. Strong hands pushed us on to the jetty, and in a few moments we were encircled by a crowd—chiefly made up of women and children—who addressed us in the language of Easter Island, Spanish, and English. Soaked to the skin by the rain and the waves, and still rather dazed by our crossing, we did not know what to say or do. Our confusion can also be attributed to the emotion we experienced at setting foot on this island that had never ceased to occupy our thoughts during the long months of the voyage. It was as hard to believe ourselves in Polynesia now, amidst this mob of women, most of them ugly, dressed in discoloured clothes that clung to ungraceful bodies, as it had been a short while before, when we first glimpsed the village of Hanga-roa through the rain.

An incident occurred to interrupt these moments of uncertainty. A young woman had approached my colleague and asked him for a cigarette. He automatically handed her a packet, which she seized with a furtive movement, making off as fast as her legs could carry her. This theft delighted us. We were at once transported into the old atmosphere of the island, as it emerges from the accounts of the first navigators. Like the sailors of Cook and La Pérouse at the same spot, we had to protect ourselves against the tendency to pilfer which the Easter Islanders had shown from the first instant of their contact with white men. We greeted the incident as a good omen, and felt more inclined to reconcile ourselves to the people and things of this little universe into which we had stumbled.

The curiosity with which the women and children crowded round and stared at us left no doubt as to the success of the spectacle we were presenting. Life is monotonous on this island, and the arrival of a ship is an event that provides a topic of conversation for months.

We saw advancing towards us a hairy little gnome dressed in clothes obviously too long for him. This curious being extended a thin, old man's hand, horny with tilling the soil, and said to us in French, '*Bonjour, messieurs*'. Then I recognized Vincent Pons, about whom I had heard in Chile and whom other travellers had mentioned in their accounts. Sixty years ago Pons, after sailing all the South Seas in schooners, had settled on Easter Island, where he took a wife. Today he is the ancestor of a whole line of strapping fellows who are reckoned among the toughest customers on the island. Unfortunately, old Pons never took much interest in the customs of his native family, and he was little help to us with our enquiries.

We proceeded slowly towards the Subdelegación—the Governor's House—followed by our retinue of women and children. In the midst of the confusion, we caught a glimpse of a face completely whitened with flour: this was one of the prettiest girls on the island, who had smothered herself with rice powder to make herself more attractive.

Two men were waiting for us near the Governor's 'Residence': Mr Morrison and Mr Smith, the administrators of Messrs Williamson, Balfour & Co, the sheep-farming company to which the island belonged. With a few polite words they invited us to take up quarters at Mataveri, the Company's farm. We accepted gratefully, knowing very well what this invitation meant to us in terms of comfort and security. At the entrance to the Subdelegación the Governor's wife, quite a pretty young woman, but with drawn features, was waiting for us with a sickly-looking baby in her arms. She gave us a slight smile, completely unperturbed at the invasion of her house by a band of men soaked to the skin. A puffy-faced, unshaven man in pyjamas and slippers introduced himself to us. This unprepossessing individual was a bankrupt Chilean businessman who had taken refuge on the island, where he exercised the dual function of schoolmaster and public scribe. Throughout our stay we always saw him in the same pyjamas, and with the same unshaven face.

As we got wetter and more exasperated by the difficulties of the landing and the way our cases were being handled, we felt our courage and our hopes ebbing. Was this the famous Easter Island —these rather plebeian faces, this mixture of servility and ready impudence?

The arrival of Victoria Rapahango—dressed in white, her long wavy hair floating round her shoulders—was enough, however, to recreate a little of that Polynesian atmosphere from which we had felt ourselves drifting farther and farther away. A long friendship did not destroy this first impression. By the distinction of her manners, her lively good-humour, and her rather sad gentleness, this woman of the royal tribe of the Miru kept alive in the heart of the decadent culture of her environment the charm of the old Oceanian aristocracies.

After a lull, the rain fell with redoubled violence. The whole island vanished beneath a thick mist and our field of vision was reduced to a muddy beach and some grim-looking rocks. Our cases were loaded up in the middle of the crowd, which was still on the jetty. We received repeated warnings to see that nothing disappeared, because 'these people are such thieves'. The incessant protestations of honesty on the part of the natives were scarcely reassuring. So we remained on sentry-go, keeping an eye both on the members of our crew and on the spectators. A few women came up to us in an embarrassed way and asked in low voices whether we had any soap. Emboldened by a friendly reply, they then dropped hints about printed fabrics and 'Pompeia', that vulgar perfume which is so highly esteemed in the island.

When dusk fell we made our way to Mataveri along a steep road bordered by mulberry trees and a low wall of unmortared stones. At the time, this country lane—which we later came to love —distressed us by its evocation of things prosaically European. When we opened the gate that gives access to Mataveri plateau, a shadow approached us, and an ungainly individual with a shambling gait thrust into our hands some stone objects that we immediately recognized as obsidian spearheads. As he handed them to us he said with an air of mystery, '*Regalo*—a present'. This was our first present, our entry into a cycle from which we were never again to escape. By accepting these modest gifts we laid the foundations of an intricate network of reciprocal obligations which, for the rest of our stay, was to tie us to so many unknown beings.

We entered a well-grown eucalyptus wood that gives the farm shade rarely found on this desolate island. Mrs Smith received us with bustling and delightful hospitality in a large dining-room. We made the acquaintance of a fair-complexioned baby that had just been born in the middle of the Pacific—no doubt the first white to come into the world in the vicinity of the great statues. These British voices, the lamp on the table, and Mrs Smith, formed a world apart, as far from Easter Island as Scotland is from the South Seas. Between these two universes there was no link of sympathy, of mutual understanding, or even of interest. Here the environment was one of simple honesty: down below a seething mass of rather disturbing humanity.

I was anxious to learn what exactly were the relations between the Company and the natives. During our stay in Chile we had been warned against the Company and had listened to denunciations of its brutality and selfishness in dealing with the natives. Many Chileans portrayed in moving terms the tragic lot of the natives confined to a corner of their own island and refused the right to move about their ancestral lands. We had also been told of the low wages paid to the few natives employed by the Company. Long experience of South America had made me familiar with the systematic ill-will that surrounds every Anglo-Saxon undertaking; but, on the other hand, I knew that commercial enterprises are not always generous to their native labour. To rid myself of any doubts, I put the question to Mr Smith, who informed me that the Company paid its workers four *pesos* plus a daily ration of meat. During shearing time the women and youngsters engaged for the occasion were paid piecework rates, that is to say, by the number of sheep that pass through their hands.

At the time (1934), these wage-levels were higher than those of Chilean peons. When I repeated to my host the remarks I had heard concerning the profits made by the Company's shop, he grew very indignant and assured me that goods were sold in it at wholesale prices, notwithstanding the cost of transport, and that it gave better value for money than could be obtained on the mainland—so much so that the crews of Chilean vessels seized the opportunity of shopping there during shore leave on the island. None the less, the natives complained of the Company's prices and at the constant increase in the sums they had to pay for the goods they bought in this shop. Unknown to them, they were the victims of the economic crisis brewing in Chile.

When I alluded to the forcible confinement of the natives to the village of Hanga-roa and its immediate environs, the Administrator of the island gave me the following explanation: 'Easter Island belongs to Chile, but in practice it is the private property of Messrs Williamson, Balfour & Co, who raise sheep on it and also, on a small scale, cattle and pigs. The pastures and climate of the island are very favourable to sheep. They multiply here, and today there are about forty thousand. They are not comparable to New Zealand sheep, but they produce quite good-quality wool. The flocks would be easy to look after if it were not for the natives, who rob us all the time. They seized the first sheep introduced by the missionaries and would have gone on doing the same thing if we had not taken precautions. So we have isolated the village and the adjoining country by barbed wire and have raised a native police force from the most honest and loyal elements. No one is allowed to cross the field-fences after sunset without a special permit. In spite of all this, we lost three thousand sheep last year. Two days before your arrival they broke into the farm and stole all the rams. We know the culprits and the police have got all the facts about the raid, but nobody was caught red-handed. All our policemen are related either closely or distantly to the thieves, and ties of blood prevent them from denouncing the culprits or arresting them at the opportune moment. If we complain to the Governor he pretends to be indignant, he threatens, promises to punish those responsible—and does absolutely nothing. Really he is overjoyed by our difficulties and does nothing to bring them to an end. The natives are inveterate rogues. At the beginning of the year they picked the lock of our shop and looted it. We have no more sugar or tobacco or soap, and the next boat is not due for six months. There is not a child in the village who does not know the culprits, but how can we get at them? We haven't a shred of proof, and even those who came and denounced the thieves will swear they said nothing and saw nothing. This time the Governor was a trifle alarmed, because he too needs our goods; but after cursing and swearing, he put the matter off till *mañana*.

'What angers us is not so much the natives' attitude to us, as the hypocrisy of which we are the victims. Chile doesn't care about the natives—she takes absolutely no interest in them. We try to stick loyally to our undertakings; we try to be humane; and the result is we are accused of the very abuses we do our best to avoid.'

The following morning we went down towards the village of Hanga-roa. On our way we met groups who greeted us with the Tahitian *ia-o-rana*. We also passed some of our sailors, astride wretched nags they had hired for a shirt and a piece of soap. Near the jetty we made the acquaintance of the man who was destined to become for us a link between present and past, an oracle we consulted ceaselessly for five months, our informant Juan Tepano. The first thing that struck us about him was his mischievous expression. He was sitting on a rock, with a cotton cap on his head and a pipe in his mouth—the very picture of an 'old salt' as imagined by romantics. There was nothing very Polynesian about his face. He struck us as being rather like certain old Parisian artists, and he was not dissimilar in character. Tepano, in fact, considered himself a skilful sculptor, although his creations were bizarre and pretty far removed from the traditions of his people.

Juan Tepano's reputation as an authority in ethnographic matters had spread as far as Chile, where he had been referred to as probably my best source of information. Mrs Routledge already speaks of him with esteem, and Macmillan Brown[1] admits being indebted to him for the better part of his (rather naïve) book on the Pacific. The previous evening, the natives whom we had told of our intentions had mentioned his name again and again. He was living history, the island's Baedeker.

After listening with a broad smile of satisfaction to a few compliments we paid him on his knowledge and reputation, Tepano said to us in his sententious voice: 'Your party will get to know all about the island and its past. Those who came before could not retain the words, but they will all be conveyed to you, I know.' He continued: 'The words of the ancients have been twisted, but you, you will receive them straight.' Looking at him as he talked to us, we were struck by his relatively young and active appearance. We asked his age, always a difficult question in a community where civil records are a recent innovation. Tepano launched out into a confused explanation from which it emerged that he must be somewhere around eighty. 'I'm the oldest man on the island,' he kept repeat-

[1] *The Riddle of the Pacific*, T. Fisher Unwin, London, 1924.

ing. Later, we learned that our first impression had not deceived us and that Tepano must have been just approaching sixty; but that day he had every interest in making himself out to be old, as old as the sculptors of the statues.

He invited us to visit his house, and in his company we entered the village of Hanga-roa. We followed an avenue of mulberry trees and came out in a little square facing the church and decorated with concrete benches. Most of the houses were built of wood with corrugated iron roofs. Everywhere we saw the same look of commonplace poverty. We might well have been in any port in the south of Chile. Finally, we reached Tepano's house, which was distinguished from the rest by having walls of unmortared stone—'like the ancient huts', he told us, not without pride, as he invited us to enter. To tell the truth, if the house was of stone, it was because he was too lazy to acquire the planks that would have enabled him to build a wooden house. He showed us into an ordinary-looking room, furnished with two iron bedsteads and a rickety table. A more picturesque sight awaited us in the next room. Round a fire burning on the floor itself, women were busy in front of cooking-pots, surrounded by a swarm of yelling brats with running eyes. In a dark corner we distinguished the vague outline of a human form. It belonged to a strange being, a kind of monster, with a thousand wrinkles, squatting on a pile of straw, who held out to us a clawlike hand. This living mummy was Viriamo, Tepano's mother, born 'in the time of the kings' and now in her second childhood. Her son, who presented her to us as though she were a museum piece or an animal in a zoo, informed us that she was already married in 1864 when the first missionaries landed on the island. He made us admire the tattooing that covered her legs, and assured us that in the old days she was in the habit of conversing with 'devils'. Finally, he declared that he owed the best part of his knowledge to her.

If we had come some twenty years earlier, this woman would still have been able to tell us of everyday life in the reed huts. She would have described to us the festivals on the *ahu* and the rites of the bird-man, and perhaps she would have remembered the songs chanted by the priests. But the poor woman was now like Easter Island itself—a body without a soul.

The news of our arrival had spread through the village; the room in which we stood was invaded by a band of young people who giggled and nudged one another as shy and derisive villagers will do anywhere. We were bombarded with questions about the goods we had brought. The moment had come to announce our intention to pay in clothing for every ancient object offered us. A few seconds later men returned with bone fish-hooks. The same evening a woman slipped into our hands, with the greatest secrecy, a splendid stone fish-hook for which she asked a piece of cloth. Once a bargain had been struck, we noticed that the magnificent specimen was a fake. The incident was a lesson to us; for throughout our stay the Easter Islanders offered us articles counterfeited with such skill that despite our precautions we were not always able to avoid being taken in. These imitations of ancient utensils were often so faithful and their patina so authentic that the forgers deserved the payment they received for their trouble.

Such was our first contact with Easter Island. Longer acquaintance did little to modify our first impression. A few days later, accompanied by Tepano and his family, which had been joined by Pacomio, we set up our first camp at the Tepeu *ahu*. We moved about at a leisurely pace, staying several weeks at every spot on the island where the statues were numerous. While my colleague Dr Lavachery measured and described the ruins, Tepano dictated to me the legends and traditions connected with the various sites we were exploring. The last two months were spent in the proximity of Hanga-roa village, completing our ethnographic material. Drapkin, our mission's doctor, devoted himself to treating the natives and collecting data on demography and physical anthropology.

A few weeks after our arrival we knew practically all the natives and were kept faithfully up to date with island gossip. Our informants spoke Spanish, but at the end of two months we were able to understand them when they addressed us in their native language. The investigation of the past, which was our Mission's chief purpose, did not leave us the time needed to make an exhaustive study of the present community of Hanga-roa. The task will undoubtedly prove extremely important, for it will make it possible to determine what aspects of the modern life of the island belong to the cultural heritage of Polynesia, and what aspects are the outcome of the years of inter-breeding and contacts with various elements from Europe and Chile. Such an enquiry would have to be undertaken by an ethnographer familiar with Polynesia and capable of discerning the old native inheritance under the European veneer.

EASTER ISLAND

CHAPTER I

Easter Island and the Lost Continent

HISTORY affords few examples of an indifference to equal that shown in 1687 by the privateer Edward Davis when, after being carried five hundred leagues west of Copiapo by the winds and currents of the Pacific, he sighted a sandy beach behind which were silhouetted high mountains. He immediately swung his ship round on to an easterly course towards Peruvian waters, without making the slightest effort to find out whether he was the victim of an optical illusion or the discoverer of a new country.

This 'Davis Land'—which was much later identified with Easter Island—confirmed the cosmographers of the period in their conviction that a continent existed in these regions which formed, as it were, a counterbalance to Asia and Europe. The peaks vaguely glimpsed by Davis henceforth cast a disproportionately long shadow over the South Seas. Many generations of navigators vainly scanned the horizon in search of them. But the shores of this 'southern continent' persistently evaded discovery. Instead of the sought-for continent innumerable islands were found dotted about the ocean, the black and brown inhabitants of which seemed to present a living image of the childhood of the human race.

The great navigators of the eighteenth and early nineteenth centuries were succeeded by the crews of the whalers, which, for more than seventy years, sailed the South Pacific in all directions. They, in their turn, were never halted in their zigzag courses by the barrier of an unknown continent.

In the end, the areas formerly occupied by the contours of the 'Terra Australis Incognita' were painted blue on maps and charts.

But people could not resign themselves to the loss of a continent. Certain minds hungry for mystery projected the existence of this world, said to have known the reign of a strange type of humanity and a civilization many thousands of years old, into a fabulous past. Of this southern land, they claimed, nothing was left but the mountain-tops, which today form the archipelagos and islands dotted about between Asia and America. By a fortunate chance, monuments testifying to the splendour of a civilization that had everywhere else been submerged by some gigantic cataclysm had been preserved on Easter Island. This explanation of the mystery of Easter Island has died hard.

But the waters of the Pacific were sounded in vain: nothing was found there but great deeps. An abyss of 1,145 fathoms extends over a ten-mile radius round Easter Island: no land could have disappeared recently and left such a depression behind it.

Just like Tahiti, the Marquesas or the Hawaiian Islands, Easter Island—far from being the roof of a submerged world—was born a few dozen millennia ago as the result of volcanic eruptions. Microscopic analysis of its rocks has not revealed the tiniest particle of any mineral derived from a continental formation. Its soil and its volcanoes are entirely composed of masses of material melted or pulverized by the former craters. All these volcanoes are now extinct, and they probably ceased to vomit their lava and scoria some thousands of years before any human being discerned them on the horizon.

The objection may be raised that these submarine eruptions which create islands may just as well destroy them with equal suddenness. In other words, Easter Island—even if it is of volcanic origin—might conceivably be a relic of a much vaster stretch of land truncated by volcanic activity. As proof of this cataclysm, some writers point to the central plain covered with stones of all sizes that seem to have been hurled forth by the ancient craters. These scattered fragments, which make walking on the island so tiresome, do perhaps suggest the action of a cataclysm vast enough to have wiped out the old civilization of the island. The collapse of the mausoleum statues has also been attributed to an earthquake accompanying this eruption of subterranean fires. Once again, geology brings us to our senses: these accumulations of basalt stones are the outcome of a process of disintegration of the lava crust, through the action of atmospheric agents, that has been going on for thousands of years. No fire, no volcanic bombardment compelled the sculptors to abandon their work.

On the other hand, the waves from which Easter Island emerged are gradually swallowing it up again. Every year they gnaw a little deeper into it, wearing away its cinder cliffs and pouring into its craters; in the course of millennia there will be nothing left of Easter Island but a reef battered by the waves and frequented, like Salas-y-Gomez, by sea birds.

This slow nibbling at the coastline was demonstrated to us with particular clarity by the state of the Ohau *ahu*, one of the finest funerary platforms on the island. Its façade is composed of delicately adjusted polished slabs. On its inclined plane lie a few statues, their faces buried in the debris. It is unlikely that this monument still raises its austere silhouette on the cliff it then dominated. For when we visited it in 1934 a gaping fissure had already detached its right wing, and a few rainstorms would have been enough to send the mausoleum crashing down six hundred feet into the sea.

This crumbling away of the cliffs might be interpreted as the continuation of a process of erosion which, over a period of thousands of years, had reduced a vast territory to minute proportions. But in fact it is nothing of the sort. Far from suggesting great antiquity, these subsidences are definite evidence of the comparatively recent character of Easter Island civilization. A stroll round the island makes it abundantly clear that the mausoleums were intentionally built on the sea-front. If they had been erected many centuries ago some of them would already have fallen victim to the waves.

In short, everything goes to show that when the Polynesians made their first landing on Easter Island it was very much the same as it is today: then, as now, it was an insignificant little island whose triangular shape recalls Sicily, but a miniature Sicily with an area of about 48,000 acres and sides measuring respectively fifteen, eleven and ten miles in length.

A different hypothesis has been advanced by Mr Macmillan Brown, a man with a mind both simple and excessively imaginative. According to him, Easter Island was once the centre of a smiling archipelago, inhabited by an industrious race, but too arid for permanent settlement—it served as a collective cemetery for the populations of the neighbouring islands. As the result of a movement of the earth's crust, the island kingdom vanished into thin air, leaving as the sole testimony to its existence this bare islet covered with funerary monuments.

There is no foundation for this hypothesis. Macmillan Brown claims that Davis Land was his archipelago, which sank between 1687 and 1722; but everything seems to indicate that Davis's eyes deceived him—unless he discovered Mangareva, to the west of Easter Island. And by what miracle could the natives, who have piously preserved the legend of the ancestral migrations and tribal wars, have lost all recollection of such a major catastrophe occurring only a few years before the discovery of the island by Europeans?

The idea of an isle of the dead for the inhabitants of an archipelago is tolerably romantic in itself. The mausoleums, to which Macmillan Brown attributes an age of thousands of years, were still being used by the grandparents of the present generation of Easter Islanders. According to him, the island's monuments could not have been carved and erected by a handful of men: their erection would have required the population of a vast archipelago. But, as we shall see later, the seven hundred and twenty people now living on the island represent only about a fifth of the population at the time of its discovery. Easter Island certainly supported a population sufficiently large to have executed these masterpieces of primitive statuary.

A monstrous pumice-stone, an enormous scoria—that is the best definition of Easter Island. It is pierced all over by caves that open into the face of the cliffs or yawn beneath the feet as one strolls amidst its black rocks. The former inhabitants utilized these clefts and subterranean galleries either as resting-places for their dead, or as refuges in time of war, or as hiding-places for their treasures.

What stories we were told about these grottoes! One of them at the foot of the high Poike cliff, we were informed, was ornamented by two giant statues carved out of the solid rock. We wanted to explore it, but no guide offered to take us here. No doubt this cavern, like many other of the island's marvels, is a myth. Nevertheless, when we sailed round the island on board the 'Mercator', we saw the entrances to a large number of these enormous holes which the natives claim, by turns, to be peopled by demons or filled with inaccessible archaeological treasures.

CHAPTER II

Easter Island—Polynesian Soil

GENEALOGICAL investigations carried out by our Mission disclosed an incredible variety of racial intermixtures in the course of the last fifty years. The inhabitants of Hanga-roa count among their ancestors Chileans, Frenchmen, Englishmen, Germans, Italians and even Americans, who have stayed or put in at the island. This interbreeding has produced some very fine results; in particular, there are some splendid specimens of humanity of mixed British and Easter Island descent. The natives who claimed pure Easter Island origin—about two hundred—did not fall short of their fellows of mixed blood in vigour and appearance.

The eighteenth-century navigators found the Easter Islanders little different from other Polynesians. They had fair complexions, straight or wavy hair, and wore beards. In short, they looked much like Europeans.

Some nineteenth-century anthropologists, judging by incomplete indices or unreliable statistics, declare that Easter skulls closely resemble those of Melanesia. Volz and Dixon went so far as to speak of an Australoid element in the island's racial composition. Even if Negroid characteristics were manifest in the Easter type, they could not be taken as proof of two successive occupations by natives of different races. The Polynesians do not constitute a homogeneous population, and in the course of their migrations they have absorbed Negroid groups, certain of whose hereditary traits have been very distinctly preserved in some islands.

Measurements taken in 1935 by Dr Harry Shapiro, using subjects of pure Easter descent, gave results that demolished the hypothesis of a Melanesian origin and threw into relief the close affinities of the Easter type with other Polynesian types. In one particular, however, they occupy a place apart: on the average, their heads are longer than anywhere else in Polynesia. This peculiarity of their cephalic index suggests that they may be the purest representatives of an ethnic layer which, having been

33

replaced in Central Polynesia by shorter-skulled invaders, continued to exist on the periphery of its former domain. Moving eastwards from Tahiti, the length of the cranium perceptibly increases, till it reaches its maximum on Easter Island.

Dark pigmentation of the skin and fuzzy hair—the most persistent signs of a Negroid heredity—are rarer on Easter Island than on the other islands inhabited by Polynesians. It is the same with noses and lips of the 'Melanesian' type.

Linguistics do not contradict the data of physical anthropology. The speech of Easter Island is a pure Polynesian dialect, free from elements borrowed from any other family of languages; it is similar to Mangarevan and Marquesan, of which it seems to be an archaic form.

Some authors have placed the beginnings of Easter Island culture very far back in the past, totally disregarding the lists of the great chiefs that have been recorded at various times. These go from King Hotu-matu'a, who discovered and colonized the island, to little Gregorio, who died at the Mission of the Fathers of the Sacred Heart in 1866. The lists do not always agree, and they often include the names of deities and even the wives of certain kings. After carefully sifting them we were able to establish that the number of *ariki-mau*, or sacred chiefs, who had succeeded one another from mythical times to the present day was about thirty. Allowing an average of twenty-five years for the duration of each reign—the accepted figure in Polynesian ethnography—this puts Hotu-matu'a's voyage somewhere in the twelfth century. It was during this century that the Polynesians swarmed from the Society Islands and the Marquesas to settle in the Gambiers, the Hawaiian Islands and New Zealand.

Even supposing—which is unlikely—that the first statues were erected shortly after Hotu-matu'a's landing, the most ancient would be scarcely seven hundred years old. This is a long way from the thousands of years with which they have rather frivolously been credited.

The far-flung migrations of the Polynesians are almost unique in human history. It has even been denied that they were possible with the means of navigation at the Polynesians' disposal, and imaginary areas of land have been made to rise in the middle of the

Pacific to explain this people's vast dispersion. Such fantasies cannot deprive the Polynesians of the glory of having discovered, in their outrigger canoes, all the islands, high and low, scattered within the immense triangle with its apexes in New Zealand, Hawaii and Easter Island.

To understand an historical event fully it is not enough to know its cause and development: we must also reconstruct the psychological climate. This is no longer possible in the case of Easter Island; but the annals of Mangareva, painstakingly noted down by Father Laval, afford valuable background information regarding the various Polynesian migrations in the archipelagos next to Easter Island.

Emigration was not merely a physical necessity imposed by a conqueror on a vanquished group: it was also the only honourable solution for men of courage whom defeat had stripped of their prestige and their lands. When a young Mangarevan chief hesitated to follow out to sea his sovereign who had resolved to leave his island, his mother improvised the following song to encourage him and make him ashamed of his hesitations:

O Tupu! O my King!
The dull groaning of the reefs makes itself heard under the wind
Behind Hararuru. It is for you they are moaning.
O Tupu! O my King!
Alas! You have disappeared with seven canoes.
O Tupu! O my King!
One of them is still left, it is the double canoe of Mapukutaora.
What is it going to do?
O Tupu! O my King!

The young chief obeyed the voice of the waves and left in search of Tupu, his king.

Another vanquished chief, Mata-puku, accompanied by his son, sought refuge with his married daughter living among another tribe. There the fugitives were ordered to go and fish: 'When Matapuku saw his son doing the work of a servant, steering the canoe, his face lashed by the waves, he was filled with grief at the thought that they were both in a state of servitude. They resolved to seek another island where the shame of defeat would no longer weigh openly upon them. They asked for a canoe, which was immediately given them, for, according to the ideas of the country, no one could live on without avenging himself or confiding himself to the mercy of the waves.'

'To the mercy of the waves'—no expression could more accurately convey the character of these maritime adventures. The emigrants sailed blindly, straight ahead, in the hope of reaching some island beyond the horizon.

Hundreds of Polynesian chiefs must have roamed the sea until their canoes were no more than hulks, filled with the dead and dying. Others perished in storms. But a few landed on 'oases of the sea', which they conquered for man.

These primitive flotillas setting out for unknown lands left the homeland amidst a joyful and festive tumult. Various stories describe the lamentations of those remaining behind, and the last wishes addressed to one another by the two parties. Those who were leaving made it a point of honour to affect an 'air of triumph and joy', to demonstrate their faith in a better destiny ahead.

At the moment of departure, everyone decked himself out in his finest ornaments and covered his hair with garlands of flowers. Decorated as though for a festival, the canoes moved slowly out to sea; at the stern, one of the priests sang and danced the 'last farewell to the fatherland', while saluting in advance the land 'they were seeking beyond the horizon'.

By what name did Hotu-matu'a greet the island he had discovered? The modern natives call their island Rapa-nui, but this name is of quite recent origin. It means Great Rapa, and was given to Easter Island by Tahitian sailors struck by certain resemblances between Easter Island and Rapa.

Many writers employ for this island, which they claim to have been the centre of an empire, the esoteric name Te Pito-te-henua, 'The Navel of the World'. This high-sounding epithet bestowed upon a little triangular rock is not, as might have been supposed, pure invention. *Pito*, the word translated as 'navel', also means 'end', while *henua* is the normal word for 'earth'. Pito-te-henua is actually the name of one of the island's three headlands and signifies no more than 'Land's End'.

A third name, Hiti-ai-terangi, has been proposed. This is the

name by which Easter Islanders being repatriated from Peru referred to their island when speaking to other Polynesians on the
boat. But the name seems to have been unknown to the native
population.

These differences of opinion on such a simple subject may
appear a trifle strange. In actual fact, the island that Roggeveen
called after the day on which he discovered it had probably never
had a name. Every one of its bays and rocks bore a name, but not
the island as a whole. As isolated on it as though they were alone in
the world, the Easter Islanders probably never felt any need for a
name by which to distinguish their country from others, of which
they had no knowledge.

CHAPTER III

The Tragic Story of Easter Island

DESTINY seems to have been bent on destroying every piece of evidence on Easter Island that would have enabled us to solve its riddles. The island was baptized with the blood of its children; and, as though this massacre had been an omen for the future, it was the scene, in the middle of last century, of one of the most hideous atrocities committed by white men in the South Seas.

On Easter Sunday 1722, the Dutch Admiral Roggeveen, on board the 'Arena', discovered an island which he took to be Davis Land—although nothing in its appearance tallied with the brief description left by the famous buccaneer. As the 'Arena' drew closer, various signs of habitation could be distinguished. It was not until the following day, however, that the first contact was made between the islanders and the Dutch. A native came aboard in the most matter-of-fact manner and without showing the slightest trace of astonishment. His friendly air and graceful movements won him universal good-will. For his part, he seemed mainly interested in the ship and its rigging. He walked up and down the deck, touching the gear and gazing curiously at the masts and cannons. There was nothing of the 'savage' terrified by supernatural beings about him: he behaved like a man absorbed by new technical problems. He lost his composure only when he caught sight of his reflection in a mirror. With an instinctive movement, he jumped forward to seize the companion whom he suspected of having surreptitiously slipped in front of him. The Dutch tried various other experiments in the hope of amusing themselves at his expense. The ship's orchestra played a tune to test his ear for music. At the first notes, the Easter Islander began to dance. So much trust and good humour gained him many presents, which he took with him when he swam away.

His example and his stories encouraged the rest, and soon the ship was invaded by a noisy band of visitors. They laughed, were delighted with everything and were getting on wonderfully with the Dutchmen, when suddenly there was the sound of a chase and of bodies diving into water. Some of the natives had robbed the sailors of their caps and jumped overboard with their booty. Then the Admiral's table-cloth disappeared through the window of his cabin. These first petty thefts initiated a tradition in relations between natives and foreign visitors that has not been lost.

In the afternoon the Dutch went ashore. The crowd massed on the beach behaved in the most incoherent manner. While some made gestures of friendship and seemed delighted by the visit, others wore a hostile expression and picked up stones. This marked contrast characterized the natives' attitude on the occasion of every subsequent European landing on the island.

The shore party were advancing calmly, when suddenly the cry rang out: 'Fire, now's the moment.' There was a crackle of musket shots, and when the smoke cleared several natives lay groaning on the sand—among them the gay companion who had been the first to venture aboard the 'Arena'. What had happened exactly? No doubt a soldier, exasperated by some petty theft or frightened by a threatening gesture, had given way to fear and provoked this senseless massacre. The crowd, which had broken up, returned, but this time timid and humble, imploring forgiveness for a crime of whose nature they were unaware. Standards were presented to the strangers in token of respect. But the latter were nervous and ill at ease on this beach they had just sprinkled with blood. They cast a glance at the huts made of branches, picked up a few tubers, and retired as fast as they could to their boats.

In the midst of the tumult and confusion, the Dutchmen had caught sight of some strange monuments which they later discussed at length. They wondered how 'naked savages' could have put up these colossi, and finally decided that these 'idols' must have been made of clay. This was the first solution offered to the mystery of Easter Island.

The island discovered by Roggeveen was forgotten for fifty years. Seafarers continued to look for Davis Land, the southern continent that seemed to recede as fast as the Pacific unveiled its mysteries. Spain, worried about her American colonies, emerged from her lethargy and sent ships to annex these territories next door to her overseas domains.

Easter Island was discovered for the second time, in 1770, by
Felipe González y Haedo, who anchored there for several days and
sent a boat party round the island, which made a very accurate
map of it. Before the Spaniards left, a shore party in full dress uniform set up three great crosses on the Poike hills. There was no
clash. The natives indulged in a good deal of pilfering, but they
made up for these misdeeds by the liberty they allowed their
women. Young girls calmly offered themselves to the Spaniards,
who were outraged by the cynicism shown by the men on this occasion.

The annexation of the island—which the Spaniards named San
Carlos—to the kingdom of Spain was proclaimed in a deed that
was read out to the natives. Following an old Spanish custom
dating from the conquest of America, the latter were invited to put
their marks at the foot of the document as a sign of consent. The
islanders readily agreed to this request. They scribbled a few lines
on the paper, doubtless in imitation of the script in which the
manuscript was written. One of them, however, drew a bird in the
style that appears on the tablets and petroglyphs.

The reception which the Easter Islanders accorded, four years
later, to Captain Cook (1774) differed little from the welcome they
had given his predecessors. They were full of high spirits, friendly,
good-humouredly and audaciously dishonest. The baskets of
sweet potatoes they offered in barter were weighted with stones,
and they filched the goods for which they had already been paid
and sold them a second time. These little tricks did not always go
unpunished: an angry officer fired on one native who had stolen a
bag from him. The women, somewhat more shy, distributed their
favours for trifling gifts 'in the shadows cast by the giant statues'.

Captain Cook's brief visit brought Easter Island the celebrity it
has never ceased to enjoy up to the present day. In the story of his
voyage the great explorer describes the giant statues standing upright or fallen flat on top of mausoleums, whose sundered stones
revealed the bleached skeletons within. He draws a vivid picture of
the contrast between these grandiose relics and the bare little
patch of land covered with scoriae and inhabited by a sparse and
impoverished population.

In 1786, a French expedition commanded by the Comte de La

Pérouse landed on Easter Island. They stayed only twenty-four hours—long enough to bestow on this strange and grim piece of land a little of the delicate and ironic charm of the dying century. La Pérouse was a sensitive soul. The true son of an age well disposed towards the 'noble savage', this courteous and cultivated French aristocrat believed that a stolen cap or handkerchief was not worth the life of the poor children of nature who purloined them with such ingenuity. He also concluded, very reasonably, that he could not undertake to re-educate them in a few hours. The best thing, he thought, was to laugh at the ruses the islanders employed in robbing him. To avoid all pretext for the violence that was always to be feared from a crew of rough sailors, he announced that he would replace the stolen caps himself. The natives took advantage of this windfall. They must have noticed the strangers' interest in their women, and they exploited their guests' weakness to the full. While the young girls were leading the sailors on, the men relieved them of their caps and handkerchiefs. La Pérouse took a lenient view of the situation. He distributed medals to those whom he took to be chiefs; but in reality these were the most arrant thieves, and although 'they pretended to go in pursuit of those who had stolen the sailors' handkerchiefs, it was easy to see that it was with the definite intention of not catching them.' Looting reached such a pitch that the Frenchmen were sometimes obliged to fire blank cartridges or small shot.

La Pérouse made a number of observations that are not lacking in subtlety and remain true of the modern Easter Islanders: 'It is certain,' he says, 'that these people do not have the same ideas about theft as ourselves; they probably do not attach any shame to it; but they know very well that they are committing an unjust act, since they immediately flee. Their physiognomy does not express a single genuine feeling: he who was most to be mistrusted was the Indian to whom one had just given a present and who appeared most anxious to render a thousand little services.' La Pérouse noticed their inquisitiveness and open minds and the lively interest they took in navigational matters. Those who came on board examined the cables, the anchors, the compass and the steering-wheel. They came back again later with a piece of string and measured the ship: no doubt there had been some discussion ashore on this subject, and they wished to clear up uncertainties.

A famous drawing that appears in La Pérouse's *Voyages* shows the natives sitting at the foot of the great statues purloining the French officers' and sailors' kit. This was the visitors' only revenge. We showed the modern Easter Islanders a reproduction of this picture. Their reaction is not without interest: first, they found the exploits of their ancestors extremely comical, and the simpletons who were allowing themselves to be robbed highly ridiculous. What struck them most, however, were the good looks of the women, whom the artist had treated according to the conventions of his period. They saw in them a confirmation of their racial pessimism: the women of days gone by were whiter and had firmer breasts and 'deeper navels' than those of today. These remarks were also an indication of the ideal of feminine beauty held in the island. Afterwards women often came and asked us to show them the portraits of their grandmothers. They gazed at them for a long time and generally commented: 'How black and ugly we have become now.'

In 1808 a crime was committed on Easter Island that foreshadowed the fate awaiting the rest of the population half a century later. An American ship, the 'Nancy', carried off twelve men and ten women after a bloody battle. These unfortunates were taken down into the holds and put in irons. The trader's intention was to land them on Masafuera Island, where he hoped to employ them as slaves in seal-hunting. When the ship was three days' sail from Easter Island, he had his captives brought up on deck and their chains removed. The moment they were free of their bonds, men and women leapt into the water and began to swim with desperate vigour. The captain, imagining that the waves would force them to come back on board, stopped his ship and watched from afar the discussion that broke out among them as to the right direction to take. Being unable to agree, some made off towards Easter Island while the others swam towards the south. Boats were lowered and an attempt made to recapture them, but they refused to come aboard and continually evaded capture by diving under the water. Tired of chasing them, the sailors left them to their fate.

It is not surprising if other ships putting in at Easter Island after this date were greeted with hostility. Nevertheless, curiosity and

trust generally regained the upper hand, and in the middle of aggressive demonstrations the natives could not restrain themselves
from giving free rein to their gaiety and their naive desire to converse with the strangers. The arrival, in 1816, of the Russian navigator Kotzebue, whose ship was the 'Rurick', was the pretext for
extraordinary scenes. The first boat to come ashore was surrounded by a group anxious to barter tubers for nails. The bargain
was struck amidst disorder and confusion, of which more than one
islander took advantage to steal everything within reach. When the
other boats ventured on to the beach, the excitement of the natives
reached fever pitch: 'They shouted and jumped about, making the
queerest gestures.' Still laughing and joking, they blocked the only
little beach on which the Russians could have landed, and forced
them to put out to sea again. The din of their chatter was ear-
splitting; they all talked at once and indulged in jokes that caused
roars of laughter from the crowd. Finally, they tired of this game
and began to throw stones at the sailors. After a shot had dispersed
them 'like a flock of sparrows', the Russians disembarked. The
uproar then became so intense that the officers had to shout to
make themselves heard by their men. The leaping and dancing of
the black- and red-painted warriors constituted an appalling spectacle that terrified the leader of the landing party. He confessed
later that he had imagined himself to be surrounded by a band of
monkeys. He gave the order to fire blank cartridges. At the first
salvo, the natives took refuge behind rocks; 'but when the noise had
passed and they realized that they were unhurt, they came out
from their hiding-places laughing and making fun of the strangers.'

Kotzebue was also unwilling at first to 'take revenge for the
pleasantries of these grown-up children', but he thought it advis-
able to beat a retreat, and even to fire a few bullets, when he was
struck by a stone. A few hours later, the 'Rurick' left Easter Island
waters. If it had not been for these incidents, Easter Island might
have left a mark on German literature, for among Kotzebue's companions was Adalbert von Chamisso, the Romantic poet.

The English navigator Beechey was welcomed to Easter Island
in much the same way as Kotzebue had been, but his account is
coloured by a few picturesque details concerning the peculiar

charm of the South Seas.

Beechey sent two boats ashore; clusters of swimmers fought to get to them and threw presents to the sailors. Yams, bananas and sugar cane rained down on them, together with wooden images and fishing-nets. The number of swimmers clinging to the oars and rudders was so great that they brought the whalers to a standstill. They all wanted to clamber aboard, especially the women. There was no provocative or coquettish gesture in which they did not indulge in order to persuade the sailors to take them on board. One of the boats ended up by being so overloaded that it almost sank; the seamen had to beat off this aquatic crowd that came back again as soon as it had been driven away. The contents of the boat were pillaged without anyone being able to arrest the looters, who dived into the water like porpoises. The women committed no thefts, but they were in league with the thieves: their job was to distract the rowers' attention by their caresses and suggestive attitudes. The Englishmen decided to take stern measures: no women were allowed into the boats except one young girl, who could not swim as well as the others and whose father lifted her into the whaler. With a kindly smile the officer let her sit beside him. The girl was wearing nothing but a grass skirt; feeling this costume to be inadequate in her present situation she calmly took possession of an officer's jacket, after which she started to sing. In no way jealous of the favoured treatment she had been accorded, the girl tried to help her friends aboard by pulling them out of the water by their hair, until she was forbidden to continue for fear the boat might capsize again.

'As our party passed,' writes Beechey, 'the assemblage of females on the rock commenced a song, similar to that chaunted by the lady in the boat; and accompanied it by extending their arms over their heads, beating their breasts, and performing a variety of gestures, which showed that our visit was acceptable, at least to that part of the community. When the boats were within wading distance of the shore, they were closely encompassed by the natives; each bringing something in his hand, however small, and almost every one importuning for an equivalent in return. All those in the water were naked, and only here and there, on the shore, a thin cloak of the native cloth was to be seen. Some had their faces painted black, some red; others black and white, or red and white, in the ludicrous manner practised by our clowns; and two demon-like monsters were painted entirely black. It is not easy to imagine the picture that was presented by this motley crowd, unrestrained by any authority or consideration for their visitors, all hallooing to the extent of their lungs, and pressing upon the boats with all sorts of grimaces and gestures.

'It was found impossible to land where it was at first intended: the boats, therefore, rowed a little to the northward, followed by the multitude, and there effected a disembarkation, aided by some of the natives, who helped the party over the rocks with one hand, while they picked their pockets with the other.'

An officer fired a shot to clear the beach, but the report had less effect than the water poured on the people in front by those at the back, who were impatient to enjoy the spectacle. The tumult on the seashore surpassed all imagination. The natives handed the Euro-peans empty sacks, in the hope that they would be given them back full of presents. At the first signs of hostility the landing party beat a retreat. Perhaps this movement was interpreted as a sign of fear or enmity. Whatever the reason, matters took a nasty turn immedi-ately afterwards. Showers of stones rained down on the sailors, many of whom were seriously injured. The young island girl in the boat, knowing her compatriots' marksmanship, showed no sign of alarm; an officer had to throw her overboard into safety. Finally, the sailors fired on the crowd, and a chief was hit. Taking advant-age of the panic, the Englishmen were able to push out their boats and jump aboard.

Thus ended the last visit that Easter Island received from a European navigator who still preserved the humane traditions of the great travellers of the eighteenth century.

Admiral Dupetit-Thouars sailed past Easter Island in 1838. He only anchored long enough to receive on board a few natives who treated the crew to an exhibition of dancing. One woman amongst the visitors had provided herself in advance with a basket in which to put the presents she anticipated from the sailors' generosity. Some years earlier, Moerenhout had anchored off the island on his way from Chile to Tahiti and had received a visit from a native who, once aboard, invited the crew to come and frolic with the women on the seashore.

Before the visits of Moerenhout and Admiral Dupetit-Thouars another crime had been committed. The whaler 'Pindos' sighted Easter Island in 1822. Boats sent ashore to procure women and fresh vegetables returned with as many girls as there were men on board. The next day they were taken off in the same boats, and when they were fairly close to the shore they were forced to jump overboard. 'The boats remained stationary, to watch these unfortunate girls swimming with one hand as they did their best to hold above water with the other the trinkets they had received for prostituting themselves, and perhaps carrying with them the germs of a disease that might cost them their lives. As they came ashore they were received by groups gathered in a crowd on the strand; it was then that the skipper, without any provocation and apparently for the sole pleasure of killing, took his gun and fired into the midst of them—as a parting gesture—with the marksmanship characteristic of the men of his country. It was immediately evident from the confusion reigning round one poor Indian who fell that the shot had found its mark. He then gave the order to row, and moved off with a smile on his lips and congratulating himself on his good shooting. . . .'

The year 1862 was decisive in the history of Easter Island. It saw the end of its civilization, most aspects of which have become for us, since the middle of the nineteenth century, as vague and far-off as though we were separated from them by the mists of time.

In 1859 exploitation of the guano deposits on the Chile coast was an extremely prosperous undertaking, handicapped by only one obstacle—the shortage of labour. Fatigue, undernourishment and epidemics decimated the unfortunate labourers compelled to do this exhausting work on arid, sun-scorched islets. The companies recruited their workmen with the aid of adventurers who employed force or cunning as occasion demanded. These new-style slave-traders made a full-scale expedition to Easter, of all Polynesian islands the closest to Peru. A flotilla arrived off Hangaroa Bay on December 12, 1862. The few islanders who unsuspectingly came aboard were immediately seized, chained and thrown into the hold. As no one else presented himself, the Peruvian slavers went ashore and drove all the natives they could find to the beach with gunshots. The islanders were too terrified to offer much resistance.

According to another version of this slave raid, the Peruvian traders attracted the islanders to the shore by a display of presents, and then, at a given signal, slew and captured a great number of them. In 1914, at the time of Mrs Routledge's voyage, there were still some old men who remembered these scenes. They described the gunshots, the flight of the women and children, and the lamentations of the captives as they were held down on the ground and tied like animals—in short, all the horrors of the slave raids in black Africa. Among the prisoners were King Kamakoi and his son Maurata.

On reaching Peru this miserable cargo of human flesh was immediately sold to the guano companies. In a few months disease, ill-treatment and homesickness had reduced the nine hundred or a thousand natives taken into slavery to about a hundred. Thanks to the intervention of Monseigneur Jaussen, the French Government—backed by the British—made representations to Peru. The Peruvian Government ordered the repatriation of the handful of Easter Islanders who had survived these months of forced labour. They were put on board a ship that was to take them back to their island; but most of them died on the way from tuberculosis or smallpox. Only fifteen regained the island, to the greatest misfortune of the population that had been left behind: shortly after their return, smallpox, the germs of which they had brought with them, broke out and transformed the island into a vast charnel-house. Since there were too many corpses to bury in the family mausoleums, they were thrown down clefts in the rock or dragged into underground tunnels. The bones we found scattered about certain caves probably belonged to the unfortunate people who died at this period.

Civil wars added their toll to the havoc wrought by this murderous epidemic. The social order had been undermined, the fields were left without owners, and people fought for possession of them. Then there was famine. The population fell to around six hundred. The majority of members of the priestly class disappeared, taking with them the secrets of the past. The following year, when the first missionaries settled on the island, they found a culture in its death throes: the religious and social system had been destroyed and a leaden apathy weighed down the survivors from these disasters.

This people without past or future, physically and morally broken, was won over to Christianity, if not without effort, at least in a short time. In Hango-roa cemetery there is a stone slab bearing the inscription:

L'ILE DE PÂQUES
AU FRÈRE EUGÈNE EYRAUD
QUI D'OUVRIER MÉCANICIEN
DEVINT OUVRIER DE
DIEU ET EN FIT LA
CONQUÊTE POUR JÉSUS-CHRIST

This brief inscription sums up the whole life of the apostle to the Easter Islanders. This earnest and deeply religious young man, who exiled himself to Argentina to pay for the studies of his brother destined for the priesthood, had a strange career. He was a mechanic by trade, but the harsh necessities of emigration compelled him to follow many occupations up to the time when he crossed the Andes and settled in Chile. There he led an exemplary life, devoting himself to the well-being of his family. The destiny of his brother—a missionary in China—fired his imagination, and he longed to join him and share his labours. One day he invited into his shop two passing priests, whom he had recognized from their appearance to be Frenchmen, and learned from them that he could dedicate himself to missionary work without having taken holy orders. He became a novice with the Fathers of the Holy Spirit and left Chile in 1862, in the company of other missionaries, to undertake the spiritual conquest of Easter Island.

The little band proceeded first to Tahiti, where they learned of the raid that had just been inflicted on Easter Island. In the face of this terrible disaster, the missionaries hesitated to embark on an undertaking that seemed to have become pointless. But Eyraud refused to be discouraged; he announced that, if necessary, he would settle alone on the island among the survivors, to prepare the way for the priests who would join him later. His proposal was accepted, and the schooner took him to Easter Island with carpenter's tools, a barrel of flour, cuttings of trees, five sheep and a bell—the last-named object doubtless being in his eyes the most important. Eyraud was accompanied by an Easter Islander named Pana, who had been carried off by slavers but had managed to escape. The two of them reached their destination on January 2, 1864. Pana wanted to be landed in the bay of Anakena, where he was born, but the master of the schooner preferred that of Hanga-roa. A Mangarevan was sent ashore to investigate. He returned in a state of abject terror, asserting that he had seen on the beach a thousand demons, their faces painted red and black, who leapt into the air shouting and threatened him with their weapons. Rushing up to Eyraud, he gasped: 'I would not go ashore again for a thousand piastres. They are horrible-looking people. They are threatening . . . and smallpox is ravaging the island. . . . You cannot possibly land, you would risk losing the boat and catching the disease. . . . The captain will take you back to Tahiti free of charge.' These incoherent words sowed panic on board. Everyone was in favour of standing out to sea immediately. Eyraud alone was opposed to this and demanded to be put ashore. The longboat was sent out for the second time, to set him down on the beach along with the native who had accompanied him. A milling crowd was waiting for them. In the uproar that broke out the moment they landed, Eyraud saw his companion's belongings looted. It had been agreed with the captain that he would make his way on foot to Anakena, where his luggage would be put ashore the following day; but the crowd would not let him leave, and every time he and Pana tried to escape they were forcibly dragged back into the middle of the throng. Pana succeeded in gaining the support of the warriors, and under their protection Eyraud was able to reach Anakena after an exhausting march across lava-fields and through tall grass.

Next day the schooner, after fetching about in sight of Anakena without coming inshore, disappeared over the horizon. For Eyraud this was a moment of utter despair. The ship was carrying away all his possessions and, more important still, 'a Tahitian catechism with which to teach the Kanakas prayers and the fundamental truths of religion'.

In the evening good news came. The missionary's effects had been landed in Hanga-roa Bay. To avoid losing them, Eyraud had to retrace his steps across the island over the fields of stones. Before setting out, he inaugurated his ministry: in the presence of an audience and with all possible solemnity he said a prayer in the Kanaka language.

The first thing he saw on arriving at Hanga-roa was his hat on the head of one warrior and his frock-coat on the back of another. The natives gathered round his portable hut were engaged in a lively argument, some saying the sections were parts of a boat, the rest attributing various other purposes to them. When the discussion became heated Eyraud saw an opportunity to regain possession of his belongings. He offered to settle the dispute by giving a public demonstration of the real function of these pieces of timber. To everyone's amazement, he put up his house. The same evening he had a dwelling-place, and everything that had not already been stolen was stowed away in safety.

Eyraud shows his perspicacity when he tells us in his letters that the toleration he enjoyed was due above all to the free spectacle he offered to public curiosity. All by himself, he was a circus and a zoo. The natives came in groups to watch him, and his every movement provoked laughter or endless comments. In disillusionment he writes: 'I am the stranger, the *papa*, whom everyone wants to know, to see working, and above all to exploit.' Nevertheless, the natives' inquisitiveness could be turned to account. He was constantly surrounded by an audience ready to listen to him, and he made use of it to spread the gospel. He even had some pupils, for whom his lessons were a new sort of pastime. He good-humouredly admits this: 'Whether you are ready or not, Mr Teacher or Brother Catechist, here come your pupils. They knock at the door; if I come out straight away, well and good, the class begins on the grass in front of the hut. But if I keep them waiting, or tell them to come back later because they seem to me more inclined to amuse themselves than to learn, they do not waste the opportunity. After knocking at the door they knock all round the house, then they sit down a little way off and throw stones, first little ones, then bigger ones, to keep the game interesting.

'Whether the catechist feels like it or not, he must show himself. So I go out armed with my catechism, sit down on the grass and say to them: "Come over here, we are going to learn some prayers." "No," reply the pupils, "you come over here." The simplest thing is to go across to them.'

Once the class was assembled they repeated prayers or the responses of the catechism in chorus. One may be sure this purely mechanical mode of instruction was well received by the islanders. The newcomer was conforming to the tradition of the *rongorongo* or pagan chanters, who taught the ritual chants. Was not Eyraud simply a new kind of priest teaching them different magic spells? The class was not always docile. The pupils quickly tired, and Eyraud often found himself alone on the beach. But he was not deserted for long, since, as he himself remarks, 'there are few occupations, few distractions; they soon knock at the *papa's* door and say: "Teach us to pray."'

There can be no doubt that those who had assimilated the prayers felt that they had gained power by learning these magic spells, and their confidence in Eyraud was notably enhanced in consequence.

One day, Eyraud went into his hut to write a letter, while a ship was sailing past the island. Everyone was convinced that he had sent his spirit to his compatriots, and they asked him in all seriousness what news he had received from the vessel.

After some months several of the islanders could spell, five or six were able to read, and a certain number of adults and children had learnt to say prayers. Brother Eyraud had a right to be satisfied with his handiwork: 'I had survived, and I was listened to.'

Life on a Polynesian island is delightful as long as peace reigns; but if the families or tribes take up arms against one another, it becomes difficult to keep outside the conflict and avoid unpleasantness.

Eyraud was annexed by a *matato'a*, a war-chief of the island. He tells us how this came about. The chief of a neighbouring bay came with a gift of three chickens. No sooner had Eyraud received them than a powerfully built man stepped forward and, without so much as a by-your-leave, took them away 'to relieve him of them'. 'He did relieve me of them,' adds Eyraud, not without malice, 'and during the nine months and nine days of my stay on Easter Island this rum customer continued, with great persistence, to relieve me on every possible occasion of everything I had brought with me, although it was not bothering me at all.'

The man who had thus burst into Eyraud's existence was Torometi, his 'evil genius', as he describes him. Evil genius? Not entirely, for in exchange for his petty thefts Torometi offered Brother
Eyraud the protection of himself and his people. His motives are
obscure: no doubt he was activated by cupidity, but reasons of
policy certainly played some part in his behaviour, for his tribe
must have derived advantages from disposing of the person of this
priest who was more powerful than those already on the island.

On the morrow of this memorable day, Eyraud had to open all
his trunks and display his treasures. Torometi modestly contented
himself with a small axe. To console his protégé for his loss, he told
him in a detached tone that he might borrow it from time to time.
Torometi hankered after the bell, but he consented to be reason-
able and merely took possession of a small hand-bell, the tinkling
of which 'subsequently won him universal applause and gladdened
all the island's echoes'.

It was not always easy to elude this tyrant, constantly greedy for
fresh gifts. If Eyraud shut his door Torometi calmly sat down
beside the hut, where he was soon joined by his wife, his neighbours and the passers-by. A terrible din broke out; stones were
thrown at the walls, and Eyraud, not without reason, judged it
prudent to give up the object coveted by Torometi, rather than
have his hut demolished or 'wait until they set fire to it'.

One day Torometi suggested to Eyraud that he should tour the
island and visit his pupils scattered in the various bays. No sooner
had Eyraud left Hanga-roa than he received warning that his dwelling was being looted. He returned home as fast as he could and
met Torometi, who told him, in the most natural way in the world,
that if his window had been smashed and some of his belongings
had vanished, it was the fault of—the wind. Eyraud was really the
kio, the servant, of the *matato'a* Torometi. If he tried to plant vegetables, they were stolen. If he wanted to make bricks, Torometi
whisked away the straw to heat his own stones.

The festival of the bird-man took place in September.
Torometi's tribe was threatened by jealous rivals and Torometi,
knowing he was incapable of resisting the other *matato'a*, decided to
quit Hanga-roa. But he did not want thereby to lose his 'servant' or
his riches. He ordered Eyraud to accompany him on his retreat.

The latter refused to submit to this final humiliation. To make sure that he would at least not lose his 'protégé's' possessions, Torometi broke into his hut and plundered it. This was the first time Torometi had used brute force. Eyraud, at the end of his tether, resolved to flee. A few natives accompanied him; but Torometi and his followers set out in pursuit, and after a long and acrimonious argument threw Eyraud to the ground, seized him by the arms and legs, and dragged him along until, after being almost torn apart, he promised to come with them. Shortly afterwards, the threats that had hung over Torometi materialized. A band of warriors gathered in front of his hut, tore off the thatch, and set fire to it. Poor Eyraud passed into the hands of the conquerors.

The humiliated Torometi prepared to seek refuge with some south-coast tribes linked to him by ties of blood. The conquerors would have liked to keep Eyraud; but the latter, moved by feelings hard to understand, chose to follow the man he depicts to us as his tormentor. He had taken only a few steps when, hustled from all sides and dazed by the uproar, he felt his hat being whipped off his head. This was the signal for a general assault. In a minute, he had been stripped of his overcoat and shoes, and his clothes had been torn to shreds. A few seconds later, Eyraud was as naked as an islander. A well-aimed stone put the finishing touch to his misery. In the evening, Torometi forced him to return to his hut and fetch the few objects that had not been stolen. Eyraud was lucky enough to find a worn-out pair of shoes and an old blanket, with which he covered himself. The same night he fled to Vai-hu.

Eyraud then gave proof of great strength of character. Unaffected by his destitution, he quietly continued his lessons in a cave by the seashore. Eight days later he heard the *karanga*, the sound that announces an important event. '*Pahi, pahi*—a boat.' The news left him almost unmoved. Many ships had sailed past the island, but none of them had put in. The following day, however, a schooner anchored before Hanga-roa, and Eyraud, with a shaggy beard and wrapped in his blanket, went down to the beach after the natives, who had forgotten their quarrels in the excitement. The schooner carried two Fathers from Chile, who had come to enquire into the fate of Brother Eyraud and to bring him succour.

The natives' impatience reached a climax: they flung themselves

into the water and swam round the boat. A woman clambered
aboard, made the sign of the cross by way of greeting, and recited
the Credo. This gesture and this prayer seemed like a miracle to
the priests, who were none the less worried by the yelling crowd.
They asked after Brother Eyraud, but the question—which was
misunderstood—gave rise to indignant denials: the islanders imagined they were being asked whether they had slit their visitor's
throat. A whale-boat was lowered and headed for the shore. Thereupon the crowd offered the same spectacle that had greeted Kotzebue and Beechey. The men yelled and danced about as though
seized with mass hysteria. But one thing had changed: in the
middle of this vociferous mob there was a white man who had lived
on the island for six months. The crew of the whale-boat signalled
to the crowd to come and help them land. Torometi, mistaking the
sailors' wish, took Eyraud on his broad shoulders and carried him
out to the boat. The oarsmen, terrified by the behaviour of the
natives, seized Eyraud and rowed away as fast as they could. After
relating his adventures to those on board the ship, Eyraud demanded to be taken back to land. The captain refused, and the
schooner set sail for Chile the same evening. Long before she
weighed anchor, a great silence fell on Hanga-roa: the crowd
—regretting the man they had tormented, or perhaps fearing vengeance on his part now that he had gone to join his own people
—had dispersed, leaving the beach deserted. Only an abandoned
little wooden hut marked the dawn of a new era.

But Brother Eyraud had not deserted either his island or his
task. Seventeen months later he returned to Easter Island in the
company of Brother Hippolyte Roussel and seven Mangarevans.
Nothing had changed. But this time Eyraud had taken the precaution of bringing with him a hut of corrugated iron. The treasures so
much coveted by the natives were placed in the shelter of these fire-
proof walls. The islanders laid siege to the little dwelling, and, in
their vexation at not being able to get in, pelted it with stones. The
noise made by the corrugated iron was a revelation to them. Immediately 'the whole multitude of grown-up children surrounded
the cabin, dancing, shouting, drumming on the metal sheets, and
every now and then sending a hail of stones rattling on to the roof'.
Everything had to be hermetically sealed, and for two months the

missionaries were obliged to light their lamp in broad daylight to read their breviary. Every time they went out they had to force their way through a crowd 'whose attitude left no doubt as to their intentions and who were watching for the moment when they could take us by surprise and strip us of our possessions.' Practical jokes were played on them; they often found it impossible to open the lock of their door, which had been filled with gravel. But, in spite of everything, the Mission was put on its feet. Timber houses went up near Hanga-roa beach, and orange, fig and mulberry trees sprouted in the Mission garden. The natives grew accustomed to the presence of these inoffensive and benevolent strangers and came in ever-increasing numbers to learn the prayers and songs. On Sundays the church was full.

The succession of unpleasant incidents was not, however, entirely at an end. One day, when Brother Eyraud was working at the bottom of a well, a native demanded that he should immediately surrender his trousers, if he did not want to be crushed in his hole. Eyraud could not have escaped from this awkward predicament if Brother Roussel had not providentially come to his rescue.

The chiefs were the only ones to offer any resistance to conversion, and they did so for a reason that has greatly retarded the progress of Christianity among peoples practising polygamy. They were unwilling to separate from wives who had shared their lives and to whom they were often very attached. In some instances they feared they would be unable to maintain their position if they lost the wives who assisted them in their functions and helped to keep up their prestige. But they, too, finally gave in. The *matato'a* of Hotu-iti received the missionaries with a solemnity that gives us some idea of the refinement of etiquette governing the old pagan society.

Knowledge of the new doctrine spread rapidly. It had reached the most distant creeks, and the moment had come to administer the lustral water. As in the old days of barbarian Europe, baptism was accorded to hundreds of catechumens gathered at the foot of the altar.

The last heathens were received into the bosom of the Church on August 14, 1868, the eve of the Assumption. Brother Eyraud, the humble mechanic who had become a 'worker for the Gospel', died a few days later. His last words were, 'Are they all baptized?' 'All,' came the reply. Then, like a good workman who had finished his task, he fell asleep to rest for ever in the sands of this beach on which he had been the first European to live and die.

The missionary, who breaks the natives' resistance and urges them to submission by promises of future bliss, is invariably followed by that other representative of European civilization—the trader. A French adventurer, Dutroux-Bornier, settled on the island with the missionaries' permission. The portrait the missionaries draw of him, and the memory he has left behind on the island, are not very prepossessing. He seems to have been violent, grasping and unscrupulous. But at the same time he was enterprising and ambitious. He bought land for a few pieces of cotton cloth, enlarging his property by force, and finally laid the foundations of a prosperous agricultural undertaking at Mataveri. He was surrounded by a native bodyguard commanded by Torometi, who was eager to take revenge on those who had once driven him out of Hanga-roa. He dreamed continually of becoming a great chief and having for his slaves 'the vanquished people of Hanga-roa and Vai-hu'.

The natives associated with Bornier and Torometi made raids on Hanga-roa. Huts were burnt, shots exchanged, and, dominating the tumult, a small cannon set up at Mataveri fired a few balls, the detonation of which has not yet been forgotten by the modern population. People were wounded and even killed. A bullet whistled very close to Brother Roussel's ear. The missionaries, exasperated by these outrages, complained to the adventurer's partner —Mr Brander of Tahiti—who came to Easter Island to investigate the position and saw nothing but burnt-out wreckage. He fled in terror without making up his mind what to do. From that moment on, the situation became so impossible for the missionaries and their flock that the Bishop of Tahiti ordered the evacuation of the island. Not all the natives, however, followed their pastor to the Gambiers. Three hundred allowed themselves to be enticed by Brander and were transported to Tahiti, where their descendants populate one of the districts of the town of Papeete. They have not forgotten their origins, and even today they exchange letters at long intervals with their relatives who stayed on Easter. In 1935 we acted as voluntary intermediaries between some of these families that had been separated for sixty-five years.

The whole island would have been evacuated by its inhabitants if Bornier, afraid of finding himself without labourers, had not seen to it that a hundred and eleven natives were left behind. The captain put them ashore before weighing anchor, 'despite their sobs'.

The four hundred and fifty natives we found on Easter Island in 1934 were the descendants of this handful of islanders who had been compelled to remain against their will. Dutroux-Bornier was destined to suffer for his brutalities. Acts of violence and the rape of women had caused him to be bitterly hated by the natives who surrounded him. One day, after he had committed a fresh excess, he was murdered. Two or three days later a French ship anchored off the island. The facts did not come to light and the visitors went away firmly convinced that Bornier had died by falling from his horse. His wife, Koreto, passed herself off as queen of the island and impressed the guests by her haughty air and evident desire to imitate European ways.

Mr Brander installed as the new manager a half-caste named Salmon, who was related on his mother's side to the Tahitian royal family. Salmon lived nearly twenty years on the island, with a team of Tahitians who contributed greatly to changes in local traditions and even introduced a number of Tahitian expressions into the Easter language. The natives took to this Tahitian who understood and did not ill-treat them. The island was subsequently annexed by Chile and leased to the British firm of Williamson, Balfour & Co. The little Polynesian kingdom was no more than a vast farm administered by breeders of Scottish sheep, without much imagination, and by nondescript Chilean officers exiled for one reason or another to this tiny colony. The Easter Islanders of today wear European clothes and have done their best to forget the past. But they have retained their language and a few elements of their former culture, and they continue to fish and cultivate the soil in the ancient manner. A few old people can still recall stories and legends of the pagan era, and the children can still croon traditional little rhythmical tunes as they play cat's cradle with a piece of string. A few matrimonial and funerary customs have been preserved in a more or less modified form, and in the evening the islanders still fear the return of the *akuaku* or spirits of the dead.

Wooden sculpture, the glory of Easter art, still thrives, but its products are heart-breakingly vulgar. They are bazaar 'curios', horrors typical of their kind. Such poverty reigns on the island that it is
impossible to speak of a transition from the primitive condition to
Western civilization. Easter Island, neglected by the Chilean
Government and disastrously influenced by the people who found
their way to it, has not fallen into decline—it has simply rotted in
the midst of a poverty from which there is no way out.

Easter Island hit the headlines for a brief instant in the course of
the present century. In 1914, von Spee's fleet put in there before
meeting its tragic fate. No one on the island had heard about the
declaration of war; Williamson, Balfour & Co's British manager
stocked up the German ships with sheep and demanded a cheque
instead of the gold he had been offered in payment. The 'Prinz
Friedrich Eitel' sailed into Easter waters and sank the French
cargo-boat 'Jean', whose crew remained on the island.

It was at Easter Island that the war on merchant shipping conducted by the crew of the 'See Adler', commanded by von Lückner,
came to an end in 1918. A few of the officers and men, who had
been wrecked on an atoll in the Society Islands, managed to capture a French schooner. They sailed it to Easter Island, where it
went to the bottom under mysterious circumstances. The rumour
is still current that it was scuttled by the sailors, who were tired of
adventure. The officers were lodged at Mataveri and led a peaceful
existence for several months, until one day they sighted a sail on
the horizon and tried to seize the vessel, in the manner of filibust-
ers; but it turned out to be a Chilean ship and, giving up their
plan, they allowed it to take them to Valparaiso.

It seemed as though the world was determined to communicate
its turmoil to this little patch of land which, more than any other,
deserved peace and oblivion. The economic crisis that descended
on Chile around 1928 caused a period of revolutions. Some politicians implicated in a *coup d'état* were deported to Hanga-roa.
They brought with them a spirit of agitation that was disastrous to
public peace. Violent quarrels broke out between soldiers and
sailors in which the natives took sides, splitting into factions as in
the days of the *matato'a*.

During this turbulent period the island witnessed another event that found an echo in the world press. We heard the story from the hero himself. A group of opposition politicians (including President Alessandri's son) had been exiled to Easter Island under the supervision of Señor Cumprido, who was appointed Governor of the island.

After a few months a schooner, which the exiles' friends had chartered to rescue them, put in at the island. Señor Cumprido had enough police to put up a resistance, but knowing the instability of political passions he speculated on the future and, not content with releasing his captives, he departed in their company. Señor Cumprido proved to have backed the right horse, and he had no cause to regret his decision.

In 1934, the year of our visit, Easter Island was undoubtedly the most unhappy of all the Pacific colonies. All the other Polynesians had adjusted themselves to modern life, and a kind of *status quo* has been established between them and their conquerors. Easter Island had been left to its own resources and received no other aid than that given by the Company's agents to its employees. In Chile the name of Easter Island merely revived sordid quarrels.

The Franco-Belgian Mission served to draw the Chilean Government's attention to the fate of the islanders. Some progress has been made in the course of the intervening twenty years. A missionary, Father Sebastian Englert, has made his home there and has used the leisure left to him by his ministry to collect texts of great interest to ethnography and folklore. A dispensary has been built at Hanga-roa, and one of the attendants named Pakomio gave us a good deal of useful information. A school has been opened by nuns and almost all the children are learning to read and write. The Chilean Government has conceded fresh tracts of land to the natives—a step rendered essential by the continual increase in the island's population. This rose from 456 in 1935 to 721 in 1947, and the increase is bound to go on, since forty-nine per cent of the natives, nine years ago, were under fifteen. Isolated and neglected as it is, Easter Island is none the less sharing in the great demographic upthrust that has developed during the present century in most of the Polynesian islands. Peoples that seemed on the point of dying out have reacted against their decline and begun to multiply again.

A medical report published in 1951 gives a favourable picture of the island's state of health. Tuberculosis is almost non-existent and, contrary to widespread belief, no veneral disease has been observed on the island. The only endemic disease is leprosy, said to have been introduced in 1889 by three natives repatriated from Tahiti. There are fifty-one lepers, and today—thanks to the efforts of the Society of Friends of Easter Island—they are housed in a leper settlement that is more comfortable than the filthy hovel to which they were confined at the time of our visit.

A native I met at Valparaiso told me that the young men were extremely keen to come to Chile to live and learn a trade. As they were forbidden by law to leave the island, a certain number stowed away on every vessel that called, in the hope of reaching the continent. Easter Island, then, is undergoing a process of modernization. The transformation is not to be regretted. It will destroy nothing that was not already in ruins, for Easter Island civilization died between 1862 and 1870. After this date the island asked nothing more of us but the fulfilment of a simple human duty: that the persons and dignity of the descendants of the Polynesians who carved the great statues and engraved the tablets should be respected by their new masters.

CHAPTER IV

How the Easter Islanders Live

*The problem of water—Domestic animals—Fishing—Cooking
—Dwellings—Dress and personal adornment*

EASTER ISLAND has too often been pictured in the grimmest light.
A bare island, a field of volcanic stones, an unproductive tract of
land incapable of supporting a population of any density—such
are the expressions most commonly used to describe it. By what
strange freak did a brilliant civilization manage to develop on this
supposedly barren rock? Is the transport of the greatest statues
conceivable without the trees required for the construction of skids
or rollers? On what did the 'armies of slaves' live who hauled these
statues over the fields of lava and along the volcanic crests?

If this picture of Easter Island as a barren rock conformed to the
facts there would be only two solutions to the mystery: either this
scrap of land is really the vestige of a vanished continent, as some
claim, or else the island's flora was destroyed and the cultural level
of its people drastically reduced by some cataclysm.

In reality, however, Easter Island's arid appearance is deceptive. Roggeveen considered it so fertile that he dubbed it an
'earthly paradise'. M. de La Pérouse's gardener was delighted
with the nature of the soil and declared that three days' work a year
would be enough to support the population.

This latter comment was entirely unwarranted, of course; but it
is none the less true that a modern botanist has spoken highly of the
richness of Easter Island's volcanic soil. Descriptions left by the
first visitors to the island often speak warmly of the natives' gardens. Their horticultural produce seemed to these voyagers not
only varied, but of excellent quality.

Then as now, the slopes of the volcanoes were green meadows;
along the shore one could see a succession of gardens and banana
plantations. Trees alone were lacking from this smiling landscape.
The inhabited areas were dotted with stunted shrubs, whose low,

twisted branches could not have been much use to the islanders. Roggeveen, González, Cook and La Pérouse were intrigued by this absence of large trees which, in their view, should have hampered the development of a culture whose savage grandeur they admired in other respects. When the first Polynesian colonists landed on the island they no doubt found there a kind of natural park, abounding in groves of *toro-miro* (*Sophora toromiro*). For centuries this dwarf shrub provided them with the wood from which they carved their famous statuettes and their ceremonial objects. It disappeared from the island during the second half of last century, destroyed by sheep and goats, with the exception of a single speciment that survived in an inaccessible spot—the interior of the Rano-kao volcano. During our stay the natives were jealously watching the growth of this tree, waiting for the right moment to cut it down and turn it into statuettes and other 'curios'.

Legend has it that the island's trees—the *hau* (*Triumfeta semitriloba*), the *marikuru* (*Sapindus saponaria*), the *makoi* (*Thespesia populnea*) and the sandalwood tree—were introduced by King Hotu-matu'a when he emigrated from his mysterious homeland of Marae-renga. There is nothing improbable about this tradition; for when the Polynesians migrated they provided themselves with the seeds or plants of useful trees, especially of the mulberry, whose bark supplied them with *tapa* cloth. Some of the species enumerated above, however, arrived before Man. They were carried to the island either by the wind, or by birds, or by other agents as yet unidentified that were instrumental in spreading the flora of the Pacific. There can be no doubt that Hotu-matu'a and his followers had on board coconuts and seedlings of the breadfruit tree; but when they planted them on Easter Island they must have suffered the bitter disappointment of seeing these two trees, whose fruits were a staple article of diet in their home country, perish in this colder climate. Today the only coconut palms growing in this Ultima Thule of Polynesia are two that were introduced recently and have become sterile.

The ancient Easter Islanders apparently preserved the memory of the coconut (*niu*) on which their ancestors had fed, for it figures among the fruits and plants whose origin is celebrated in a creation chant. The line in question runs: *Atua-metua ki ai kiroto kia Rirituna-*

rai. ka pu te niu ('Parent-God by copulating with Angry-Eel produced the coconut'). It would be unintelligible to anyone who did
not associate it with the old Polynesian myth that the coconut palm
issued from the head of an eel buried in the ground by a god. The
modern natives give the name *niu* to the seeds of the *makoi* (*Thespesia
populnea*), which do indeed look like small coconuts.

Little could be obtained from the shrubs growing on Easter
Island but statuettes, spears and adze hafts. Fortunately for the
natives, the ocean currents often brought them pieces of driftwood.
These were treasures of inestimable value, which they attributed to
the favour of some ancestor. A dying father frequently promised to
send his children a tree from the kingdom of shades.

The Easter climate, so unpropitious to coconut palms and
breadfruit trees, was more favourable to the taros, sweet potatoes,
yams, bananas, sugar-cane, *ti* (*Cordyline fruticosa*) and turmeric
(*Curcuma longa*) brought by the first colonists. These plants flourished and allowed the population to increase. Although each of
them is represented on Easter by only a single species, the islanders
distinguish a strikingly large number of varieties and forms which
they know by different names. This aimlessly minute classification
is based on insignificant details, such as a patch of colour on the
leaves, the peculiar colour of certain tubers or of the fruit, or some
anomaly in the growth. Such refinements of nomenclature are
proof of great familiarity with plants and indicate a long agricultural tradition. They are also an expression of that spirit of observation and analysis which so-called primitive people often bring to
their vision of nature.

About half a mile from the Te Peu *ahu*, the crust of the basalt is
cracked like a loaf of brown bread the baker has allowed to rise too
much. Beneath this lava skin gape immense cavities that are today
filled with luxuriant vegetation. A drop of a few yards is enough to
take one down from a blackened and rocky plain into a tangle of
verdure that emits an odour of rotting vegetation and sap reminiscent of a greenhouse. In these sunken gardens the natives, as in
days gone by, grow bananas and other plants that cannot with-
stand the cold blast of the sea winds.

Easter Island has been cultivated and inhabited across almost
the whole of its length and breadth, with the exception of the Poike

headland and a few areas in the interior.

Once it could easily have fed four or five thousand inhabitants, since the 720-odd natives that make up its present population are able to live in comfort in a district covering about six acres round the village of Hanga-roa.

The soil of Easter Island is, therefore, fertile; but in extolling its richness we tend to neglect the island farmer's labour. His task was a hard one. He had to clear his fields of stones, raise a little heap of earth for every potato or taro he planted, and hold back the invading weeds. His agricultural implements were rudimentary: his hoe consisted of a sharpened stake or, in default of this, a long, pointed stone. There being neither a stream nor a river, he had to keep the vegetable beds moist and prevent the sun from burning up the crops. To this end the fields were covered with a thin carpet of grass. Certain plants demanded special measures. Taros were made to 'suffer', as the Easter term has it, by being planted among stones, which protected their tubers from the sun and retained the moisture. These apparently unpromising sites helped the plants to grow larger and better. Furrows drawn across the slopes of the volcanoes temporarily held the rainwater.

Some plants, such as the paper mulberry, that were liable to be destroyed by the wind, were grown either in natural or artificial hollows of varying depths. In addition they were protected by low walls of unmortared stone. These enclosures are numerous near old dwellings. Vegetable waste accumulated through the ages has finally formed a thick layer of extremely fertile humus. Hence, the natives continue to use these enclosures for growing taros and the tubers of ti (*Cordyline fruticosa*), which thrive there with no effort on the part of the cultivator.

'Body full of water,' it is said, was a serious insult addressed, out of jealousy, to those who prided themselves on the fine appearance of their gardens. The implications of this expression are obscure, but the old-time Easter Islanders nevertheless considered it a grave taunt which they were ready to avenge in blood. The circumstances under which it was used bear witness to a feeling that is also manifested in other ways—love of the land. The frequent allusions in the old travellers' tales to the regular arrangement and meticulous tidiness of the fields, and the symmetry of the furrows, leave no doubt about this attachment to the soil. The banana plantations set out in quincunx (alternate rows of different spacing) seem to have been a particularly pleasant sight. Work in the fields was not monotonous drudgery. It provided an opportunity for joyful reunions of friends and relatives, who came to offer their assistance to the head of the family; and at the end of the day the latter regaled them with a copious meal taken piping hot from the underground ovens. The feast ended with songs and dancing. With the coming of the Whites, the Easter Islanders lost this element of joy harmoniously interwoven with the tasks imposed upon man by nature.

The future harvests were preserved from theft, and even from the impatience or greed of their owners, by a tabu pronounced by the king himself or by some priest of the royal line. Any violation of the interdict brought sudden death or a disease that rendered the transgressor an object of pity and horror. A little heap of stones or a few branches arranged in a certain manner warned passers-by of the danger.

When the time came for harvesting, the tabu was lifted by the same exalted personage who had imposed it, and the produce of the fields was restored to the profane world once the first-fruits had been offered to the gods.

Drinking water has always been a difficult problem for the natives. Easter Island has no river, and the little ravines that furrow the slopes of its hills are volcanic in origin: the rain quickly soaks into the porous soil and forms underground water tables that flow into the sea at beach level. Thin trickles of water may be seen oozing from the rocks at several points along the coast. Unfortunately, these rivulets emerge so close to the sea that their water is brackish. The ancestors of the modern natives sought to prevent salt water from mingling with the fresh by constructing walls that formed a kind of reservoir; salt water still seeped into the water that accumulated at the foot of the walls, however. The Easter Islanders disregarded the brackish nature of the water and quenched their thirst at these beach pools, to the great surprise of the first mariners, who imagined that, like the albatross, they were drinking brine. At low-lying spots along the coast the natives also dug stone-lined wells, which are now dry or partially filled with mud.

The largest reserves of fresh water are the lakes at the bottom of the craters; but they are difficult, and even dangerous, of access. Today as in the past the natives only draw water from them under the pressure of extreme necessity. There are a few springs of low output, but perfectly pure, a certain distance from the shore and even at two points inland. In days gone by, these springs were the centres of important hamlets (Puna-marengo and Via-tara-kai-ua, for example), as the numerous traces of houses and ovens (*umu*, see page 72) in their vicinity testify. Elsewhere, the natives had to be content either with slightly brackish water, or with water that collected in natural cavities or caught in calabashes or stone receptacles. Square holes cut artificially in the rocks were—if the natives of our own day are to be believed—little reservoirs that served in days gone by to catch rainwater.

Pigs, dogs and chickens are the three domestic animals the Polynesians took with them on their migrations. They did not always succeed in bringing them safely to land. The first settlers on Easter Island must have lost theirs at sea, for their descendants had no other domestic species than the chicken and were astonished and frightened by the dogs and pigs shown them by the eighteenth-century seafarers. Chickens constituted an important source of nourishment for a population whose diet was essentially vegetable in origin. They seem to have been a symbol of wealth and the outstanding instrument of exchange in the system of reciprocal obligations and ritual gifts that characterized ancient Easter Island society. The chickens were shut up by their owners every night in niches constructed in platforms of unmortared stones, where they were safe from theft. To get at them a thief would have to shift the stones, and the resulting noise would inevitably have raised the alarm. Last century, when the majority of the villages were abandoned, some chickens reverted to a wild state and settled at the bottom of the craters, which still echo with their cackling.

The rat is not a domestic animal, but, like the fowls, it was introduced into Easter Island by its first colonists, to whom it was a delicacy. The modern islanders still remember the taste for these rodents displayed by a few old people they knew in the past. They are rather ashamed of it, and the epithet 'rat-eaters', like that of 'cannibals', calls to mind the barbarous age from which they flatter themselves they have escaped. The black rats that invaded the island at the same time as Hotu-matu'a and his followers have now given way to the grey rats that arrived with the European vessels. This breed has overrun the island, where it wages war on the chickens and devours foodstuffs. The innumerable walls of unmortared stones provide them with nests, and they carry their effrontery to the point of showing themselves in broad daylight.

The waters round the island abound in fish, especially the waters round the rocks of Motu-nui which, for this reason, are frequented by thousands of sea birds. The present generation of natives take little advantage of this abundance, preferring their eternal diet of mutton to fish. We had very few opportunities of eating fish during our stay on the island, but it is true that it was winter, a season not considered good for fishing. In ancient times fish were the object of a tabu during all the months of the southern winter. Tunny fishing still enjoys some favour and is practised in the open sea during summer. It is the speciality of a few individuals who possess two boats in common. The rest of the population rely on their generosity or on reciprocal obligations that compel the fishermen to distribute their catch.

Although today fishing occupies only a secondary position in the island's economy, such was not the case in the past. This is proved by the number of stories and legends with fishermen as their heroes, the multitude of fish-hooks to be found in the caves, and the frequency with which representations of fish and other marine species occur among the petroglyphs collected by our mission. Important as fishing was for the Easter Islanders, it was never as vital to them as to the Tahitians or Marquesans. Easter Island is not, like many other Polynesian islands, encircled by a coral reef that attracts fish and makes them easier to catch. By limiting the number of canoes at their disposal, the lack of timber forcibly reduced the fishermen's scope. For the most part they confined themselves to catching fish from the top of the reefs or within a short distance of the coast. Large fish were caught with stone hooks, several of which came into our possession intact. In elegance of shape and perfection of polishing they are master-pieces of Neolithic art. The discovery of several unfinished speci-mens enabled us to reconstruct the different phases in their manufacture. A pebble was sought whose natural shape suggested the hook-to-be. It was then submitted to prolonged and meticulous polishing until it had attained its final outline. To hollow out the centre, a large hole was drilled and constantly enlarged, until nothing was left but the hook itself and the shank. The latter part of the operation was the most delicate, and it could happen that at this stage the stone broke, wasting weeks of effort. The number of broken fish-hooks we recovered near former villages proved that such accidents were not infrequent.

The big fish allowed themselves to be caught with stone hooks, but the small fry, and even the medium-sized species, would only bite more delicate fish-hooks.

According to legend, the first inhabitants of the island used none but stone hooks, with which they only caught tunny. The other fish swam round the bait without touching it. Catches were few and the fishermen could not understand their ill-fortune. A hero with visionary gifts, Ure, had a dream. His soul entered a hut at Tirako-ka, where it saw a bone hook hanging on a wall. The soul returned into the body it had temporarily left, and when Ure awoke in the morning he went in search of human bones, of which he made a fish-hook. During the day he joined the fishermen, who had been casting their stone hooks in vain since dawn. Ure's success was im-mediate. He drew in a fish at every cast; the other fishermen —surprised and jealous—tried to worm his secret out of him with questions. 'How do you do it?' they asked. 'What bait do you use?' Ure replied modestly: 'I fish just like you, with a hook of stone.'

In the end his companions, suspecting some trick, seized him and discovered his bone hook. Angered by his lies, they beat him severely and left him in his canoe bleeding profusely.

In this small Polynesian world, where the dead became gods and every outrage inflicted on their remains was inflicted on the whole group, this manner of using bones represented the most odious humiliation. The half-sawn fragments of femur or humerus that are found in the caves enable us to glimpse a background of bloody wars, vengeance and profanation. The fish-hook carved from an enemy's bone participated in his *mana*, that is, in his mystic power. The warrior who used it could imagine that his victim had become his slave and was helping him to obtain food, thus increasing his strength. The power emanating from the hook was supposed to attract the fish and create a supernatural association between the food and the dead man. For a cannibal Polynesian, no insult was greater than to refer to a man as being 'food'—this was to defile his *mana* and reduce him to the level of an animal: to eat a fish caught with a hook made of human bone was tantamount to eating the owner of the bone himself.

The tunny fishers used as bait little fish called *ature*, which they crushed between two stones. The pulverized flesh was attached to a stone that acted as a sinker. When the hook had reached the desired depth the fisherman released the bait and the stone with a jerk. Attracted by the flesh, the tunny swam around the hook and eventually took it. Sometimes the fisherman would use two hooks at the same time, a small one baited with crushed *ature* flesh and a larger one baited with a whole *ature*. One line was attached to his belt, the other to a transverse stick in the canoe by a knot that the fish undid when it tugged at the line. The fisherman let it swim out to sea before drawing it in.

There were also a wide variety of nets, from little spoon-nets to great draw-nets 100 to 130 feet long. Each type and size was used for catching a particular species of fish. The *ature* were caught in huge bag-nets into which they were lured by crustaceans attached to the opening.

Analysis of an ancient draw-net preserved in the Washington National Museum has shown that the meshes were made of fibres of the paper mulberry. This detail is important, for it tells us what the ropes used to haul the great statues were made of.

Net-fishing has lost much of its importance. The collaboration of a great number of individuals was required to manage the large draw-nets, and modern Easter Island society is broken into too many small units for the team spirit to have been preserved. This is one of the reasons why individual fishing has superseded the collective undertakings of the past. The modern islanders catch the crayfish that are common round the island, either during the day by diving along the reefs or at night by torchlight.

Women and girls made daily visits to the beaches and the foot of the cliffs to gather sea-urchins, crabs, shellfish and seaslugs. They also ventured out at night, when the fish were sleeping in the rock-pools, to catch them with pointed sticks. This shore fishing was the special prerogative of the women, and most of the adventures that befell women and are related in stories and legends happened to them when they left their houses to go out on the reefs.

Turtles have become rare, but they are depicted in several petroglyphs and frequently mentioned in legends. We discovered in a cave turtle-shell ornaments that confirmed what we had been told about them. When turtles were sighted offshore the islanders pursued them in their canoes; when they caught up with them they dived down behind them and drove them into a net with a strong mesh. The Easter Islanders prized turtles so highly that certain structures of unmortared stone—known as *tupa*—standing on the seashore are said to have been look-out towers on which watchmen were posted day and night. The rooms adjoining these towers are believed to have been the watchmen's dwellings.

Fig. 1. Easter Island canoe with outrigger: after an original sketch by Blondela, 1780. *Archives du Ministère de la Marine, Paris.*

The ancient Easter Islanders' boats were constructed on the same model as those of other Polynesians, but because of the scarcity of timber they were neither as large nor as strong. They were made of small planks 'sewn' together at the expense of much effort and much patience. Stability was provided by an outrigger of a type rare in Polynesia, but also found in the Marquesas. The float was attached to two slender booms fastened to the flat gunwale of the canoe. The prow and the poop, shaped like a duck's bill, rose above the water in the manner of the Eastern Polynesian craft (Fig. 1). These boats carried not more than two or three people. The paddles were of the most unusual type: they consisted of a heavy blade with a high median flange attached to a handle. At the time of Brother Eyraud's arrival in the island, the natives had not entirely forgotten the long canoes in which their ancestors crossed the sea. In 1860, their contacts with Europeans had re-awakened their enthusiasm for navigation; they wanted to be able to put out on the waves without fear of capsizing and without having constantly to bale out their little craft. They therefore insisted that their missionary should immediately build them a great bark. Eyraud offered as excuse the lack of timber. 'Timber!' cried the natives, 'we've got more timber than we need.' Making off in all directions, they came back and laid at the feet of the unwilling shipwright every piece of timber—straight, warped or rotten—they could lay their hands on. 'At the end of a fortnight,' writes Eyraud, 'the savages could see something resembling a boat made of a hundred pieces of wood. I had only one fear,' he adds: 'that I might be chosen to command this new and dangerous vessel.'

Recalling that the boats which had occasionally put in at the island were manned by crews wearing shirts and trousers, the islanders thought of dressing in uniforms. Eyraud had of course, to supply the costumes, and this provided a fresh opportunity of plundering him. Here is his own account of the launching of this national ship:

'The vessel was dragged roughly across the stones and quickly reached the water's edge. This was the crucial moment. Everyone wanted to lend a hand and contribute to the long-awaited operation. But alas . . . as the ship entered the sea, the sea entered the ship . . . Farewell pleasure trips, excursions and expeditions of all kinds . . . The national canoe had sunk.'

The five or six canoes which the natives of Hanga-roa possessed in the eighteenth century enabled them to reach certain areas of the sea that they identified with the aid of landmarks on shore. One of the latter was the stone statue of Pou-haka-nononga, which the 'Mercator' took with her at the end of our stay on the island and which now graces one of the rooms of the Musée Royal du Cin-quantenaire at Brussels. A magical link existed between this statue and the shoals of tunny to which it guided the fishermen; this led one of our informants to say that the statue was the 'divinity of the tunny fish'.

The shortage of wood raised the problem of fire. Investigators wondered where the natives obtained the fuel needed to cook their food. Like their modern descendants, the ancient Easter Islanders burnt brushwood, sugar-cane stems, the dried trunks of banana palms and dry potato leaves. Formerly they produced fire by the classic method of Oceania—by moving a stick to and fro along a groove in a piece of soft wood. After a minute or two, the shavings accumulated at the end of the groove began to smoke and then glow. All that was required then was to put some easily inflammable substance to it.

Food was cooked Polynesian fashion in an *umu*, that is to say, a pit with a fire at the bottom. Stones were heated in this pit and taken out as soon as they had reached a high temperature. The bottom of the pit was then lined with banana leaves on which the food was placed in layers one above the other and covered first with hot stones, then with leaves and finally with earth. A few hours later, the food was dug up. It was cooked to perfection without the slightest loss of juice. These ancient ovens, which are very numerous in the vicinity of archaeological sites, are lined with four or five slabs of stone that prevent the contents from coming into direct contact with the earth.

Contemporary Easter story-tellers delight in introducing into the legends of their island a detailed enumeration of the dishes that constituted a traditional ovenful. In addition to yams, taros and potatoes, these lists—which have become a positive *leitmotif* of folk-lore—mention chickens, eels, spiny lobsters and various species of fish. These were, of course, banquets or meals which a hero —following the custom of the islanders themselves—offered to someone who had promised his aid, both to show his gratitude and to bind his guest to him by the magic of the gift. The diet of the ancient Easter Islanders seems to have been very well balanced and not to have been lacking in any element essential to health.

True, it is difficult at this stage to determine the proportion of each foodstuff in the daily menu. Then as now, sweet potatoes were the staple food. Brother Eyraud complains in one of his letters of having to eat them all day long. An Easter Islander who wished to give me an idea of the monotony of life on his island once said to me: 'Here, we are born, we eat sweet potatoes, then more sweet potatoes, and then we die.' However, it must not be forgotten that peoples condemned to eat the same article of food all the time eventually develop a refinement of taste that enables them, for example, to prefer one variety of tuber to another, where our sur-feited palates can detect no difference.

The savour of food cooked in underground ovens has been too often extolled by voyagers, and even by tourists, to require fresh praise. Nevertheless, Easter cooking, like that of many Poly-nesians, is marked by the absence of salt. The natives absorb the salt intake necessary to the organism from the sea air they breathe and the seaweed they eat raw, not to mention the sea water they drink when swallowing the flesh of the molluscs which they pull off the rocks on the shore.

We owe to Father Zumbohm, one of the first missionaries on the island, a description of a banquet served according to ancient custom. He had been invited by one of the great chiefs of Hotu-iti, who, despite his hostility towards Christianity, did not want to lose face by a display less ostentatious than that put on by his rivals.

A few days before, the host had sent one party of his men fishing and others to the fields to fetch potatoes, bananas, sugar-canes and chickens. He had had a large oven dug, which was lit on the morning of the day the feast was to take place. Etiquette de-manded that the guests should take their places on stones round the oven; and they had to conform, in spite of their desire to rest in the shade. The host asked them if they were ready to begin, and when they replied in the affirmative he gave a sign to some ten men, who hurried to the trench, removed the earth and grass covering the food, and placed the best portions on mats at the feet of the guests of honour. Other choice morsels were brought to the chief and his friends. The European guests were astonished by the dexterity and despatch with which their hosts disposed of the chicken. They noticed with surprise that no one drank water, but that they refreshed themselves by sucking sugar-canes. The remainder of those present took no part in the banquet, but competed with one another in their zeal to serve the feasters. Only when their chief gave the word did they fling themselves on the remnants of the repast. The bestial appetite they displayed doubtless provided an amusing spectacle for the watching chiefs, and to please them the subjects exaggerated their voracity.

During the course of this feast, one of the chiefs present complained that he had not received the full respect due by etiquette to his rank, which had been under-estimated. His followers supported him, and the argument degenerated into a violent brawl. Calm was finally re-established and the incident resulted only in the loss of a few potatoes. The meal was followed by games and dances, watched by the guests softly cushioned on the grass in the shade of a rock.

Neither women nor children were admitted to this revelry. If any choice dish—such as fish or chicken—was served, nothing was left for them but the scraps.

Before the missionaries gathered the Easter Islanders together at Hanga-roa, there was no village properly so-called on the island. The natives lived in isolated huts or tiny hamlets. The ground-plan of the ancient huts is still traced in the earth by the line of stones that formed the foundations. These are wrought basalt curbs, all the same size, set on edge in an oval or ellipse. Sticks and stems of *ti* (*Cordyline fruticosa*) inserted in holes in the upper edge of these curb-stones constituted both the uprights and the rafters. They were fastened to a thin ridge-pole and as each one crossed the corresponding upright on the opposite side they formed a series of arches, decreasing in height from the centre towards the two ends. This fragile frame was covered with mats and bundles of reeds carefully overlapped. These dwellings bore a certain resemblance to an overturned boat with an upward pointing keel. In front of the door, which opened in one of the long sides, lay a few slabs of stone supporting a small porch or vestibule. Statues of wood or stone sometimes flanked the threshold. The porch was so low that it could only be entered on all fours. The furniture consisted solely of reed mats, stone pillows and calabashes containing all the family treasures. These huts were generally empty during the day, but everybody crowded in at night to sleep. The atmosphere quickly became stifling and sleep was constantly interrupted by children crying and the coming and going of the occupants.

As the inhabitants liked to spend their leisure in front of their huts, the entrance and the immediate precincts were often paved with large rounded pebbles and occasionally decorated with small pieces of coral.

On the average, the huts were thirty to fifty feet long and five to seven feet across, but some were much larger. The hut visited and described by La Pérouse's expedition was more than 300 feet long by thirty feet wide, and housed two hundred people. We discovered the foundations of a dwelling whose major axis measured about 120 feet.

The fragility and rusticity of these habitations seemed to us out of keeping with the imposing masses of the mausoleums and statues. The natives could have made up for the lack of wood by using stone, as was done at Orongo. This contrast is due to ideas of comfort that differ from ours, and also to traditional habits going back to the time when the Easter Islanders' ancestors lived on islands with a richer flora. Unimpressive as they may appear, these huts none the less bear witness to an ingenious adaptation to the scanty resources of the environment.

Simple shelters erected beside the ovens did duty as kitchens.

Are the underground chambers that occur at various points on the island close to the mausoleums to be regarded as permanent habitations? Their original purpose is unknown to the modern natives, who describe them as places of refuge in which women and children shut themselves up in time of war. This interpretation must be treated with reserve, to say the least of it: how could these cellars with unconcealed entrances have afforded safe hiding-places? The underground chamber behind the Vaimata *ahu* is the best preserved and finest in the island. Its location is marked by a paved undulation of the ground, beside which opens a long tunnel—lined with well-polished stone slabs, but extremely narrow—leading into a fair-sized chamber formed by a natural cavity extended by walls of very carefully finished masonry. La Pérouse describes a chamber of the same type that he visited near the Hanga-roa *ahu*. M. Bernizet, who entered this vault, tells us that the natives used it to store their provisions, their tools, their wood and, in fact, everything they possessed.

The fact that many of the island's numerous grottoes have been converted into temporary or permanent habitations is evidenced by the platforms constructed in their sides to serve as beds. Some of these caverns are most impressive. The cave at Punamarengo, the strangest of all, is one of the local curiosities. It opens in a mass of reddish scoriae and communicates by various passages with several subterranean chambers. The halls of this natural palace contained skeletons, and as if the atmosphere were not already sufficiently haunted, the air forced through the porosities by the waves fills the chambers with eerie groans.

A few Easter Islanders live like cave-dwellers in crevices between the rocks or beneath overhanging ledges, which they turn into narrow cells. Statues that have fallen on the inclined surfaces of the mausoleums have become the roofs of shelters that have been inhabited for varying periods.

The men used to wear nothing but a wide belt of beaten bark, one end of which was passed between the legs and hung down over the abdomen. To keep off the cold, or merely for the sake of elegance, they cast about their shoulders a rectangular cape stained with turmeric. The women wore a similar belt and sometimes a short skirt. They also liked to wrap themselves in a bark cloak.

The hair of both men and women fell loose to their shoulders or was knotted in a tuft on top of their heads. In a love song a woman's top-knot is compared to the fin of a fish:

> *Young girl, you are dying of love.*
> *You are a crab living under Akurenga mausoleum,*
> *You are a fish with a top-knot.*
> *You make for the shore,*
> *Little fish, O my friend!*
> *Down there is seaweed*
> *That is good to feed you.*

There was little scope for personal vanity in clothes or hair-style;

this found expression in the tattooing that made some men's bodies real works of art. Loti and other travellers made drawings of the patterns which the Easter Islanders tattooed on their persons. In the variety and intricacy of its motifs and their unexpected and ingenious arrangement, Easter Island tattooing falls little short artistically of that produced by the Marquesans and Maoris—the peoples who have carried this art to the highest degree of perfection.

Easter tattooing is characterized by the important rôle of areas of geometric form spread over the face and other parts of the body. Another of its peculiarities is the frequent use of naturalistic motifs, representing birds, plants and implements. The native whose tattooing was copied down by Stolpe bore on his arm a picture of the Orongo statue being carried off by the sailors of the 'Topaze'. Close perpendicular lines tattooed on the thighs and lower legs gave many natives the appearance of wearing stockings or breeches.

These works of art were produced by experts who supplied their services to those who could afford to pay for them. An individual's rank and affluence were often indicated by the extent and beauty of the patterns covering his body. The operation was slow and carried out at intervals of several years. For tattooing to be perfect when the subject reached adulthood, it had to be started early —generally at the age of eight. The tattooist's instrument was a little bone rake, which he tapped with a mallet to drive it into the epidermis. The pigment was charcoal made from *ti* stems mixed with *poporo* (*Solanum nigrum*) juice. These sessions were painful, and some children—such as Viriamo, whose tattooing remained unfinished—were unable to endure them. The chief source of our knowledge of Easter Island tattooing are two *tapa* images now in the Peabody Museum, Harvard. They are covered with painted drawings which reproduce with great care the most common tattoo patterns (Fig. 2).

The effects of tattooing were enhanced by painting the body with red, white and grey earths, and especially with powder extracted from the turmeric. The popularity of this latter root was due not only to the orange pigment obtained from it, but also to its perfume. The scent it emits is regarded by Polynesians as particularly

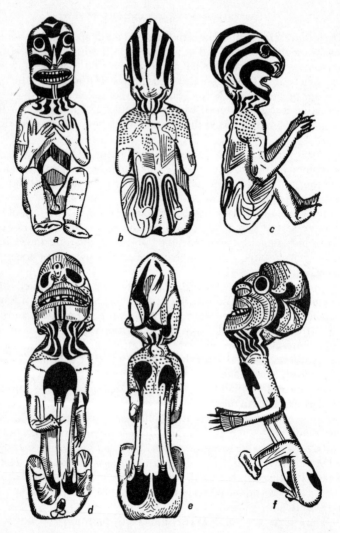

Fig. 2. Images made of bulrushes covered with tapa cloth painted so as to show patterns of body painting and tattooing. *Peabody Museum, Cambridge, Mass. 53543.*

delectable, but Europeans are insensible to it. In olden times the
perfumed emanations of the Rano-raraku turmeric attracted two
spirit-women who were living *i te hiva*, in a foreign land, and who
flew to Easter Island to see these marvellous plants. The myth adds
that it was they who taught the islanders' ancestors the delicate
method by which the famous *pua* powder is prepared.

Red and black were the favourite colours of the men. They
smeared their faces with alternate stripes in these two colours.
Men blackened from head to foot made a tremendous impression
on the first Europeans who saw them, as may be gathered from
Beechey's account.

Easter Island might have been called the 'Land of the Long-
Eared Men'. The natives described by the first voyagers had the
lobes of their ears widely perforated to make room for the insertion
of a heavy ornament made of shark's vertebrae or wood. This practice was abandoned at the period when native culture vanished,
and the last old people with deformed ears died at the beginning of
the present century.

The finest ornaments were cock-feather diadems of various
shapes and colours, and especially reed helmets covered with feather mosaic. The women wore strange wicker-work hats, wide and
rounded at the sides and with turned-up points at the back and
front.

The old Easter Islanders had a passion for headgear and to satisfy it they risked the retaliation of the Europeans whose caps they
stole. This taste sometimes had comical results. Eyraud relates in
one of his letters that there was no object of which they would not
make a hat. A calabash, half a melon, the carcass of a bird
—anything would do. One native even proudly set on his head two
buckets one inside the other. The most amusing case, however, was
that of a man who, having found a shoe, shod his head. These sar-
torial extravagances came to an end after the period of assimi-
lation.

The portrait of an old Easter Islander in gala dress is incomplete
until the wooden ornaments with which he decorated himself have
been enumerated. If he was rich and noble he hung on his chest a
large crescent (*rei-miro*), whose carved horns represented bearded
men or cocks. Others attached to their shoulders *tahonga*, a sort of

wooden 'heart', which some writers have interpreted as stylized coconuts. These objects for indicating wealth have never been seen displayed by a modern traveller. We know them from the accounts of the living natives and the specimens that have found their way into our museums.

Tepano took delight in enumerating these wooden treasures. They are the subject of the same legends as are current regarding the tablets. During our stay, more than one islander, inspired by a dream, set out to look for caves full of *rei-miro, tahonga* and statuettes, for dreams of wealth are still nourished by the memory of these wooden adornments.

We have accompanied the ancient Easter Islander into the fields and out to the sea; we have studied his dwelling and his costume. It remains for us to get to know him in his creative activities.

The raw materials at his disposal were limited in number on an island that was not rich in anything except volcanic rock. The settlers to whom this meagre heritage fell must have known days of worry and discouragement, when they found themselves deprived of the majority of the plants upon which their basic crafts depended. The poverty of the environment created problems which they had to solve, if they were not to impoverish their traditional culture and deprive themselves of its most essential benefits.

The following are a few of the difficulties by which they were confronted. In the islands of Central or Eastern Polynesia, from which they came, the ancestors of the ancient Easter Islanders had woven their baskets and mats from the leaves of the pandanus or coconut palm. On Easter Island they lacked not only these resources, but any natural substitutes. They got out of the difficulty with great ingenuity: bags and baskets were made from banana leaves cut in strips and interwoven according to their basket-making technique. These strands were not always suitable for the manufacture of the large mats which served them as beds and which they needed to cover their huts. They had recourse to the reeds that grew at the bottom of the craters, but being unable to plait them they sewed them together with thread.

The colonists succeeded in getting the paper mulberry (*Brousson-etia papyrifera*) to grow on the island, and so were able to go on making their cloth from its bark. They preferred that of the young stems, which they soaked in water after scraping its gnarled surface with an obsidian knife. The strips of bark were then beaten with a wooden mallet on big polished stones. Unlike the other Polynesians, who joined the different pieces simply by beating them, the Easter Islanders sewed them together with bone needles. In this way they produced cloths that were relatively thick and durable.

Nature favoured the Easter Islanders in one sphere only: it provided an abundant supply of obsidian. Thanks to this volcanic glass, the natives were able to manufacture extremely effective knives, awls and weapons with a minimum of effort. The *mataa* or javelin heads, which are to be found in hundreds above ground, have the characteristic ace-of-spades shape with sharp, rounded edges. The unfinished or broken specimens that abound in the vicinity of the Mount Orito quarry show the various stages in their manufacture: a large flake of obsidian was detached from a slab of the rough stone. The final shape was imparted by retouching with a bone instrument, by means of which smaller flakes were split off by skilfully directed pressure (Fig. 3, page 101).

The value attached by the Easter Islanders to the smallest scrap of wood is reflected in their folklore and in certain incidents observed by the first mariners. The swimmers who ventured aboard Admiral Dupetit-Thouars's 'Vénus' shouted loudly for planks; fearing they might not be understood, they employed an extraordinary dumb show, disdaining all other presents and even refusing the food and drink offered them.

When our informant Tepano had nothing to do, he would fetch his adze and start hacking a piece of wood that developed into some monster, or simply a human figure with protruding ribs. His tools, although he claimed to have inherited them from a famous sculptor, were of good polished steel. He refused to believe that his ancestors could have carved wood with stone adzes, although he had picked up large numbers of them. The Easter Islanders of today are perfectly willing to believe that the great tufa statues were produced with the aid of stone axes and mallets, but the operation seems to them impossible in the case of the wooden images. The products of the modern natives show the effects of using iron

tools and have neither the finish nor the polish of the images labori-
ously cut out of a *toromiro* trunk with a basalt adze.

We often watched these wooden images—the last survivals of
Easter Island art—come into being before our eyes. The sculptor's
first act is to check the cutting edge of his adze; then, with regular
blows, he whittles away the wood until he has removed the superfluous parts and obtained the rough shape he requires. Reducing the force of his blows, the artist now works with quick, precise
touches until his creation has acquired its final form. Lastly, the
statue is given eyes: a ring of bone for the cornea and a tetrahedron
of obsidian for the pupil. The last stage consists in polishing the
carving and getting rid of the little facets with which it is covered.

In olden days, the carving of an image was an absorbing and
pleasant occupation that was intentionally prolonged. There was
no fear of not having enough statues to sell if a ship should put in.
The image the artist was fashioning was destined to become the
tabernacle of a spirit or an ornament he would wear round his neck
during festivals. This purpose does not, however, explain either the
sculptor's patience or his meticulous workmanship, which spring
from a deeper emotion—the joy of creating a perfect work of art.

The same desire for perfection characterizes the products of
stone-masonry. A stone hammer without a handle is a clumsy tool
with which to turn a block of basalt into a polished slab that will
exactly fit against its neighbour. Teams of obscure workmen
devoted long days, perhaps months, to this unrewarding task. The
results were those few gems of primitive architecture which, like
the Vinapau *ahu*, present a surface as smooth as a marble slab.

The arts and crafts reviewed above almost all belong to a bygone
age. They have not entirely disappeared, for they have left behind a
certain tradition of craftsmanship which the islanders have
adapted to different techniques. A relic of the respect that formerly
surrounded the wood-carver may be seen in the current predilec-
tion for joinery, which involves the same precious material.

CHAPTER V

A Cannibal Society

*The two confederations—The social hierarchy—The king—The priests
—The craftsmen—The warriors—Commoners and slaves—Social relations—War and cannibalism*

IF ANY inhabitant of Hanga-roa village is asked the name of his
tribe, he will unhesitatingly reply Marama, Tupa-hotu, Nga-ure
or Miru, as the case may be, even if his father is British or Chilean.
If pressed, he will give the tribal affiliation of his mother and even of
his grandparents, and will point out the approximate boundaries
of the ancestral territory. Thirty years ago, some old people were
still able to name the sub-tribes of each district with their respec-
tive sanctuaries.

This, unfortunately, is the limit of our knowledge of Easter
Island's social organization as it was less than a century ago.

The significance of the hierarchy, the ties of family and tribe,
were broken first by the chaos that followed the sudden disappearance of part of the population in 1863, and then by the epidemics that decimated the remaining inhabitants of the island.
The concentration of the survivors in the village of Hanga-roa,
after their conversion to Christianity, destroyed the last vestiges of
the social order. Tribal patriotism alone was strong enough to live
on, in an attenuated form, in the memory of the present generation.

A list of names, geographical frontiers, and vague allusions in
legends do not provide much of a foundation on which to reconstruct a political and social system of some complexity, but they
sufficiently indicate the general outline.

At the beginning of the nineteenth century the population of
Easter Island was divided into ten 'tribes' or *mata*, whose members
considered themselves descendants of eponymous or name-giving
ancestors, who, in their turn, were held to be the offspring of the
first king, Hotu-matu'a.

Legendary history has it that on his deathbed Hotu-matu'a

divided the island among his sons. The eldest, Tu'u-maheke, inherited the title of *ariki-mau* (king) and received the stretch of coast between Anakena and Mount Teatea; Miru had the lands between Anakena and Hanga-roa; Marama, the seaboard south of Akahanga to Vinapu; Koro-orongo, the lava fields round Mount Ranoraraku; Hotu-iti became master of the whole eastern section of the island; finally, Raa had to be content with the territories to the north and east of Mount Teatea. The Hau-moana do not figure in this distribution, which assigned to each tribe its hereditary district, but the king-lists contain a ruler of this name who seems to have been the name-giver of this tribe.

A few new tribes formed at various times by breaking away from another tribe, of which they were only a sub-division. By splitting up, a family could give birth to a sub-tribe or lineage which sooner or later claimed its independence. An example of this process of segmentation is to be found in the myth of the origin of the Raa and the Hamea, who lived in the territory of the Miru.

In the course of one of their wars with the Tupa-hotu, the tribe of the Miru was cut to pieces and suffered great losses. Two young men, Taka and Parapuna, succeeded in escaping from the carnage along with Taka's wife, who was pregnant. When she was about to be delivered they took her to a cousin who lived in enemy territory. When his wife was recovered, Taka gave her to Parapuna so that he, in his turn, could beget a child. The woman passed from one brother to the other every year, until each of them had had by her a large number of sons and daughters who became respectively the ancestors of the Raa and the Hamea. For this reason these two tribes consider themselves closely related to one another and to the Miru, from whom their ancestors issued.

The Tupa-hotu, the Ureohei and the Koro-orongo had no territory of their own, but were scattered at random over the region called Hotu-iti, in the east of the island. This geographical name is also that of Hotu-matu'a's youngest son, which suggests that he may have been the eponym of a tribe that later split up and formed three new tribes. This hypothesis would explain the use of the collective term Hotu-iti for these three tribes, and their close association in one and the same district.

The political geography of the island was complicated by the fact that, by the time the historical period opened, the members of a tribe no longer lived exclusively in their ancestral territory. For example, many Miru families were living in the Marama district. This interpenetration of the tribe by another, surprising as it may appear, is explained by intermarriage and the system of adoption, which enabled children to retain their rights to the lands of their true father or to inherit from their mother. Those seeking refuge with neighbours after a defeat in battle were entitled to settle amongst the latter while still preserving their affiliation to their own tribe. Easter Island was too tiny a world for groups to remain isolated in watertight compartments, in spite of mutual hates and hostilities.

Tribal territory was divided among the descendants of the various ancestors grouped together to form *mata-iti*, that is, sub-tribes or lineages corresponding to the *hapu* of the Maoris. The lands belonging to the *mata-iti* were narrow strips stretching back from the coast towards the centre of the island. The areas nearest the sea were the most densely populated and also the most important from an economic point of view. The closer it lay to the middle of the island the lower was the value of the land and the less heed was paid to the boundaries of each property. The *uta*, that is, the centre of the island, was left to the vanquished, who—dispossessed of their lands—eked out a miserable existence far from the ocean and its treasures. It was also the realm of spirits.

The link between the lineage and its territory was symbolized by an *ahu* that stood near the shore and was both the group's cemetery and its common sanctuary. These ruined mausoleums that succeed one another all the way round the island are the last tangible expression of the territorial rights exercised by the ancient sub-tribes, now no more. The great mausoleum of Anakena belonged to the Honga sub-tribe, which gave the island its kings.

In the old days the natives tended to live communally in large huts. Even today, although the modern houses are of modest dimensions, it is quite common to find them occupied not only by the owner and his family, but also by his brothers and cousins. This cohesion reveals a type of family organisation known as the extended family (*ivi*). It might be composed of several brothers living together with their wives and children, or of various families belonging to different generations but grouped round the grand-father or great-grandfather. It was doubtless this personage, the chief and representative of this social unit, who was honoured with the title *tangata-honui* (respectable man, man of importance).

The rôle of the extended family in the overall social structure is unknown to us. By analogy with the rest of Polynesia, we may sup-pose that it possessed lands in common and that its members co-operated in agriculture and fishing. War united them in a single bloc. Legends have transmitted to us an echo of this family solid-arity. In accounts of battles we always see brothers acting in con-cert or going to one another's aid.

Above the tribes, the lineages and the extended families that formed the skeleton of society there existed a broader organization, political in origin. The ten tribes or *mata* were split into two groups that were probably nothing more or less than two hostile confed-erations. The tribes of the west and north-west were generally re-ferred to as the people of Tu'u, the name of a volcanic cone near Hanga-roa. They were also known, for obscure reasons, as the 'great tribes' (*mata-nui*). The tribes of the east or 'little tribes' appear in historical legends as the 'people of Hotu-iti'.

This dualism was probably the expression and consequence of a constant state of war between the tribes occupying the two ex-tremities of the island. Legends frequently allude to the hatred and wars between the Tu'u and the Hotu-iti, whose struggles con-tinued, with varying fortunes, for many generations. The victors unified the island until the moment when the vanquished felt strong enough to renew the conflict. This secular antagonism eventually manifested itself in the religious sphere. The sacred places common to all the tribes were divided into two sections, cor-responding to the island's two factions. The rock of Motu-nui, for example, was divided in two by a statue that served as a boundary mark. In the course of the national festival of the bird-man, the chanters of the east refused to intone their sacred chants in concert with those from the west.

The sense of hierarchy, as manifested in the past, is completely dead. A century ago, however, this society was as rigorously stratified as that of New Zealand and the Society Islands. At the top of the ladder was the *ariki-mau*, or great chief, whom we have referred to as the king of the island. Below him, it is said, came the priests (*ivi-atua*) and the *ariki-paka* or nobles. The latter title is still given to all members of the Miru tribe, without distinction. It seems strange that all the individuals belonging to such a large tribe should have been honoured with the title of 'chief', when there is no question of an *ariki* in any other tribe. This is an anomaly contrary to Polynesian traditions. To resolve this contradiction, I often tried to explain to our informants that, in my opinion, all the Miru could not have been nobles; but this supposition was always indignantly rejected. 'All the Miru were *ariki-paka*, and they were the only *ariki-paka* there were.' In one sense, being of the king's tribe and descendants of Hotu-matu'a, the Miru had a claim to the title of nobility; but how is the absence of *ariki* in the other tribes to be interpreted? The only parallel to such a system in the whole of Polynesia is afforded by the *Nga-ariki* of Mangaia: all the priests of this island had to belong to this tribe. In any event, the position of the nobles in Easter Island society is far from clear. According to the evidence of one missionary, they occupied a secondary place in the social order to the priests, but the latter were no doubt recruited from their class.

The *matato'a* or warriors came fourth in the social scale. At the very bottom of the ladder we find the *kio*. This word, which may be translated, according to the context, as 'vanquished enemy', or 'servant', or 'farmer', was applied to individuals in subordinate positions. The craftsmen, technicians or experts, who belonged to a guild, held a distinguished rank; but in the present state of our knowledge we cannot place it exactly in the social hierarchy.

This gradation of social classes is misleading when we are considering political power. The *matato'a*, who were not nobles, were not on the same social plane as the king or the *ariki*, but they were none the less the wielders of authority. In the following pages I shall try to outline the precise functions and prerogatives of each of these classes.

One day, when we were examining a petroglyph representing turtles, in the company of Tepano, we asked him whether these creatures were still hunted as in days gone by. He replied in a voice tinged with melancholy: 'The turtles stopped coming here after the kings died.' Then he added: 'Many other things vanished with the kings. There used to be a variety of yam that was bigger and more succulent than the yams of today. It too died out with the lineage of the kings. The sandalwood tree, of which King Hotu-matu'a brought a shoot in his boat and which flourished on the island, no longer grows here. The kings are gone, and the sandalwood is gone.'

These reflections on the part of our informant made us think of the last *ariki-mau*, little Gregorio, who died of tuberculosis at the Catholic Mission around 1867. Easter Island's decline was, in a way, symbolized by the rapid decline of this frail descendant of the gods. The only function left to surviving royalty in the charnel-house which the island had become, lay in the mystic link uniting the *ariki-mau* to the fertilizing forces of nature. After the harvest the natives still came in procession to pay tribute of the first fruits to the heir of Hotu-matu'a. The bearers of the yams headed the procession, followed by two files of young men carrying standards made of *hau* branches, peeled and stained black. They advanced to the sound of hymns mingled with exclamations of respect.

It is in this last tribute offered to the little king, as in the association with the plants and turtles, that the essence of royalty is best expressed. As in the Marquesas and Tonga, the king was a sacred being whose magic power influenced nature and assured his people a regular supply of food.

This power over the vegetable and animal kingdoms was the outcome of the king's mystic force, his *mana*, which had been transmitted to him by his divine ancestors. (It is probable that the Easter Island *ariki*, like many Polynesian chiefs, were held to be descendants from the gods Tangaroa and Rongo. This, at any rate, is the most likely interpretation of the occurrence of these two names among the first kings of the island.)

This power is celebrated in lyrical terms in a hymn collected on Easter Island in 1886. The transcription was full of errors and arbitrary omissions, while the translation was not merely free but fanciful. I was able partially to reconstruct the original version, thanks to the combined efforts of my native informants and experts in Polynesian languages.

What does the king make fertile in the country?
Mars comes up, appears in the sky. The king makes the shoots
*   of the white sweet-potatoes grow in the country.*
He makes the sweet-potatoes favourable, the sky favourable,
*   the ancestors favourable.*

What does the king make fertile in the country?
The crayfish, the po'opo'o fish, the conger eels, the nohu
*   fish, the moss, the ferns and the kavakava-atua plants.*

What does the king make fertile in the country?
The mosses, the ferns, the kavakava-atua plants, the king
*   makes grow in the country.*
He makes the mosses favourable, he makes the ferns
*   favourable, he makes the roots of the kavakava-atua*
*   favourable.*

What does the king make fertile in the country?
He introduces the tunny fish, the atu fish, and the ature fish.
He makes the tunny fish favourable, he makes the atu
*   favourable, he makes the ature favourable too.*

What does the king make fertile in the country?
The turtle, its abdominal shell, its legs—these he makes
*   grow in the country.*
He makes the turtle, its abdominal shell and its legs favourable.

What does the king make fertile in the country?
The stars, the sky, the heat, the sun, the moon, the king
*   increases their strength.*
He makes the sky, the heat, the sun, and the moon favourable.

What does the king make fertile in the country?
He sends the dew, the heat, the sun, and the moon.

What does the king make fertile in the country?
Worms, earwigs, beetles, the king makes fertile in the country.
He makes the worms, the earwigs, the beetles favourable,
  he makes them grow in the country.

This power over nature was concentrated in the eldest son; but sometimes it developed such intensity that it risked becoming the source of numberless evils. The legend of the little prince Rokoro-kohetau, son of the third wife of King Nga'ara, affords a famous example of this. The case is particularly curious because this king's son had, by birth, no right to royal dignity. His entry into the world was accompanied by wonders such as generally announced the birth of a great chief. Many people were devoured by sharks, and sea beasts appeared on the shore and attacked those who ventured there. Finally, white fowl—hitherto unknown—began to multiply. These miraculous events were manifestations of Rokorokoheatu's *mana.* In the hope of averting these disasters and saving his people, the reigning king had his son taken away and shut up in a cave on Mount Rano-aroi. In vain—because his subjects, convinced of the sanctity of the little chief 'with the diadem of white feathers', refused to carry before the legitimate heir the standards symbolic of royalty. In the end Nga'ara had his son, whose mystic power had such baleful effects, put to death.

Another legend, unfortunately obscure and incomplete, deals with the dangerous manifestations of royal *mana.*

Tangaroa [does this refer to the god of this name or to a king?] was walking along the southern shore with his brother when he found a hen and copulated with it. He killed it, plucked it, and put it in a basin. An old woman passed by this place and heard a child crying from inside the stomach of the hen in the basin. She took the child to her home, cared for him, and named him Tu-ki-haka-he-vari [Curled-up-as-a-chicken-in-an-egg]. He grew up and stayed with her at Hakarava. One day he asked the old woman, 'Where is my father?' She replied, 'There, where there is a dark cloud.' Then the boy called to the people, 'Make a litter to carry me to Tu'u.' Many men came in relays to carry him, but those who touched his litter fell dead 'because of his *mana*'. Near a place called Pare, the king caught sight of two very ugly girls. He called out to them, 'Go back, O you ugly women. You are throwing dust in the eyes of King Tu-ki-haka-he-vari.' [With this ambiguous sentence the legend ends.]

The king carried in a litter, contact with which kills the common people, is a typical sacred chief of Polynesia, the Easter Island equivalent of the Tahitian *arii*, who travelled on a man's back so as not to communicate their *mana* to their subjects' land.

The *ariki-mau* was isolated from his subjects by numerous tabus which, on the one hand, stressed his divinity and, on the other, protected mortals from contagion by his *mana*. His head was the most sacred part of his person, that which was surrounded by the strictest tabus. It may have been enough for him to call an object 'my head' to render it untouchable. He wore his hair long, for no hand was holy enough to cut it. When the missionaries wanted, for reasons of hygiene, to shave the head of the young king whom they had taken under their protection, the child rebelled and only yielded to threats. His hair was cut by a Mangarevan catechist, but popular indignation was so intense that the sacrilegious foreigner was very nearly stoned.

Although many activities were forbidden them, these sacred leaders could indulge in the pleasures of fishing and were permitted to make their own tackle. They might be seen sitting in front of their huts rolling on their thighs the mulberry-bark fibre, with which they made fishing lines, or weaving nets with the aid of a shuttle. But woe betide anyone who touched the objects that shared their *mana*.

The king lived alone in his hut, which he did not share even with his wife, who occupied another hut next door. Two sorts of servant, belonging to the Miru tribe, ministered to his needs. The *tu'ura* cultivated the fields of the royal domain and accompanied him when he went fishing. The *haka-papa* prepared his meals and served him at table. When these servants left the king's presence, they walked backwards. Those who wished to communicate with the king entrusted their messages to them.

Only the intricacy and extent of his tattooing distinguished the king from other Easter Islanders. No doubt he also wore a longer and better-painted cloak than his subjects and especially fine ornaments of wood and shell.

When Easter Island had appeared in a dream to Hotu-matu'a in the country of Marae-tenga, he sent six young men to reconnoitre and take possession of it. As they were leaving, he requested them to look for a sandy beach, on which he would establish his residence. These scouts paddled all round the island, putting in at all the coves; but they were not satisfied with any of them until they came to Anakena, which alone seemed to them worthy of the king. Here Hotu-matu'a landed and here his first son, Tu'u-ma-heke, was born. Anakena is still closely associated with memories of the ancient *ariki*. Every time our excavations brought to light a skull, the workmen remarked, 'There's the head of another *ariki*'.

Anakena cove is the pleasantest spot on the island, the place most deeply impregnated with the melancholy charm peculiar to certain Polynesian landscapes. The sea here is transparent and slightly green. The sand, formed of pulverized shells, crackles beneath the feet, and on all sides rise volcanic eminences, gently rounded heaps of reddish scoria. To the rear of the beach stand rows of royal mausoleums, lined up like so many bastions to defend its peace. Some are barely visible in the midst of lapilli, others are half buried by sand. The wind uncovers statues and whited bones, only to inter them afresh as the whim takes it.

It was in this privileged cove, where one can swim at leisure without fear of the waves and reefs, that the Honga lineage resided, whose chief was the *ariki-mau*. Avenues bordered with sticks bearing garlands of feathers led to it, but only the king and the queen or queens and their servants were entitled to go on the beach. It was a tabu zone, and those who ventured into it were put to death. One of the present natives of the island had been told by an old man that in his youth the king's son had invited him to come and play with him on the beach. Some men who had seen him threw themselves upon him to kill him, but he managed to run away. The king's son ordered the guards not to pursue him.

A rather vague tradition has it that the king's eldest son was brought up in a village adjoining the Papa-o-pea *ahu*, which is in a good state of preservation. After becoming king, the young chief resided at Ahu-akapu, near Tahai, on the west coast. It was only when he had relinquished his title in favour of his eldest son that the king returned to Anakena to end his days.

In conformity with a custom frequent in Polynesia, the king lost his rank on the birth of his eldest son. The *mana* that had been in him passed into the little being, who became in his turn the intermediary between the tribe and the gods. In point of fact, the king retained his power in his capacity of regent until his heir was old enough to fulfil his functions. This date was determined by his marriage; after which the old king sank into oblivion.

Our knowledge of the king's powers and duties is very incomplete, but one of his functions was to impose and remove tabus. No house could be occupied before the *ariki-mau* or an *ariki* representing him had entered, no doubt to perform some propitiatory rites within. The same applied to boats, which had to be 'inspected' by the king before being launched on the sea.

During the winter months sea-fishing lay under an interdict. At this period only the king and his family could eat fish without being poisoned. They were kept in isolation, because their flatulence was a danger to their entourage.

The tunny caught by the fishermen on the first sea trip at the beginning of summer were brought to the king, who ate them in the company of his family. The delivery of the first catch, and this meal, lifted the tabu on fish and rendered them *noa*, that is, profane. Thereafter, they could be eaten by everyone. In time of drought, prayers for rain were addressed to Hiro under the king's auspices.

Tradition also shows him to us making tours of the island to inspect the schools for priests and listen to recitations of the sacred chants associated with various economic and social activities.

All these functions are religious in character and make it plain that the king was head of the college of priests, but we do not know whether he was compelled to learn the genealogies and chants that constituted the science of the priesthood.

The political authority of the *ariki-mau* is not clear. On this point we are reduced to conjecture. Although he was the civil leader of the Miru, he was not regarded by the other tribes as more than an extremely sacred personage. The respect in which he was held did not spare him the fate of a captive when the Miru were defeated by their rivals.

During the first half of the nineteenth century King Nga'ara was a prisoner of the Hotu-iti for several years and forced to live in the district of the Nga-ure.

Political power seems to have fallen into the hands of the *matato'a*, who formed an aristocracy of happy warriors. Royalty would doubtless have disappeared if the king had not been invested with the *mana* necessary for the continuance of natural processes and the prosperity of the island.

It is as though an obscure presentment of things to come united the destiny of this society to that of its kings. When little Gregorio died, the old civilization vanished with him, and 'the turtles went away, never to return'.

Religion was too intimately linked with the life of Polynesian societies for the prestige of the priesthood not to have been close to that of the nobles. In point of fact, the two orders were so nearly related that it is difficult, if not impossible, to distinguish priest from aristocrat in the island's traditions. This confusion is probably due to the fact that the members of the royal family and the servants of the gods were subject to the same tabus and lived in the same mystic atmosphere. Moreover, we may be certain that the high priest was chosen from the immediate family of the king.

Even the word for priest—*ivi-atua* (family of the gods)—expresses their relationship with the dieties. They were the vessels, or, to use the Polynesian expression, the 'boats of the gods'. They formed a hierarchy whose degrees are totally confused in the recollection of the Christian generations. Every rite or act relating to religion is indiscriminately attributed to the *ivi-atua*, who are described at one moment as vulgar sorcerers, and at the next as agents of a more lofty cult.

Priestly functions must have been specialized. Those who officiated at the royal sanctuaries were the bearers of traditions both sacred and secular. This is proved by the collapse of the island's religious tradition that followed the brutal kidnapping of the members of the priestly caste in 1862.

The priests whom the missionaries met in the island had more

modest functions. They presided over domestic festivals on the occasion of the birth of a child and exorcized spirits from the bodies of
the sick. The lowest members of the hierarchy were the humble
priests or magicians who ministered to the needs of the poor.

Were the highly-placed priests wealthy? Undoubtedly, for they
disposed of the offerings of fowls, fish and tubers that were made to
the gods. Their power may have been formidable, for the high
priests appointed the victims of the human sacrifices.

The rank occupied by local priests, medicine-men and sorcerers,
is difficult to determine. They probably fell within the category of
commoners and their prestige depended on the success of their
cures and charms.

In his capacity as a 'technician' in divine matters, the priest was
related to the specialists in other fields. The craftsman also had to
possess traditional tricks of the trade and be acquainted with the
rites and charms that would render his work effective and guard it
from danger. The same word, *tahunga*, often designated both the
priest and the craftsman in other Polynesian languages.

In the current dialect of the island, every expert craftsman, of
whatever type, is a *maori*. The word *tahunga* is unknown to the present generation, although it existed in the ancient vocabulary. It
figures in a fragmentary chant, the meaning of which is obscure.

He naunau no ta Puku-naunau. There is a sandalwood tree in
Puku-naunau.
He rongorongo no ta Orongo. There is a chanter at Orongo.
He tahonga no ta Puku-tahonga. There is an expert craftsman
in Puku-tahonga.
He kiakia no ta Puku-kiakia. There is a *kiakia* bird in Pukukiakia.

The craftsmen were probably banded together in guilds with
traditional skills and a traditional cult. Their social position naturally depended on the importance of their activities to the island's
economic life. One of the few guilds whose existence is historically
certain is that of the sculptors of the statues, who enjoyed great
prestige. Fifty-odd years ago some Easter Islanders still spoke with
pride of their ancestors who had carved the great images. One of
them, who was Thomson's guide, lost no opportunity of recalling

that his grandfather, a certain Uratahui, had been a celebrated sculptor.

The son of a craftsman was initiated by his father in the practice of his art, and succeeded him. The guilds were nevertheless open to all those who gave proof of talent. The master craftsman received the orders and supervised their execution. There were also associations of high-seas fishermen, who used large nets and owned boats in common.

The *matato'a* or 'warrior' is a familiar figure in historical legends. The word 'warrior' only partially expresses the rôle of these personages, for the *matato'a* was above all a warrior who inspired terror, the leader of a band. Like the South American *caudillo*, he was both a civil and military leader. The *matato'a* is a common Polynesian type: in the Marquesas, the *matato'a* were the military leaders of these warlike people. The *kaia* or man-eater is his equivalent on Mangareva, where he assumed the political power of the *ariki*.

In a society as turbulent as that of Easter Island the *matato'a*, taking advantage of the fear they inspired, finally exercised power, first over their own tribe and then over other tribes. The most famous of these great warriors was Kainga who, beginning as chief of the eastern tribes, eventually established his authority over the whole island.

The political position of the *matato'a* on Easter Island was much stronger than that of the warriors in the rest of Polynesia, where they were subordinate to the *ariki*. Once again, Mangaia affords a parallel; for there, just as on Easter Island, power might be in the hands of the warrior who had won a decisive victory.

Certain obscure occurrences that took place on Easter Island before the eyes of the missionaries acquire a meaning if they are interpreted as attempts on the part of *matato'a* to surround themselves with the religious prestige due to the king. Some *matato'a* had the first catch of the fishing season presented to them just as if they were the *ariki-mau* himself. The Orongo ceremonies bestowed divine sanction on their hegemony, for the *matato'a* whose servant found the first *manu-tara* egg became the 'vessel' of the great god Makemake.

Commoners were called, as on Mangareva, *huru-manu*. That is all we know about them. The position of the *kio* or serf is better known. The members of a vanquished tribe scattered or hid in caves to avoid massacre. Once the fury of the battle had died down they were spared, but became *kio*, and the victors took them to their lands, which they were compelled to till. At night they were herded into a cavern under an armed guard. Those who were sent back to their own district were liable to have their crops appropriated by their masters. Discouraged, they planted only what was strictly necessary to satisfy their basic needs.

The term *kio* was also applied to a farmer who had placed himself under the aegis of a warrior, to whom he paid regular 'protection money'. Those who farmed for a wealthier individual, because they had no land of their own, fell into the same category.

It is doubtful whether social relations as they may be observed in the village of Hanga-roa give an accurate idea of individual behaviour in the pre-European communities. The families formed larger groups, and those who were united by ties of blood had a greater sense of solidarity and avoided mutual quarrels or robbery. The Polynesians who colonized Easter Island no doubt preserved those habits of courtesy and hospitality so often described in connection with other South Sea islands. These mercurial and whimsical people were capable of giving free rein to violent passions and even of committing acts of cruelty; but once the outburst was over, the guilty parties recovered the lighthearted and friendly disposition that still characterizes their descendants.

We can catch no glimpse of relations between individuals save the exterior forms and tokens of politeness. The Easter Islanders paid great attention to good manners. Every member of the upper classes had to know how to behave on every occasion. Certain words had to be avoided if they constituted allusions to some misadventure that had befallen the interlocutor or his family. Any reference to a case of cannibalism of which a person's family had been the victim constituted one of those insults that might unleash an armed conflict. The susceptibility of a Polynesian aristocrat sometimes assumed morbid proportions. Even today an unfortunate word uttered without malice may cause a violent outburst of anger.

When a chief paid a visit to the chief of another tribe he was met along the road by groups of warriors, who formed an escort. On these occasions no doubt the chanters recited long genealogies, as is still done on the Tuamotus. The two chiefs advanced to meet and pressed the wings of their noses together, inhaling deeply, as though to absorb the breath of the guest or friend. This salutation is called *hongi*. Today the word is used to describe the European kiss, which the islanders have borrowed from us. Nevertheless, mothers still express their tender feelings towards their babies by running their noses over their bodies and sniffing their brown flesh.

A European who was present at the welcome accorded to a long absent relative or friend, a century ago, would have been both shocked and surprised. First, he would have observed total indifference on both sides. The newcomer's mother would not look at him, even if she passed close by him, but would hurry to join a group of relatives and friends who suddenly broke out into lamentations and allowed floods of tears to pour down their cheeks. The individual who was the object of these manifestations joined the weepers and showed every sign of utter despair. This outburst of grief lasted up to half an hour; then the weepers dried their tears, assumed a joyful expression, and each in turn rubbed noses with the traveller. Then everyone gave free rein to his joy and the absent one regained his place in the group.

The motivations for these lachrymose welcomes are hard to determine. They probably vary from one culture to another. It has been said that the absent one was regarded, until he had proved the contrary, as a spirit, and that—as a precaution—his death was mourned to placate him. Other writers have asserted that the natives were expressing their sympathy with the traveller for the trials and tribulations he had endured. Reference has also been made to maleficent influences emanating from every individual returned from foreign parts, pernicious effluvia which the tears were intended to exorcise. In Polynesia, such a welcome seems to form part of mourning: the relative returning to the bosom of the family is invited to weep for those who have died during his absence, and his tears express his participation in the griefs of the members of his group.

Those who have left their country for a long period may be received in a manner that, to our way of thinking, is even stranger and more unintelligible. Parents and friends are not content with weeping, but indulge in outright assault: the traveller, instead of receiving the Polynesian equivalent of a kiss, is beaten or chased away under the threat of blows. These aggressive actions are not the expression of any sort of animosity: they convey the affection of the people who are reproaching him with having forsaken them and perhaps of having caused, by the mere fact of his absence, all the misfortunes that took place before his return.

This is the correct interpretation of an incident related by one of the French Fathers. An Easter Islander, who had been absent a long time, returned to the island on board a whaleboat; his relatives and friends recognized him before he had even jumped out of the vessel that was carrying him ashore. Instead of running to greet him, they began to throw stones at him and prevent him from setting foot on the island. The stoning did not stop until the voyager's wife had rushed into his arms and covered him with her body. The missionary who reports the scene explains it as due to the fear felt by the natives on seeing the apparition of a man they perhaps believed dead. These acts of violence may also be constructed as an excess of courtesy signifying to the relative or friend who has returned the bitterness caused by his long absence.

The Easter Islanders, like many Polynesians, weep very easily. The slightest object that recalls someone who is dead is capable of moving them to tears. An Easter Island girl recognized in Thomson's book a photograph of her father, who had died while she was still very young; she none the less shed bitter tears every time she saw it. When she came to see us she said, 'Show me my father's picture so that I may weep,' and as soon as it was given to her she sobbed as though her heart would break.

The Tahitian *Ia-o-rana* has replaced the ancient greeting, *Ka oho mai repa rivariva* (Come here, good-looking young man or young girl), to which the reply was, *Ka koe* (You too). Parents greet their children with the words *Aue poki* (Ah, my child). These phrases are uttered in a trembling, tearful voice. We heard them on the lips of the old queen whenever we visited her.

War, like music and dancing, must have been a powerful diversion in a world where existence tended to become monotonous. This feeling is not unknown in our own culture and was certainly even commoner in a society wherein distractions were few and unvarying. Social life demanded that passions should be held in check, and accumulated rancour inevitably found an outlet in military expeditions.

The political life of Easter Island, as we glimpse it through legends and accounts left by missionaries, was a perpetual succession of wars and rivalries between tribes—particularly between the eastern and western tribes.

The main causes of these conflicts were often insignificant; but once blood had been spilt the struggle might go on for several generations. Easter Island sensitiveness is illustrated by a tale that is perhaps only half legendary. A young boy, having seen an eel close to the beach, asked a man standing nearby to help him catch it. The latter came and frightened away the eel by poking it with a stick. The boy went away vexed and angry. As soon as he had gone, the man caught the eel with a running noose attached to a stick. The child saw him and came back to claim the eel that he had been the first to discover. The man took no notice of his demand and walked away in the direction of his hamlet, followed by the boy, who continued to pester him with his protests. He entered a *hare-hui* (a large feasting-hut) where, amongst other things, a dish of eels was about to be prepared. When they were cooked and ready to be served, the child claimed his portion; but he was only given the tip of a tail. Then he went away and complained to his father: 'I come from the interior of the island, from a big hut where a feast is being celebrated, but I was only given the tail of the eel that I was the first to see. The man who caught it refused to give it to me.' Without a word, the father took his cudgel and went to the place of the feast, where everyone was sleeping, drowsy from the banquet. He took advantage of this to club the thief and his guests to death. This massacre unleashed a war that went on for several years.

The power of the *matato'a*, of which I have spoken above, is itself a testimony to the warlike nature of Easter Island society. When hostilities had opened, the warriors stained their bodies black and spent their last night at home preparing their weapons and hiding

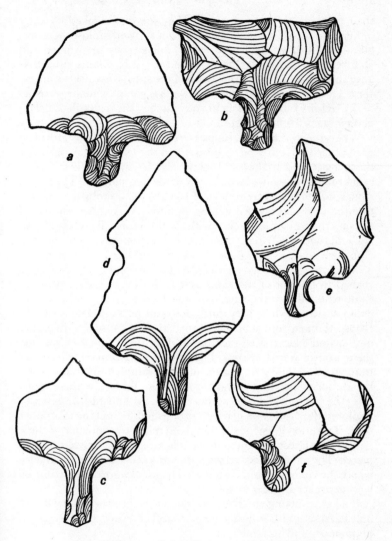

Fig. 3. Types of obsidian spear heads (*mataa*).

their most precious possessions. They ate food cooked by their fathers in a separate oven. They were not allowed to close their eyes all night. At dawn the troop set out, followed by the women and children. On the way, charms were recited or chants sung that gave courage and turned the wrath of the spirits against the adversary. The procession of non-combatants accompanied the warriors to the vicinity of the battlefield and watched the triumph or defeat of their party from the top of a hill.

When the two hostile troops were face to face, they provoked each other with outrageous insults and then started the battle by throwing stones. In the hands of the Easter Islanders these were a redoubtable weapon, of which they made frequent use. The hail of stones was followed by volleys of javelins, whose obsidian points tore the skin and opened gaping wounds. After this exchange of missiles the warriors attacked with the little short, flat club, identical with the New Zealand *patu*. Some, however, preferred the long club with sharp edges. Blows fell thick and fast until one group, having lose some of its warriors, fled from the field. The victors rushed in pursuit of the vanquished, slaying or taking prisoner those who fell into their hands. After this, they entered their enemies' territory where they burnt down the huts and laid waste the crops. Women and children were led into captivity. If earlier battles had exacerbated passions and created a spirit of revenge, the prisoners were tortured. Their skulls were broken with blows from an adze, they were buried alive, or trampled upon until their bellies burst and their entrails spilled out. To escape these reprisals, the vanquished fled across the island and hid in caves or implored the protection of relatives or friends belonging to another tribe. Traditional legends of the island relate the outcome of these battles in almost stereotyped sentences: '. . . They were cut in pieces. The vanquished, seized with panic, took refuge in caverns, where the victors sought them out. The men, women and children who were captured were eaten.'

If a high-ranking chief figured among the prisoners, he was not only eaten but his skull was burnt, to inflict a supreme outrage on his memory and his family.

The attraction of these military expeditions was rendered even greater by the prospect of banquets consisting of the corpses of the enemy. After all, man was the only large mammal whose flesh was available.

Victoria Rapahango told us that in her youth she had known the last cannibals on the island. They were the terror of little children. Every Easter Islander knows that his ancestors were *kai-tangata*, 'man-eaters'. Some make jokes about it, others take offence at any allusion to this custom which has become in their eyes barbarous and shameful. According to Father Roussel, cannibalism did not disappear from Easter Island until after the introduction of Christianity. Shortly before this, the natives are said to have eaten a number of men, including two Peruvian traders. Cannibal feasts were held in secluded spots, and women and children were rarely admitted. The natives told Father Zumbohm that the fingers and toes were the choicest morsels.

The captives destined to be eaten were shut up in huts in front of the sanctuaries. There they were kept until the moment when they were sacrificed to the gods.

The Easter Islanders' cannibalism was not exclusively a religious rite or the expression of an urge for revenge: it was also induced by a simple liking for human flesh that could impel a man to kill for no other reason than his desire for fresh meat. Women and children were the principal victims of these inveterate cannibals. The reprisals that followed such crimes were all the more violent because an act of cannibalism committed against the member of a family was a terrible insult to the whole family. As among the ancient Maoris, those who had taken part in the meal were entitled to show their teeth to the relatives of the victim and say, 'Your flesh has stuck between my teeth'. Such remarks were capable of rousing those to whom they were addressed to a murderous rage not very different from the Malay *amok*.

One of the most dramatic spectacles Easter Island offered in days gone by was that of the rites of vengeance observed when a murder had been committed. The body was carried to a mausoleum and a priest stayed with it all night, brandishing a palette of wood and bone and reciting incantations and spells. From time to time he went to the dead man and turned him over. The family gathered behind the priest mingled its lamentations with the funerary chants and waited for the moment when they could wreak vengeance on the murderer's relatives.

CHAPTER VI

From Birth to the Tomb

Birth and childhood—Games and sports—Adolescence—Sex life and marriage—Death and funerals

AT THE third or fifth month of pregnancy, but never in the fourth or sixth—even numbers being reputedly unlucky—the father-in-law would offer his daughter-in-law the contents of an *umu* (underground oven), called the *umu-takapu-kokoma-moa*, 'the ceremonial oven with the intestines of fowls'. This name referred to the fact that the intestines roasted on the glowing stones of the oven were given to the expectant mother as titbits. The rest of the food was distributed among the members of the two families allied by marriage. If the woman's father was rich he invited his son-in-law's family to a banquet, but this was a simple courtesy without ritual significance. The ceremonial meal (*rae*) bore a resemblance to the presentation of the first-fruits to the chiefs. A mystic link existed between the food eaten on this day and the child to be born: the latter's life was endangered if a rat came and gnawed the food scraps left behind at the site of the feast.

A woman gave birth squatting or kneeling on the ground. She was supported by her husband or some other person who pressed her belly with his hands to hasten delivery. A stone heated to white heat and wrapped in rushes, which was credited with a beneficent influence, was placed beside her.

The umbilical cord was severed with the teeth by a man or woman, and knotted according to a precise rite by a priest who was called in at this moment. This ceremony owed its importance to beliefs regarding the navel. In a man a 'good navel'—that is to say, a prominent navel—was in a way the symbol of his courage and vigour. It was displayed with pride. In tying a newborn child's umbilical cord, the priest was enclosing in his body a vital force (*mana*), which would otherwise have escaped from it. Every one of the ceremonial actions performed on this occasion was governed

105

by strict rites and a mistake might have had serious consequences for the child.

In the opinion of the Easter Islanders, this rite dated from the day when the boat of the *ariki* Hotu-matu'a touched Anakena beach. No sooner had she disembarked than the king's wife gave birth to a son. *Ariki* Tu'u-ko-ihu, a relation of the father and a very learned priest, cut the umbilical cord and performed the rites destined to strengthen the child's *mana*, to call forth his 'royal halo' as the original text puts it. The magical value of the knot binding the navel cord has survived to the present. There was also a mystic link between the child and the priest who officiated at his birth. The dreams the latter dreamed the night before the birth were interpreted as revealing the destiny of the newborn child. The cock the priest received as a fee could not be killed, lest the baby's *mana* be spoiled.

The dried umbilical cord was placed in a calabash and consigned to the waves by the child's maternal grandmother, with the simple injunction, 'Go away, be lost in a foreign country'. The cord could also be hidden under a rock in a consecrated place. In this case the formula of farewell was slightly different: the cord was enjoined, 'Stay here, in this country, and be strong'. The ground in which umbilical cords had been buried became tabu, and anyone walking over it was liable to develop ulcers.

The baby was washed in a large calabash filled with water heated with hot stones. Hot, flat stones were applied to the stomach of the mother after childbirth to prevent the development of ugly folds; but this precaution—if still practised—seems ineffective, for Easter Island women are invariably afflicted with such folds after several childbirths.

On the day of the child's birth, the father gave a banquet to his wife's family. The first mouthful of this repast was reserved for the young mother or, if she had no appetite, for her husband. This feast had a clearly ceremonial character. Certain dishes—sweet potatoes, among others—were strictly excluded, and the scraps had to be very carefully hidden. It was probably on this day that the child received its name, which was given by a paternal aunt or uncle. This feast was the first of a cycle that marked every stage of a child's life up to adolescence. On reaching the age of seven or eight months, his hair was cut with an obsidian knife by one of his paternal uncles. On this occasion he received a gift of fowls sent by one of his maternal uncles. A similar present was given when he took his first steps or put on his first breechcloth of tapa. At the age of seven or eight years, the child's legs were tattooed. The solemnity of this event demanded the celebration of a feast, in the course of which one of his mother's brothers made him a present of some thirty fowls. These were tabu for the boy and his family, but there was nothing to prevent their being exchanged on the occasion of some other ceremony.

Sports occupied a place of honour in former times, as they did in all other Polynesian societies. Surf riding, so popular on the beaches of Honolulu, is still practised on Easter Island. Children swim out to sea armed with a plank and wait for a big wave. The moment it comes they turn round, seize the plank in both hands and, with legs outstretched, allow themselves to be carried at full speed towards the shoals. An incautious child, unable to stop in time, might be hurled against the reefs with their knife-edged ridges. In the old days, when wood was scarce, conical bundles of reeds were used instead of surf-boards. Surf-riding demands great skill and even courage. The bolder spirits disdain to mount the wave at the moment it breaks, but go far out from the shore into the heavy surf, where they can catch great unbroken swells. In the magnificent story of Heru and Patu, the heroes reveal their divine origin by defying the submerged rocks and choosing the highest waves to carry them towards the shore. Children vied with one another in audacity and speed. For the malicious pleasure of seeing their companions 'dumped', they used to recite the following chant, which had spell-binding power:

> *A Pua e, O Pua-te-oheohe e pua!*
> *At the top of the wave there is a young man*
> *He rises towards the sky*
> *The sun, the foam*
> *Ruahie*
> *The wave breaks*
> *It breaks, it has lost its force.*

The children used to like sliding down the sides of the volcanoes on toboggans of *ti* leaves, a sport that was very popular in all the high islands of Polynesia.

The youngsters also used to indulge in sham battles. They divided into rival bands and attacked one another with harmless javelins; but sometimes, carried away by warlike ardour, they threw stones at each other, which they learned to dodge with great agility. According to a legend, the discovery of obsidian weapons was the outcome of one of these childish tussles. A boy belonging to a band that had been routed cut his foot on a splinter of obsidian while in flight. The accident gave him the idea of tipping his javelin with a piece of this volcanic glass. His companions imitated him, and the following day they attacked the victors of the previous day and scored an easy, but bloody, victory over them. Their success provoked reprisals and these mock combats gradually degenerated into real battles.

Perhaps no game is as widespread throughout the world as that which consists in making symbolic figures by interlacing with the fingers a piece of string knotted end to end. On Easter Island this pastime presents the peculiarity of being associated with short poems that were recited, rocking to and fro, when the string figure had been successful. Almost all the popular poetry that has been preserved by the modern population is connected with these cats'-cradles. Even the poems included in their tales and legends are to some extent illustrated by these figures. The natives attribute a mnemotechnic value to the string figures and liken them to their ancestors' wooden tablets.

The children also used to chant verses, which were perhaps spells for the success of the game, when they spun their tops of nuts, clay or stone. Here is one of them:

> *Spin the tops made of makoi shells that you gathered at the foot of the cliff.*
> *Oh, but these tops of wood are no good!*
> *Let us spin tops made of red clay from the Rano-kao.*

Kites, called *manu hakarere* (flying birds), probably came from Asia with the ancestors of the Polynesians. They were made of thin rods covered with tapa cloth on which was painted a bird.

These are ancient sports still remembered on Easter Island.

The first signs of puberty appear in the girls between the ages of ten and eleven, and in the boys between twelve and fourteen. The transition from childhood is not, at the present day, invested with any ritual significance. It does not even coincide with the beginning of sex life, which starts at a relatively tender age. Nowadays few girls reach the critical age without having had some sexual experiences with other children or even with adults, who, we were told, have recourse to various methods of seduction or even to force. The little boys are precocious and at an early stage imitate the frolics in which they have seen their elders engaging. As far as we could judge, parents take very little notice of these early sexual activities. Among the Easter Islanders puberty is a purely physiological state, unaccompanied by any emotional crisis or marked changes in the mode of life.

The transition from childhood to adolescence may not have been so imperceptible in the framework of the ancient civilization. Polynesian societies did not normally surround the phenomenon of puberty with a set of rites destined to initiate the adolescent in the social and religious life of adults. For this reason I hesitate to interpret as initiation rites the *poki-manu* (bird-child) ceremonies, of which the natives retained a faint recollection twenty years ago. Most of the information we received on this subject came from old Viriamo—the oldest woman on the island—and is unfortunately incomplete. The young boys had their heads shaved and had to present an egg to a man called the *tangata-tapu-manu*. The children went with this man, who acted as their sponsor and mentor, to Orongo. The ceremonies that took place at Orongo have been almost entirely forgotten. They are said to have included dances in front of the statues of Taurarenga, the reciting of sacred chants, and the offering of fowls.

The ritual said to have been observed in the case of girls seems to me a product of the lascivious imaginations of the present-day islanders. One of the rocks at Orongo is covered with symbolic drawings of the female sexual organs, a very common motif in local art. Our informants claimed that these drawings were cut in the rock during the initiation of girls. Old Viriamo also told us of a ceremony in which she had taken part at the time of her own puberty:

110 EASTER ISLAND

her mother stood beside her holding a fowl in each hand, while a priest intoned a chant.

The life of adolescents, as we have been able to glimpse it through folklore and the letters of missionaries, was one of complete idleness. Little effort was demanded of them. No doubt they carried out certain light tasks, but they passed long periods of leisure in the *hare-nui*, huts built by some generous individual in preparation for a family feast. Young men and girls gathered there to rehearse the chants and dances they were to perform at forthcoming festivities. These huts, which became reception halls on the feast-day, served the youngsters as a sort of club-house, where they spent their time discussing their fellows, composing poems or making cat's-cradles.

These long periods of confinement in the *hare-nui* were also intended to preserve the pale complexion which ranks so highly in the Polynesian conception of beauty. Nobody would have liked to appear at a dance with his skin blackened by the sun. Two legendary figures, Kaharoau and Kakoniau, were so ashamed of their bronzed bodies that they dared not attend the feast to which all the rest of the population had gone. But by immersing themselves in the fountain called Vai-a-repa ('The water of the handsome young men'), they became so white that they were greeted with murmurs of admiration and envy.

One particular cult of physical beauty may be observed in most Polynesian societies. Young people do not shrink from any procedure, however unpleasant, that will enable them to acquire a fair complexion and plenty of fat. On Mangareva wealthy families used to shut their children up in huts or caves and force them, under pain of a whipping, to over-eat. On feast-days the recluses who had attained the desired weight showed themselves in all their splendour, adorned with a belt and with a cloak of orange tapa cloth about their shoulders.

The crowd thronged round to admire them, and shouts of enthusiasm greeted the palest and most corpulent. These victims of vanity were often so fat that they had to lean on friends in order not to collapse under their own weight.

This custom possibly explains Easter Island traditions concerning the *neru*. As I understood it, there used to be young men and girls whom their parents confined in caves where they lived in total idleness, so that their nails grew immensely long. They let their hair grow and observed certain dietary tabus that must not, however, be interpreted as fasting. Their parents took great pains to provide them with food, but tradition does not refer to a fattening diet. There is nothing in the surviving recollection of the *neru* to suggest that it was a custom dictated by religion; on the contrary, a few allusions in a poem and a story stress the charms of these *neru* and imply that their confinement increased their beauty. These analogies with Mangareva perhaps justify us in interpreting the seclusion of the *neru* as a purely aesthetic measure.

The following poem addressed to a recluse by a young man makes this clear:

> *You are secluded, O recluse, in the cave.*
> *Against the wall hangs the gourd filled with red ochre.*
> *You have been secluded for a long time, O recluse.*
> *I love you.*
> *O you, who are a recluse,*
> *How white you have grown in your retreat, O recluse!*

The gourd hanging in the cave contained the colour with which these girls painted themselves. The story of the 'Talking Bananas' describes the day of one of these beauties: in the morning her mother washed her, deloused her, combed her hair, smeared her with saffron, and pulled her clitoris to make it longer.

Adoption, a custom widespread in Oceania, was practised by the Easter Islanders on a vast scale. The sway of this tradition is well exemplified by the case of Victoria Rapahango who, having had several children by a manager of the British Company, 'gave' one of them to an old Italian with whom she was on friendly terms. The rules governing this system of adoption have become obscure; nowadays the children are generally confided to their godparents. If the adoptive mother can suckle the child it is given to her immediately after birth; otherwise the transfer takes place at the time of weaning. No distinction is made between the adopted children and the rest. They receive exactly the same affection as though they had been born into the family. They bear the name of their new parents and inherit from them. This fact often complicated our task when we were trying to establish genealogies, since our informants refused to make the slightest distinction between legitimate and adopted sons. 'We brought him up, so he's our son,' they told us when we tried to explain the difference. The parents devote no further thought to the child they have given away. They rarely see it and show it no particular affection.

A child's head, especially that of the eldest son, is still surrounded by tabus. The mother takes care not to eat while holding her baby in her lap. Victoria Rapahango, free as she was from most of the ancient prejudices, shared this fear. One day, while in the fields, she had inadvertently put some sweet potatoes in her little boy's cap. She was obliged to throw them away: through the agency of the cap they had become contaminated with the *mana* of the child's head. A mother likewise cannot eat food that has come into contact with her eldest son's back or hand.

It is difficult to reconstruct the life of children as it was lived in the ancient pagan society. There can be no doubt that it was more varied and richer in training and activities than that of the modern children.

During these early years the children, by imitating in games the activities of their elders, familiarized themselves with the skills and knowledge that would later enable them to play their part in the life of the community. The boys went out with the fishing crews, tried to cut and polish statues or stone tools, learned the sacred hymns and spells, and gained military skill in mock battles. The girls carried babies, helped their mothers with domestic chores, and amused themselves by beating the mulberry bark or weaving little baskets.

Of all the aspects of a vanished culture, the most difficult to reconstruct is everyday behaviour. Patient observation is required to recreate the moral climate in which a society functioned. Too many things have changed on Easter Island in the course of a century for us confidently to deduce the past from the present. Traditional morality has been affected by other rules borrowed from our moral code, and the sanctions by which life was formerly governed have disappeared. At most we can trace in the morals of today certain general trends and attitudes inherited from the ancient culture. There can be no doubt, for example, that the sexual freedom still prevails which made such an impression on the first voyagers. During the visits of Cook, La Pérouse, and Beechey, those who landed on the island were the object of all sorts of attentions on the part of the women. The Easter Islanders were so anxious to see the foreigners respond to the women's advances that they made the nature of their solicitations abundantly clear by unmistakable gestures and pushed the young girls into the sailors' arms. These accounts have led to the belief that the ancient Easter Islanders were almost totally indiscriminate in matters of sex—the expression 'sexual communism' has been used in this connexion. One significant fact has, however, been too frequently overlooked: the number of women encountered by Europeans was always very small. In the course of his stay on the island, Cook and his companions counted only fifty or so, and other visitors saw even fewer. Various hypotheses have been advanced to explain this disproportion between the sexes, but in all probability it was only apparent and the majority of the women had hidden on the arrival of the strangers. The only ones who remained on the beach were those who could profit by their charms without injury to their rank and condition. This moral liberty, which has so frequently been discussed, did not extend to the whole feminine population. The women of the *ariki* class were doubtless expected to behave with greater discretion. The recluses, of whom we spoke above, were kept under very strict supervision. There is a story in Easter Island folklore which relates the elopement of a girl who had been seduced. The wrath and indignation of the mother are so vividly described that it is easy to see that virginity was not a matter of indifference. These few details hint at limitations to the moral laxity generally attributed to the ancient Easter Islanders.

The modern population of Hanga-roa can scarcely be called puritanical. The Easter Islanders I knew accepted the capricious play of the passions as something perfectly normal, the subject at most for a smile and some good-humoured gossip. In their opinion, every normally constituted man had a right to a regular sex life, and prolonged continence aroused some surprise. The villagers did not fail to attribute erotic adventures to every visitor to the island, even those who, by virtue of their characters or functions, should have been above suspicion.

No opprobrium attaches to unmarried mothers, of which there are a great number in this society. They almost all end up by marrying, presenting their husbands with a progeny as abundant as it is varied.

When a ship drops anchor in the Hanga-roa roadstead, the crew are surrounded and cajoled by a group of women who offer themselves without the least shame for a few pieces of soap or a little cloth. This soliciting on the beach is generally confined to poor women. Well brought up girls of families in easy circumstances do not readily give themselves to the first-comer. They are not unappreciative of gifts, but demand a more discreet courtship. Few girls make much fuss about their chastity, but there are certainly some who keep themselves for lovers of their choice. In general, the women show preference for the good dancers and gay companions. These village Don Juans are sometimes unbearably conceited.

It does not seem as though the different groups into which the population of the island was subdivided practised exogamy. The members of the aristocratic Miru tribe preferred to marry among themselves. The only obstacle to marriage was consanguinity, but the interdiction did not go further than third cousins. Incest with a prohibited cousin was apparently a serious crime, for legendary history cites the case of a war between two tribes provoked by a certain Taropa who raped his cousin. He had courted her for a long time unsuccessfully. One evening, finding her alone, he ravished her despite her protests and despairing reminders of their family relationship. The whole of the girl's family took up arms and inflicted a crushing defeat on the family of the young man. The girl's father sought the culprit everywhere. When he finally discovered him, hiding in a cave, he drove a bone dagger into his throat and drank the warm blood that flowed from the wound. He was not so much avenging the outrage committed against his daughter as the defilement of incest inflicted on his lineage.

The superstition of purity of blood, and also the desire to avoid the dispersal of landed property, compelled the *ariki* and the wealthy landowners to treat marriage as an instrument of policy. As it was not always easy to find a bride or bridegroom answering to all the requirements, recourse was often had to unions between children or between an adult and a child. Infant betrothal was so common that it came to be regarded as an essential preliminary to every marriage. A father, especially if he was a chief, chose for his son a little girl who was destined to become his wife when she reached puberty. The little fiancée lived with her future parents-in-law, who brought her up as their daughter. When she was given to her husband, the latter's father said to him: 'Do not strike her, that her eyes may never be blackened by blows. Do not make her suffer, except by giving her children.' The son who refused the fiancée chosen by his father risked the latter's anger, for he had to placate the parents of the rejected girl with a feast and gifts.

The opposite situation could also arise: an adolescent girl might be promised to a small boy and have to wait for him to reach manhood. The marriage ceremony consisted essentially in exchanges of food between the two families.

Polygamy was only practised by those sufficiently wealthy to support more than one wife. The missionaries complain in their letters that the Easter Island kinglets hesitated to become Christians because they did not want to abandon their wives. Today the natives are astonished by the polygamy of their ancestors, which they judge to be almost impossible because of the jealous and quarrelsome nature of women. They explain this custom by assuming that the husband kept his wives in different huts. This was probably not the case, since old Viriamo, as a young woman, used to live under the same roof with the other wife.

Polyandry may have existed *de facto*, if not *de jure*, during the tragic period of the decline in the population, when there were twice as many men as women. The only case of polyandry still spoken of is that of the two brothers Hamae and Rae, who are said to have shared the same wife for several years. This form of marriage used to exist on the Marquesas, whence the Easter Islanders originated. Was it continued on Easter Island? No answer can be given to this question.

The women of Hanga-roa are generally well treated and enjoy great influence. They never hesitate to express their opinions freely during discussions, but they dare not oppose their husbands' will too openly. Tepano's wife, Maria Ika, when her husband ordered her to leave us, excused herself with the words, 'I'm only a woman,

I have to obey.'

The domestic quarrels that I heard spoken of were all due either to conjugal infidelity or to some trifling dispute. A few couples are strongly united. We were told of one exceptional example of conjugal love: a young woman in perfect health, rather than leave her leprous husband, followed him to the leper colony, where she soon contracted the terrible disease. Attachment between a man and a woman to the point of death is the theme of the following anecdote: There was, in the old days, a married couple famous for the good terms on which they lived. During one of the periodic famines, the young woman's father came and fetched her because he had a store of provisions at home. The husband was out looking for food. When he returned and found his wife gone he imagined she had left him; such was his grief that he shut himself up in his hut and starved himself to death.

The division of labour between the sexes is equitable. The women do not give the impression of being overworked. They do the housework and cooking, help to harvest the taros and yams, and fish or gather shellfish on the shore. They weave baskets and formerly they used to beat the mulberry bark to make tapa cloth. The rhythm of their activities has undoubtedly remained the same throughout the centuries. The missionaries who commiserated with them on their fate were blinded by prejudice. The only example they give of this alleged servitude is especially badly chosen. They relate that a chief was very indigant at being ordered to help his wife, who was bending under an excessively heavy load. Anyone who knows how sacred are the head and back of a Polynesian chief will understand the full gravity of the insult represented by this demand. If the chief had obeyed the missionary not only would his *mana* have been irremediably destroyed, but this defilement might have had the most serious consequences for himself and his family.

In many Eastern Polynesian societies men and women eat separately. This tabu may not have been observed on Easter Island, but custom demanded that the men should be served first. The women and children had to be content with the scraps left over.

Divorce was easy. It often had no other cause than a minor tiff or a passing mood, and was effected without any formality.

Christianity has done nothing to strengthen the bonds of matrimony. A very large number of individuals, although legally married, had settled down with other women and had children by them; an official who, in a moment of untimely zeal, tried to compel separated couples to live together again, soon had to reverse his decision when he realized that he was causing a vast change of partners that would have thrown the whole village of Hanga-roa into confusion.

In olden times an adulterous woman was not punished by death unless she was the wife of a nobleman. In the other social classes she risked only repudiation or a beating. This, at any rate, was the impression we gained from our conversations with the oldest of our informants; but if the legends and stories reflect the morals of the past, not every cuckolded husband was equally forbearing. They sometimes took hideous revenge on their erring spouse, but in the story we were told concerning one such case it was hard to say whether the husband's fury was due to his wife's unfaithfulness or to the insults she addressed to him.

The numerous cases of adultery that have occurred in recent years have had no consequences other than divorce or a thrashing.

Such was the life cycle on Easter Island while it was still a closed world. Now we have reached its end. The little Easter Islander whose navel-cord was ceremonially cut has become a pleasure-loving adolescent; he has married, he has cared for his family, and to feed it he has tilled his country's stony soil. He has known the terrors of war and perhaps he was a *matato'a*, a respected warrior. Now he is dead. The medicine-men did not succeed in drawing out of his body the demon that was tormenting it, and his soul has departed. If he was the head of a large family and if his name was pronounced with respect, he may become first a benevolent demon and then a god who, at the call of the priest, will become incarnate for a few moments in the statues on the mausoleums or in the wooden images. His body will go to rest with his ancestors in the *ahu* that he himself may have helped to build to please the tutelary deities and outshine and humiliate neighbouring groups.

Only his bones will be placed in the open vaults of the *ahu* or on its surface that slopes down towards the village. First his flesh will have rotted away on a platform of wood or stone. Wrapped in a mat and firmly tied with ropes, his corpse is exposed in front of the *ahu*, where it will remain for two or three years. His soul, roaming in the vicinity, can hear the laments of hired mourners, men and women, who are celebrating the virtues of the deceased and averting his anger by singing his praises:

> *Alas, alas, what will become of us?*
> *Alas for us, father, O father who brought much food,*
> *Many fish, many yams, many sweet potatoes,*
> *Many eels, much sugar cane, many bananas,*
> *O father who did not go begging to the houses of others.*
> *Now you are lost to us.*
> *O father, great fisherman, your taut line sung.*
> *Alas, alas, what will become of us?*

While these lamentations are ringing out, a vague sense of fear descends on the assembly. The men squat on the ground discussing the event in low voices. They mention the tabus the deceased may possibly have violated and which may have caused his death. Uncles and cousins bustle about round the oven in which they will cook the food provided for the multitude of guests. The funeral meal is governed by very detailed rules. The close relatives of the deceased prepare the *umu papaku*, the 'dead man's oven'. The 'master of the corpse', that is to say, the dead man's nearest relative—his son or father—cannot touch this food himself, but he distributes it to the guests. The more distant relatives, or even neighbours, cook small ovenfuls of food—the *umu rikiriki*—which represent their share in the mourning. The 'master of the corpse' must abstain from these too. His meal is cooked separately with stones that have not been used in the other ovens: if he omitted to take this precaution he would die in the course of the year. The funeral rites, still observed on the island, demand that the 'master of the corpse' makes a symbolic gift of the tomb to his neighbours before inviting them to the banquet.

As stomachs become filled melancholy is dissipated. The guests feel fortified and enlivened by the good food and good company. Conversation grows animated, and soon the monotonous lamentations are succeeded by songs and dances. A man or woman rises and performs a few dance steps. People crowd round to watch, and the visitors or distant relatives begin to move their arms and legs to the rhythm of songs that are now slow and plaintive, now fast and violent.

The place where the corpse had been left to rot, and the adjoining sea-front, used to be placed under a tabu that was indicated by a heap of whitened stones or a few sugar-canes tied in a bundle. No fire could be lit in the proximity of the dead man. That is why González's sailors were asked not to smoke near the great statues. Fishing was strictly forbidden in the waters off the section of coast on which the mausoleum stood. No insult was so deeply felt as a breach, even if involuntary, of these tabus. Death was the only possible punishment for such an affront.

At any time when mortality on the island was high, the coast was lined with stretchers bearing decomposing corpses waiting for the moment when their whitened bones would be transferred to the family mausoleum.

The souls of the dead, it was believed, wandered about nearby and begged food from the living. If they were not kept by any desire for revenge, and if the funeral rites had been performed according to custom, they probably made their way to the westernmost extremity of the island and from there flew towards the *Po* (the Night), whence their ancestors had come in boats to meet them, and where their children would later join them. The dead retained their social rank and continued to live in the world of the shades the life they had been used to on earth.

The bones of the dead, or their dried bodies, were deposited in a vault constructed within the *ahu*. These sanctuaries were the island's commonest and most characteristic monuments, and also, when they were surmounted by the giant statues, the most imposing. They occur at short intervals all the way along the coast. Some consist only of large, semi-pyramidal cairns; others resembled caissons constructed of neatly fitting blocks (*ahu-avanga*); others again are elongated in form and represent ships with curved, raised ends to suggest the bow and stern (*ahu-poepoe*).

The Te-Peu *ahu*, one of the best preserved, will give us an idea of the general appearance of these mausoleums. Imagine first a parapet or bastion—the military term springs to mind the moment one looks at this cyclopean wall with its salient and its ramp, on which reposed the village dead. What has wrongly been designated the 'façade' of the *ahu* is actually the rear of the monument: a wall about seven feet high, whose masonry of unmortared stones is concealed behind huge slabs of basalt dressed in such a way that they fit together with the precision of a dovetail joint. The statues, which came from the Rano-raraku quarry—to be described later —used to stand on a platform about a yard and a half across at the top of the parapet. Today they lie flat on the ground, their faces buried in the soil or broken against the stones.

The position of the statues, all of which had their backs to the sea, was long considered a 'mystery'. The explanation is simple, however. The mausoleums were all built along the shore, or, like Te-Peu *ahu*, at the top of a cliff. Their statues were the objects of a cult and formed part of a religious edifice: they naturally faced the worshippers and not the waves.

In olden days the statues were approached up a ramp consisting of a huge mound of lava blocks and large boulders. It was in this heap of stones that the vaults containing the skeletons were placed. Five of these are visible in the Te-Peu *ahu*, and there are others hidden by the rubble. This sloping pile of stones held in place by a retaining wall of slabs set on edge is prolonged at ground level by a paved space. The main body of the mausoleum was flanked on either side by slanting wings.

Some twenty yards behind the *ahu* there used to rise a rectangular structure, the remains of which consist of an accumulation of stones and earth held in position by slabs set in the ground. It was on this terrace that the corpse was exposed.

The mausoleums were also the sanctuaries on which offerings were made to the gods and to which the ancestors were reputed to return in order to protect their descendants and preserve them from danger. The *ahu* were to Easter Island what the *marae* were to the Society Islands or the Tuamotu, and the *mea'e* to the Marquesas.

CHAPTER VII

Religion and Magic

Major gods—Creation chants—The bird-man cult—Tabus—
Sorcery

MEMORY OF the great Polynesian gods only survives in incomplete myths and vague traditions almost unintelligible to the new generations. The names of the most celebrated deities—Rongo, Tiki, Maui—awaken no echo in the recollection of present-day Easter Islanders. This oblivion is not due solely to the island's Christianization. As early as the mid-nineteenth century, the missionaries speak of this singular falling-off in the pagan cults. They congratulate themselves on it at the same time as they express surprise at the natives' indifference. Brother Eyraud declares in one of his letters that he has never observed any outward manifestation of religious sentiment. He is exaggerating, as other passages in his reports show; but it is none the less true that Christianity met little or no resistance. It is difficult to escape the impression that even before the evangelization of the island the rites, the sacred chants and the legends of the gods—which, in Central Polynesia, are held in such profound veneration—had lost their prestige, and that the major themes of the ancient cosmogony were already half forgotten.

The minor dieties, the mischievous and familiar spirits, have resisted Christianity and time better than the majestic 'Lords of Space' of the classical pantheon. As in the past, they haunt the solitary shores of the island and trouble the sleep of its inhabitants. In vain the church bell rings morning and evening, in vain the crosses stand at the parting of the ways—fear of the ancestral spirits is as much alive as ever. People do not like to speak of them at the hour when they are reputed to glide by the dwellings of the living, but in broad daylight the Easter Islanders have no hesitation in complaining of their spiteful tricks. Any expression of doubt as to the existence of these nocturnal visitors unleashed vigorous protests on

121

the part of the many individuals who had a bone to pick with them and swore to having seen them with their own eyes.

The most dreaded spirits are those that appear in the hideous guise of half putrefied corpses—the nostrils drawn down, ribs protruding beneath dried skin, the belly emptied of its entrails and looking as though it were threatened by the hooked breast-bone. The artists of the pre-Christian era were inspired by these horrific visions to carve the little wooden images, the *moai kavakava*, that are among the finest creations of Easter Island art and authentic masterpieces of primitive statuary.

The conventional picture a society draws of the supernatural world inevitably impresses itself on the subconscious of its individual members and colours their dreams and hallucinations. Thus, a few days before we left, a young girl told us she had seen her grandfather in a nightmare. When he turned to smile at her, she noticed that his ribs were showing and that in the hollow of his belly his bowels were seething with worms. This dream, inspired by the conventional descriptions of ghosts, was interpreted by the young woman as an augury of misfortune. Her terror was pitiful.

Nowadays all supernatural beings are called indifferently *akuaku* or *tatane*—the latter expression being derived from our 'Satan'. In fact, however, the emaciated ghosts and the benevolent spirits that help mankind belong to separate categories.

The folklore abounds in stories of *tatane*. They are often beautiful girls or valiant young men, who have nothing in common with the terrifying spectres described above. But even the dead are not necessarily to be feared as harmful. In former times some of them became the benefactors of their families and overwhelmed them with gifts. They took advantage of the powers conferred upon them by their spirit state to send their children turtles or driftwood. On this subject the following legend is told:

An old man named Rano, knowing that he was dying, said to his son: 'Eight days after my death you will observe a tree with its roots and branches floating in from the sea.' He died shortly afterwards. His son buried him in an *ahu*, lit an oven and gave a splendid funeral banquet.

On the eighth day he went to the Ana-Havea cave, where he

saw a tree with large branches washed up on the beach. Some men were in the process of chopping it up. The young man cried to them, 'Men, leave my tree.' But they replied, 'Here's your tree, little boy; take it,' and they made an obscene gesture.

The boy returned home. He took a white chicken and went back to Ana-havea. He waved the fowl and cried, 'My father, stand up.' The tree began to move and finally stood upright. The men who had taken possession of the tree said, 'Child, don't do that, leave the tree alone.' But the boy did not listen to them. He cried once more, 'O my father, stand up and go away.'

The tree was soon floating out to sea again. The young man's relatives came and implored him, 'Call back the tree for us, your relatives.' The young man said, 'All right, I will,' and the floating tree came back and was washed ashore. This time it stayed and the relatives cut it up to make statuettes, *ao* (dance paddles), pendants, paddles and cudgels.

It is, therefore, difficult to distinguish between spirits of the dead, demons, and lesser gods. Were the spirits that watched over a family or an individual deified ancestors or demons related to the great divinities of the pantheon? The tutelary genius of the Rapahango family was a spirit of the same name. He and his companion Tare, watched over the whole of the Tupahotu tribe. These two deities carried their benevolence to the point of hiding food from the neighbouring groups in order to give it to their protégés. In return, the Tupahotu invited them to their meals. No one touched the dishes until the head of the family had thrown a morsel over his shoulder, pronouncing as he did so the following formula: 'What I am giving is for the *akuaku* Rapahango, who comes from beyond the seas.' Some say that the spirits contented themselves with the essence of the food, but others are convinced that they require a more substantial diet.

Familiar spirits were very willing to talk with those who gained their confidence. They predicted the future, warned them of imminent dangers, and told them many secrets. Tepano's old mother had been in the habit of conversing for hours on end with two *tatane*. Our friend had not forgotten the high-pitched, piercing voices of these visitors and imitated them for our amusement. He had never had the courage to look at them, however—a fact on which he congratulated himself. Spirits do not like to be seen, and when they are present in a hut anyone who enters has to crawl in backwards.

Every district, every bay, every hillock had its guardian demon or familiar genius. The lists of *tatane* or *akuaku* dictated by the natives contain about a hundred names, and they are far from exhaustive.

The spirits that figure in myths and stories are often so human in character that their true nature may be overlooked. They marry, have children, suffer and die like human beings. Their supernatural power only manifests itself in the speed with which they can transport themselves from one place to another.

Some spirits have animal shapes or are the personification of natural phenomena or objects. Then they bear names like 'Landslide', 'Rain with Heavy Drops', or 'Big House with Stone Foundations'.

The ancient Easter Islanders ascribe important discoveries to these demons or minor gods. Thus the two female demons 'Lizard Woman' and 'Gannet Woman' are said to have taught them to prepare *pua*, the dye extracted from turmeric (*Curcuma longa*). The first bone fish-hooks were made by Ure, a strange and visionary hero of Easter Island folklore who introduced many technical advances. One legend tells how a bird spirit brought a farmer a new variety of yam. The beneficent actions of demons are a frequent theme of myths and legends.

In addition to these benevolent demons there were mischievous and murderous ones. At the dawn of time thirty demons, who were terrorizing the island's inhabitants, were destroyed by the hero Raraku in a moment of reckless courage due to a temporary fit of madness.

The beliefs and practices discussed in the preceding section are the scattered vestiges of a popular religion that was accessible to all, and hence has been slow in disappearing. They contain pointers —unfortunately few and far between—to much more refined religious observances and a more complex cult. It would have been surprising if the ancient Easter Islanders had not preserved, or even enriched, the heritage of myths and rites that had come to them from their Eastern Polynesian ancestors.

The Polynesian pantheon comprises three categories of supernatural beings: the great uncreated gods and their sons; local gods and deified ancestors; and finally the anonymous host of good and evil spirits.

No Polynesian god enjoyed a prestige equal to that of Tangaroa, the god of the sea. In the Society Islands and Samoa he was considered the greatest of all the divine personages and the creator of the world. The ancient Easter Islanders had certainly not forgotten him. In fact his name appears in the list of kings, and one *ahu*—on a desolate headland on the south coast—bears his name in conjunction with those of Papa, the Earth, and Hiro.

Simon Riroroko, a native belonging to the Miru lineage, dictated to me a strange myth that may refer to the ancient sea god:

The king Tangaroa-mea said: 'I shall enter the water like a seal and go to a country where I shall be king.' The king, his brother, said 'You will die, it is a distant country, you cannot go quickly. I can go there and return the same day.'

They quarrelled. Victory was Tangaroa's and he went to Easter Island. His *mana* was over the sea, in which he was like a seal. The *mana* of his brother was over the land.

He landed at Tonga-riki, and he was seen by the people. The clamour resounded: 'People of the land, a seal has landed at Tonga-riki.' People said: 'He has seal's feet, seal's hands, but a man's face.' They wanted to kill him. The king Tangaroa said: 'I am the king Tangaroa. I am not a seal. The people said: 'No, he is a seal with a voice.'

They assaulted him with stones. They shouted: 'Haul him to the shore.' They carried him to Pito-kura. They dug out an oven, put Tangaroa inside, and closed it with stones. Later they opened the oven, but the meat was still raw. They covered the oven again and they stayed there waiting. They opened the oven again, and the meat was not cooked.

The people said: 'It was true, he was really a king, he was Tangaroa and not a seal. Therefore he is half raw.'

The brother of Tangaroa, Teko-of-the-long-feet, saw that his

brother did not come back in one month. This king of a foreign
country cried for his brother. He went to search for him. He
landed on the islet. He put his foot at Retu (near Vai-tea). He
was looking for his brother. 'Where is Tangaroa, the king?' he
asked at Ranokao, again at Retu, and at Pui. The men of the
land were afraid. He lifted his foot again at Puku-puhipuhi, the
place Where-Teko-planted-his-digging-stick. He again lifted his
foot beyond Poike. He asked again, 'Where is Tangaroa, the
king?' He asked for the last time for the king, Tangaroa. He
turned back, he disappeared to the foreign country. His feet
trampled on the earth, but his head reached the sky. He was
always asking about Tangaroa, the king.

Hiro, the great navigator of Polynesian myths, was the god of
rain on Easter Island, as this fragment of a hymn for rain shows:

> O rain, long tears of Hiro,
> Fall,
> Strike the ground,
> O rain, long tears of Hiro.

On the northern coast, near the Mahatua *ahu*, there is a stone
pierced by a natural hole called by the natives 'Hiro's Trumpet'.
The north wind is said to draw from it a dull, melancholy sound
like that produced by a conch shell. An aura of superstitious
respect surrounds this rock, which is covered with innumerable
symbolic representations of the female sexual organs. In olden
days it was credited with the property of causing clouds of flying
fish to leap on to the strand every time it was shaken.

As to the other great gods of the Polynesian pantheon—Rongo,
Ruanuku, Atua-metua (God the Parent)—they are little more
than names appearing in the royal genealogies and in a creation
chant that will be discussed later.

One of our expedition's surprises was the discovery of numerous
petroglyphs representing a mask with large eyes, identified by the
natives as the god Makemake.

The god's face shows an astonishing likeness to that of Tiki,
which is one of the most characteristic motifs of the art of the Marquesas. The shape of the Marquesan Tiki has been interpreted as

View of the Rano-raraku volcano

An Easter Island native selling curios

Beating tapa cloth

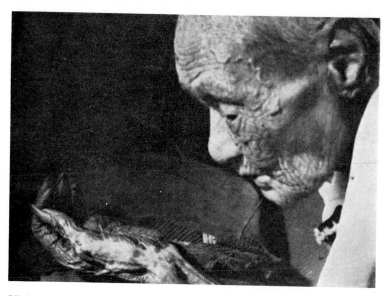

Viriamo, who was born about 1845, before the coming of the French missionaries

Juan Tepano, our informant, carving a wooden image

A girl on her way to church

Playing cat's cradle

Victoria Rapahango, descendant of kings

Petroglyphs of the bird-man

A petroglyph of a shark

A *tupa*, probably a shelter for fishermen

Stone houses at Orongo, used as shelters by pilgrims

The head of an ancestor image

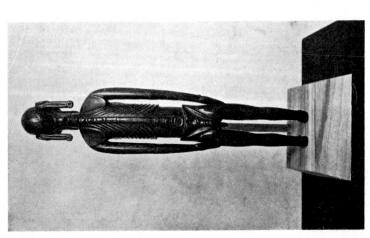

Ancestor image, back view

Portion of the tablet Aruku-kurenga (Museum of the Congregation of the Sacrés Cœurs du Picpus, Braine-le-Comte, Belgium)

Two views of a female ancestor image

Stone statues on the slopes of Rano-raraku

Recumbent statue in the quarry where it was sculpted

Unfinished statue

Head of fallen statue, crowning the Ahu Tonga-riki

Stone 'hat', lying near statue on which it once stood

Seaward façade of Ahu Tepen, showing curbstones from house foundations

Fallen statues on an *ahu* of the south coast

Seaward façade of Ahu Vinapu, built of dressed slabs

Another view of the façade of Ahu Vinapu

Statues on the slopes of Rano-raraku

Statue on the slopes of Rano-raraku

portraying a skull, and the same probably applies to the symbol of the god Makemake, as the following myth suggests:

There was a priestess watching over a skull on a rock in the bay of Tonga-riki. One day a big wave came and swept this skull out to sea. The priestess leapt into the water to recover it. The skull floated rapidly away on the water and she swam after it to get it back. After swimming for several days, she landed on the island of Matiro-hiva. Then the god Haua appeared to her and asked: 'Where do you come from?' 'I am looking for my skull,' she replied. Haua said: 'It is not a skull, but the god Makemake.'

The priestess stayed on the island with Makemake and Haua. The gods brought her the fish they caught. One day Makemake said to the god Haua: 'What would you say to our driving the birds to Easter Island? For that purpose I came here.' Haua answered: 'It is good, tell the old priestess to prepare herself and we will leave for Easter Island. There she shall reveal our names to the inhabitants and teach them the rites with which they must worship us.'

So the two gods showed the priestess the rituals they wished her to teach the inhabitants of the island.

Then Makemake said to Haua: 'Now we must go.' They set out, driving the birds in front of them, in search of a place where they could leave them to nest. They stopped for three years at Hauhanga with their birds; but the spot was badly chosen, for men discovered the eggs and ate them. Then they brought the birds to Vaiatare, but here again the inhabitants came and took the eggs and ate them. Finally Makemake and Haua said to one another: 'We shall have no peace until we find a place where men cannot reach us.' So they established their birds on the islets of Motu-nui and Motu-iti.

During this time the priestess was travelling about Easter Island initiating its inhabitants in the cult of the gods Makemake and Haua. She said to them: 'Before beginning a meal, when you take food out of the oven, set aside the portion of the gods and make them an offering of it, pronouncing these words: "Makemake and Haua, this is for you!" ' Do the same when you are about to eat sugar-canes, fish, tunny, and eels. Never forget the portion of the gods.'

In addition to being symbolized by a skull, Makemake was also represented as a man with the head of a bird, the famous 'bird-man' of Easter Island art. It was in his capacity as god of the 'denizens of the air', as the guardian of the birds on the islets of Motu-nui and Motu-iti, that Makemake was worshipped during the annual festivals of the bird-man.

The name Makemake undoubtedly conceals the old New Zealand deity Tane, the god of forests and the friend of birds. Like Tane and Tiki, Makemake embodies the fecundating forces of nature. He is the creator of mankind, despite the difficulties he encountered in this task.

'Makemake found a calabash full of water. He masturbated and his semen spurted into the water. Flesh appeared on the water. But it was no good. He copulated with stones, which still show the holes the god made in them. He thrust his member into clay and masturbated. From this were born Tive, Rorai, Hova and the noblewoman Arangi-kote-kote.'

These successive copulations are one of the most famous themes of Polynesian mythology. When Tane or Tiki wish to procreate human beings they mate with all sorts of queer objects, to the great delight of the story-teller's audience, who are highly amused by the gods' simple-mindedness.

Makemake was probably the most important god in the Easter Island religion. He was the only one of whom the missionaries heard when they enquired about the pagan deities. He was the supreme *atua* and the Creator of the Universe. The Makemake cult has, however, left few traces in the island's traditions. Only the feast of the bird-man, which was held in his honour, can still be reconstructed in its broad outline. The disappearance of a large proportion of the priesthood during the slave-raid of 1862 would explain this sharp break in religious tradition and forgetfulness of the ancient cults.

Makemake, Haua and the other gods received offerings of fowls, fish, sweet potatoes and pieces of tapa cloth. These gifts were handed to the priests, who undertook to convey them to the deity. The god Makemake demanded human flesh. Children stolen by the priests from their parents were sacrificed to him, as well as prisoners of war and people who had incurred the wrath of the *ariki*. The first French missionaries relate that at the beginning of their stay on the island women came and thanked them for saving the lives of their children, who, without their intervention, would have been sacrificed to the god.

The prisoners destined for these thanksgiving sacrifices were shut up in a hut facing the *ahu* belonging to the family of their captor. Their bodies were devoured at a feast that followed the religious ceremony. The English voyager Palmer, who visited the island in 1867, describes cylinders of red tufa that he took to be the altars on which the victims were placed and on which their ashes were preserved. We did, in fact, find some cylinders corresponding to Palmer's description behind the south-coast *ahu*. But they seem to have been pillars on which corpses were left to decompose.

A few old people still remember the rites formerly carried out to induce rainfall. This ceremony was performed on the initiative of the *ariki-mau*, who sent a high-ranking priest—generally a member of his own family—to undertake this magical operation. The rainmaker, his face painted half black and half red, went to the top of a hill, where he buried a piece of coral that was still wet and covered in seaweed. He then addressed a prayer to the god Hiro, begging him to shed tears on the thirsty earth. Sure of the result, he awaited the downpour; as soon as it came, he ran across country to oblige the clouds to follow him and discharge their waters on the territories of all the tribes.

Polynesians were profoundly imbued with the aristocratic spirit. Everyone's rank depended on the purity of his blood and the number of his known ancestors. Such an attitude produced an almost morbid interest in genealogies. No feast was celebrated without the recitation of the complete list of ancestors of all the chiefs present. In salutations between *ariki* it was obligatory on each party to enumerate the other's forbears.

The value attached to genealogies infected religion and literature. The gods themselves were provided with a pedigree and presented as the fruit of a long series of unions between imaginary beings. This mania even extended to nature: minerals, plants and

animals, in their turn, were credited with parents. It would be pue-
rile to look upon these sacred genealogies as lists of deities. These
couples are pure abstractions or imaginary objects chosen more or
less at random because of the consonance of their names. There is
nothing here but empty verbiage, with no other significance than a
desire to honour the gods in the manner of the *ariki*.

By a fortunate chance one of these genealogical chants explain-
ing the origin of gods and natural objects was taken down from the
mouth of old Ure-vaeiko by the American traveller Thomson. It
was dictated to him as the text of one of the tablets. Thomson's version has reached us so mutilated by errors of transcription and
printing that it is almost unintelligible. My efforts to re-establish
its original form were not entirely successful, but it was possible to
translate fragments so that the general character of the hymn is in
no doubt. Alongside personified abstractions, we find references to
some of the great mythical personages of Eastern Polynesia—the
Lord Tiki and his wife Hina, who was moulded from clay, for
example. This religious text tells us nothing about the island's
past, except that its oral literature drew inspiration from themes
common to many Polynesian cultures.

God-of-the-angry-look by copulating with Roundness produced
the *poporo* [*Solanum nigrum*].
Himahima-marao by copulating with Lichen-growing-on-the-
soil produced the lichen.
Ti by copulating with Tattooing produced the *ti* plant.[1]
Elevation by copulating with Altitude produced the inland-
grass.
Sharpness by copulating with Adze produced obsidian.
Twining   by   copulating   with   Beautiful-face-with-
penetrating-tongue   produced   the   morning-glory
plant.
Parent-god by copulating with Angry-eel produced the coconut.[2]

[1] *Ti* is here regarded as a deity who produced the plant of the same name. The
ashes of *ti* provided a pigment used in tattooing.

[2] An allusion to the eel whose head, thrust into the ground, produced the coconut
palm.

Grove by copulating with Trunk produced the ashwood tree [*Sapindus saponaria*].

Dragonfly by copulating with Bug-that-flies-on-the-water produced the dragonfly.

Stinging-fly by copulating with Swarm-of-flies produced the fly.

Branch by copulating with Fork-of-a-tree produced the beetle-living-in-rotten-wood.

The Lizard Woman by copulating with Whiteness produced the gannet.

Hard-soil by copulating with Layer-of-earth produced the sugar-cane.

Acridness by copulating with Bad-taste produced the arum.[3]

Killing by copulating with Flat-one-of-the-white-tail [the sting-ray] produced the shark.

Tiki-the-lord by copulating with Stone produced burning-red-meat.[4]

Small-thing by copulating with Imperceptible-thing produced the fine dust in the air.

Tiki-the-lord by copulating with the Woman-of-sand produced Hauhara.

The island's greatest religious festival, the only one concerning which circumstantial details survive, was that of the bird-man, intimately linked with the cult of the god Makemake. The long mystic drama enacted every year on the Orongo cliffs was not only of great religious significance, but also profoundly affected the island's social life.

The aim of these rites, which were repeated every year and gave rise on every occasion to the most violent passions, was the discovery and possession of the first egg laid by the *manu-tara* (*Sterna hirundo*), the sooty tern, on the islet of Motu-nui. This purpose may seem out of proportion to the sum total of the effort expended to attain it and the risks taken by those who coveted this meagre booty. But only those ignorant of the power of symbols can smile at such endeavours. The egg was the incarnation of the god Make-

[3] The arum is a species of taro that is extremely bitter when insufficiently cooked.

[4] An allusion to the Polynesian myth in which Tiki copulates with various objects before creating the first woman.

make and the tangible expression of religious and social forces of great intensity. The stake in this struggle for the possession of an egg was nothing less than divine favour and the sanction of political power.

The ceremonies leading up to the proclamation of the bird-man can only be understood within this framework.

The two centres of the cult were Orongo and the islet of Motu-nui. The village of Orongo, which was occupied by pilgrims during the festival of the bird-man, stands on the crest of the Rano-kao volcano, on top of a cliff that separates the bottom of the crater from the ocean. This thin wall is the last remnant of the southern slope of the volcano, the rest of which has been worn away by the waves. If any of it caves in, the waters of the lake will pour out into the sea and the former crater will become a cove encircled by steep slopes.

The ruins of the houses are covered over by grass and would be unnoticeable but for their low, narrow doors. These buildings used to rise in several tiers on the lip of the crater, coming to a stop at a group of basalt blocks on which there were sculptured images of the bird-man. These rocks rose at the extremity of a narrow ridge looking out over the reed-filled lake and the foam-fringed islets of Motu-iti and Motu-nui.

The houses of Orongo, forty-six in number, were built of schistous slabs modelled after the thatched huts which the worshippers had originally erected, but which had been blown away by the wind. Artists have covered the slabs retaining the wall-fillings with paintings representing Makemake—the god with the big eyes —sacred objects, such as dance paddles, and European ships. The majority of these frescoes have been removed by the crews of the German vessel 'Hyaena' and the American 'Mohican', who did not hesitate to destroy the houses of which they formed part. The great statue that stands today beneath the portico of the British Museum also comes from the village of Orongo.

The results of excavations carried out by Mrs Routledge in the Orongo huts were disappointing. The best find was an anthropomorphic pillar that decorated the entrance to one of the narrow passages leading to these dwellings. The niches in the interior walls were empty, as were the paved pits in front of the doors.

These were doubtless *umu* or earth ovens in which the pilgrims cooked their food.

On the other hand, the detailed study of the petroglyphs undertaken by the Routledge Expedition and by our own clearly demonstrated the importance of the bird-man symbol, which is portrayed no less than 150 times, very often with an egg in its hand. Some rocks bear very realistic representations of the frigate bird. The aesthetic value of these sculptures varies greatly. Some of them have been carved by the hand of a master with great purity of style; others, on the contrary, are clumsy and crude. There is no orderly arrangement in the way these petroglyphs are grouped and it would be vain to seek any over-all plan. They are the products of isolated efforts on the part of generations of devout worshippers, who, by this pious labour, sought either to win the favour of the bird god or to thank him for his aid after victory.

The choice of Orongo as the centre of the bird-man cult was due to its proximity to the islets of Motu-nui, Motu-iti, and Motu-kaokao, which have always been refuges of sea birds. They hardly ever leave this vicinity and are rarely found in other parts of the island. As Makemake and Haua had hoped, they are seldom disturbed by men in search of eggs. Motu-kaokao, covered in guano, shoots up like a white needle amidst the waves. The two other islets are accessible, but to land on them requires a calm sea and some agility. They are both covered with tall, straight grasses, some species of which belong to the ancient flora that has now disappeared from the main island. This vegetation conceals the entrances to subterranean chambers whose clay walls have been decorated with engravings. One of them represents the profile of a bird, from whose open beak streams a kind of ribbon that seems to symbolize its cry.

When we visited the islets we explored several of these caverns, which must have served as shelters for the hunters of *manu-tara* eggs. One of the chambers presented a spectacle worthy of the atmosphere of Easter Island. The entrance was narrow and steep, so that only a dim light could penetrate the cave. When our eyes grew accustomed to the darkness, we distinguished on a platform a skeleton still wrapped in its rush mat. Above the dead man, as though watching over him, an enormous head painted in red stared at him with its great round orbits. In the soft clay covering the wall were drawn a dance paddle and a two-headed bird, partially effaced. Mrs Routledge states that she found in this grotto four other skeletons, which have since vanished.

These are the various décors against which the drama of the bird-man was enacted every year. The first phase in this cycle of festivities comprised a halt at Mataveri, at the foot of Rano-kao volcano, where two or three large huts stood—in roughly the position now occupied by the buildings of the British Company. These huts were only occupied at the time of the bird-man feast. The pilgrims stopped there to rehearse their dances and prepare the ornaments and accessories used during the ceremonies. Revelry and cannibal feasts are also associated with this initial period in the recollection of the present-day natives, but it is possible that our informants ascribed to this first stage on the way to Orongo the colours and details properly belonging to the apogee of these festivities, when the triumph of the bird-man was celebrated at the same spot.

The pilgrims went up to Orongo in July. Their faces painted black and red, with diadems of feathers on their heads and brandishing dance paddles (*ao*), they set out to the accompaniment of shouts and chanting on a path that is still called the 'road of the *ao*'.

The decisive moment was at hand: in a few weeks, a month at the most, the sooty terns would lay, and the possessor of the first egg would receive the god. So much was at stake in the quest for this symbol that it aroused deep emotions and intense excitement throughout the island.

The competitors were generally war chiefs, the *matato'a*, whom we have already discussed. The title of bird-man (*tangata-manu*) seems to have been so coveted that only those who possessed some political power could lay claim to it. Power was not the only condition for taking part in the competition. The participants had also to have been designated by the god. The candidates were those whose image had been seen or whose name heard by some priest in a dream. These visions were considered a promise of victory. When the victor had been proclaimed, the unsuccessful competitors naturally turned on the false prophets. But the latter were never at a loss for an answer: their dream, though it had proved misleading on this occasion, presaged victory in some distant future, or even referred to a descendant of the individual concerned.

Aspirants to the title and rank of bird-man entrusted the task of finding the first *manu-tara* egg to servants, the *hopu*, who were sent to the islet of Motu-nui to watch the birds. This task was dangerous and onerous. The team of bird-nesters had first to swim across the shark-infested arm of the sea separating the Rano-kao cliff from the three islets. To scramble ashore on these islands amidst the reefs and breakers that protect them was a feat which can hardly be contemplated without shuddering. To make this crossing, the *hopu* employed conical floats made of rushes, inside which they placed the provisions they took with them in anticipation of a long stay. The anguish of the swimmers was expressed in a long semi-magical invocation, the text of which is unfortunately lost. The gods occasionally took the trouble to warn some priest of the danger threatening the *hopu*. Those *matato'a* who, although warned of his danger, still exposed their servant to the risk of death, may be reproached with a certain callousness. As a precaution, they sent a second servant to take the place of the one who was going to be devoured by sharks.

The *hopu* lodged in the grottoes described above. They spent their days watching the movements of the *manu-tara*, in the hope of seizing the first egg laid. During these weeks of waiting, they were sometimes entirely cut off from the main island by stormy weather. Foreseeing this possibility, they carefully preserved the skins of their bananas and potatoes and dried them in the sun, to be eaten if they were subsequently short of food. If the sea was calm their revictualling was taken care of by their relatives or masters, who sent other servants with provisions wrapped in rush floats.

The tribes established at Orongo were meanwhile extremely active. The servants on the island were only the blind instruments of the god. Their quest was vain if their hand and eye were not guided by Makemake. If Makemake did not wish a *matato'a* to become a bird-man, his servant would not see the first egg even if he touched it with his foot. Success depended on the zeal shown by the candidates and their families in winning divine favour. They set to with a will.

The village hummed night and day with the rhythmic chanting of the *tangata-rongorongo*. Food offerings were brought to the god

Makemake, his companion Haua, and even to the priestess who disseminated his cult. Prayers were also addressed to Vie-Kana, a bird god who lived at Mataveri.

Our informant had these details from his uncle Rue, who was one of the last bird-men. While telling me of the activities of the pilgrims, Tepano suddenly uttered a series of piercing cries or yelps, which he assured us were a faithful imitation of the voices of the gods when they took possession of the priests. These contacts between man and god were made in the darkness of the stone houses, from which the inhabitants had been temporarily ejected. Offerings to the gods were accompanied by the formula which they themselves had revealed to men: '*Ka to'o ma Haua, ma Make-make* . . .'

At the beginning of September the *hopu* on the island of Motu-nui redoubled their vigilance. They scarcely slept and never took their eyes off the flight of the *manu-tara*. Suddenly one of them found in the grass a speckled egg. He forthwith leapt on to a rock called the *Rangi-te-manu*, the 'Cry of the bird', and shouted at the top of his voice: 'So-and-so, (the name of his master) shave your head!'

This cry of triumph was heard by a sentinel who had been listening during all these critical days in the shelter of a cave in the Orongo cliff called Haka-rongo-manu (Listening-to-the-birds).

Immediately this signal had been given, the *hopu* prepared to leave the islet. But before going they waited for the servant who had found the egg to perform a brief ceremony. He dipped the precious object in the sea, then bound it to his forehead. Thereupon they all threw themselves into the water and swam for the shore. The return swim was reputedly less dangerous than the outward journey, since the swimmers were under the protection of the sacred symbol. If they kept close to its bearer they had nothing to fear from the sharks, the swell or the breakers: the god would not allow the man he had favoured with his grace, and who shared in the sacred aura of his person, to perish.

The *hopu* with the egg on his forehead climbed the high Orongo cliff as fast as he could, and ceremoniously handed the egg to his master. This act brought his functions to an end, for—apart from a few exceptional cases—it was not he, but his master, who became a bird-man.

As soon as the name of the new bird-man had been proclaimed by the sentinel, the elect of the god Makemake shaved his head, his eyebrows and his eyelashes. A priest tied a piece of red tapa cloth round the arm that had received the sacred egg, and slipped a sliver of sandalwood underneath it. During this investiture the chanters intoned hymns and prayers, and the victor's relatives manifested their triumph in wild dances.

The bird-man, his face covered with red and black stripes and with a bird—probably a wooden one—attached to his back, placed himself at the head of the pilgrims of Orongo, who formed a tumultuous procession and descended towards Mataveri. He is said to have been escorted by other warriors who had also received *manutara* eggs, no doubt collected by their servants before they left Motu-nui. The god's anointed carried the egg in the palm of his hand, covered with a piece of red tapa. He intoned an incantation in a quavering, tearful voice of which Tepano gave a wonderful imitation, although he could remember none of the words. The bird-man's demeanour betrayed extreme agitation and distress. He behaved 'like a god', that is to say, like someone who had become the vessel of the deity. Here, in Tepano's own words, is his description of the dancers and the appearance of the crowd that made its way to Mataveri: 'The men leapt about, twirling their dance paddles. They wore wigs made of women's hair. Others wore turbans of tapa or garlands of leaves. Some were ornamented with hair. They brandished their dance paddles and made their bodies tremble.'

The procession stopped at Mataveri to celebrate joyously the presence among them of a new bird-man. Human victims designated by the priests or the bird-man were sacrificed to Makemake. Their bodies, cooked in enormous ovens, provided the food for noisy banquets interspersed with dances and chanting. The relatives and friends of the Elect, carried away by his triumph, mocked their rivals or enemies. These acts of bravado degenerated into outbreaks of violence that led first to raids, then to fire-raising and pitched battles.

Letters from missionaries on Easter Island contain frequent references to the excitability to which everyone was prone during the period of this '*Campus Martius*'. How long did this state of anarchy last? We do not know. Calm may have been re-established when the bird-man departed to live in seclusion in a hut near Ranu-kao or, according to other authorities, at Anakena or in a village adjoining some important *ahu*. The tabus surrounding this hence-forth sacred personage lasted a year. He could not leave his retreat, was forbidden to bathe, and was forced—on pain of death—to practice continence. He was provided with a special servant who cooked his food in an oven reserved for this purpose. The only external sign of his distinction was a peculiar head-dress, a sort of wig made of women's hair.

The *hopu* or servant who had found the egg was likewise sub-jected to religious interdicts. He withdrew into solitude for several months and could not touch food with the hand that had been ren-dered tabu by contact with the sacred object. The sanctity with which he was impregnated also contaminated his wife and chil-dren, who, for a certain time, were treated like pariahs.

The *manu-tara* egg was blown, filled with tapa, and hung in the bird-man's hut. It was venerated for the great magical virtues attri-buted to it. It was believed to bring abundance. 'The egg was a magician,' Tepano explained to me. 'It gave potatoes, chickens, fish, eels and crayfish.' Fishing in the open sea began soon after its discovery.

In the present state of our knowledge we can see no relation be-tween the apparent object of these ceremonies and the exceptional position this egg hunt seems to have held in the islanders' social and religious life. For a period of seclusion subject to uncom-fortable tabus would not appear likely to stir the ambition of war chiefs.

The religious sense, and the prestige attached to being the 'lord's anointed', are undoubtedly potent stimulants of human action in themselves; but they only partially explain the passionate rivalries that came to light during these festivities. Did the bird-man derive material or political advantages from his position? It seems extremely likely.

To begin with, he had the satisfaction of giving his name to the new year. This name was not the one he had borne up to then, but another, more sacred one, that was revealed to him in a dream. Thus Tepano's paternal uncle, Rue, took the name of Rokunga, which he subsequently gave to his nephew. The year 1866 or 1867, when he emerged victorious from the egg hunt, was called Rokunga. During their seclusion the bird-men fed at the expense of different tribes, and those who refused to bring their contribution were liable to have their huts burnt down.

The nature of the bird-man's authority is not clear. Only his economic privileges are mentioned in our sources. He had a right to claim more than his fair share during family festivals. Missionaries describe these personages as birds of prey, ready to pounce on their victims and strip them of their possessions. No one dared complain too openly, so much were they feared.

This tyranny of the bird-men perhaps explains the nature of their function. In their capacity as the war chiefs or *caudillos* of a tribe possessing the hegemony over part, or even the whole, of the island, they held political power. The discovery of the egg invested them with a sacred authority. They became, like the *ariki*, god-men. Strong in the presence of the deity, they could—without fear of sacrilegious opposition—seize property and enjoy advantages which, at other times, they would probably have had to fight for.

These rights to plunder were doubtless more theoretical than real, for, if they had been universally recognized, it would be difficult to explain the state of war that seems to have reigned during the Mataveri assemblies—at least during the early period of the island's Christianization.

The human sacrifices that took place at Mataveri, and the cannibal banquets that followed them, had a great deal to do with the warlike mood that developed at the end of the festival. The victims' families would have had to be crushed and completely humiliated if their resentment was not to find expression in acts of war.

Tepano showed us the bird-man's dwellings at Rano-raraku. Nearby are the remains of Orohie *ahu*, in which the bird-men were interred.

The funeral rites observed in their honour differed from those of ordinary mortals. Representatives of different tribes attended their funerals and all the other bird-men honoured their *confrère* with their presence. They kept apart from the crowd, and their rôle in these ceremonies was to release the ten cocks that had been tied to the dead man's toes. They passed on these birds to the dead man's son, for whom they became tabu, as did any fowl that had touched the soil of the *ahu* in which the bird-man's remains reposed.

After a year the magic egg lost its power. It was thrown into the sea or placed in a crack in the rock along the Rano-raraku cliff.

Soon after the Mataveri festivities a team of young men returned to Motu-nui to obtain fresh *manu-tara* eggs and, if possible, chicks. These eggs had not yet joined the ranks of profane objects. They were offered to the gods, and those destined to be eaten were given to the *mata-kio* or slaves, whose deaths were of little importance. Some young *manu-tara* were kept in captivity until they could fly. A strip of red tapa cloth was then tied round their wings and they were released with the words: '*Ka oho ki hiva* . . . Go to a foreign country.'

There is no equivalent to the feast of the bird-man in the rest of Polynesia. In many respects it recalls the ceremonies which, in other parts of the world, establish a mystic relationship between the fecundating forces of nature and a man who became a temporary king. These are the god-kings discussed by Frazer in *The Golden Bough*. The parallels that can be traced between the bird-man and these sacred personages are striking: the same connexion with spring, the same importance accorded to the first-fruits, the same insistence on the king's seclusion, the same brevity of his reign. One of our sources referred to obscene dances performed at Orongo by naked women. This detail is strangely reminiscent of the fertility rites that accompany the whole magico-religious complex of the god-men.

The drama enacted on the flanks of Rano-kao, overlooking the green lake at the bottom of the crater, is perhaps in its deepest essence a replica of the ancient rites celebrated in the groves of Lake Nemi, among the Alban Hills, to ensure human being their daily bread.

The concept of the tabu or religious interdict, so deeply ingrained in Polynesian cultures, could not fail to leave its imprint on Easter Island. Ninety years of Christianity have not wiped it out. Today stomach disorders still threaten every plebeian who marries a Miru woman, ulcers eat into the legs of those who walk on land formerly placed under an interdict, and mothers take great care not to eat above the head of their children.

Thanks to Father Englert, we know some of the tabus affecting the manufacture of fishing-nets. Nobody—especially no woman —was allowed near the patch of beach where the experts gathered for this work. Children were permitted to sit beside them so as to learn their art, but they were forbidden to play games and above all to pass under the nets. The craftsman charged with beginning the net had to finish the first row of meshes before sunrise. He was supplied with an ovenful of food by the future owner. The work could not be interrupted until the net was completely finished. Furthermore, it had to be delivered into the owner's hands by those who made it. They used it for three days before handing it over to the client or clients who had ordered it.

The first missionaries to the island draw attention to these tabus, which they were determined to wipe out, and complain of the resistance they encountered over this point. In vain they demonstrated the emptiness of the natives' fears by walking on tabu ground and by trampling on the mounds of earth or branches that indicated the sanctity of some particular spot. Their ostentatious violation of tabus made no impression on the Easter Islanders, who merely concluded that the strangers' *mana* protected them against the magic action of the interdicts. On the other hand, they turned their wrath against those of their compatriots who ventured to imitate them.

A violated tabu could bring death. We have already seen that fish lay under an interdict during the winter months. Those who ate them during this period were supposed to die an agonizing death. The tunny or *kahi* was particularly dangerous. To destroy what they considered an absurd prejudice, the French Fathers encouraged the natives to eat fish during this season. A few Easter Islanders overcame their terror, but a messenger came to announce that a boy who had swallowed a few mouthfuls of tunny was writhing on the ground in the death agony. The missionaries hastened to the spot, greatly alarmed by this turn of events. They triumphed in the end, however, by laughing at the victim's apprehensions until they had convinced him that they were groundless and that he had nothing to fear from his audacious gesture. The poisoning of which the young man was dying

was of a psychosomatic nature; not finding in the priests' attitude the sympathy that would have confirmed his terror, he
escaped from the emotional and physiological disturbances that
would otherwise have shortly caused his death.

Tabus guaranteed respect of ownership. Anyone who wished to
reserve to himself the right of fishing on the shore adjoining his
property had only to place three stones one on top of the other. The
same symbol, or the branch of a tree, protected fields from tres-
passers; but, to be valid, the sign of the interdict had to be put in
position by a chief or some influential man. Crops were subject to
royal tabu until the moment when the first fruits had been presented to the *ariki-mau*.

Violation of a tabu not only calls down a supernatural sanction,
but also arouses the deep resentment of whoever has placed his
person or possessions under its protection. His dignity is at stake
and he may take up arms to avenge his honour.

The *ahu* were probably tabu, for the natives showed great an-
noyance when European visitors went close to examine them.

The first voyagers were highly intrigued by cairns of stones
crowned by a sort of white hat, which they observed at various
places on the island. These humble monuments were *pipihereko* or
tabu symbols. They were often erected on the occasion of funerals.
This fact may explain the mimicry in which the natives indulged
when asked to explain the nature of these objects by signs. At Vaimata one of these cairns stands on the *ahu* itself. Perhaps it was left
there after the funeral of the last man to be interred in this mausoleum.

The distinction between priest and medicine-man, always difficult
to draw, has been entirely blotted out from the memory of the present generations. Medicine-men and sorcerers are also described by
the term *ivi-atua*, although the words *tangata-taku* or *koromaki* seem
to have been especially reserved for them.

All the important or common acts of life were accompanied by
spells and incantations, which gave those who pronounced them
the sense of security necessary for the success of a risky undertaking.

We have seen the priest in his rôle of a magician exorcizing evil spirits. White magic has its counterpart in black magic.

This is the procedure for killing a man, as described to us by Carlos Teao: take a cock and bury it head downward in a hole. Trampling on the spot where the bird is dying of suffocation, pronounce a charm naming the intended victim. The result is certain —he will die, unless some more powerful magician comes to his assistance.

It is also possible to influence other people's actions, or even to make them ill, by a simple incantation. The following is an example of one such formula: '*Ka oho ki te kokoma manava, ka taviri, ka tavara*—Go and penetrate his entrails, he staggers, he falls.'

The agent of death thus despatched is no doubt a tutelary spirit employed by the magician to carry out his will. Teao assured us that the intermediary was an animal depicted on the tablets. This is doubtful, but it is an interesting idea, for it would explain the superstitious terror in which these pieces of engraved wood are held: the signs may well be regarded as so many little devils waiting to be launched against their prey.

The magic of words, in the most literal sense, has always been very clearly perceived by Polynesians. Their constantly alert sensibilities predispose them to snatch at the slightest phrase casting a slur on their dignity or vanity. If they find a threatening implication in a sentence, their reaction is terrible. Brother Eyraud has left a vivid account of one episode among his misfortunes on the island that may serve to illustrate this. Wishing to warn his 'evil genius', Torometi, that he would have to answer for his iniquities in another life and to remind him that he was mortal, but being still unfamiliar with the language of the island, he used the phrase '*E pohe oe*—you will die'. He had no sooner uttered these words than Torometi behaved as though struck by lightning. He turned pale, he trembled, and his gestures betrayed the most abject terror coupled with growing rage. 'The Father said, "*E pohe oe*",' he cried to the crowd, who were no less horror-stricken by the mealediction than he himself. Realizing the full significance of his unfortunate phrase, the missionary did his best to pacify those who had been shocked by the brutality of his imprecation.

Religion and medicine were inseparable. This was a very natural association, for most of the diseases from which the natives suffered were attributed to the malevolence of demons or gods who took possession of their victims' bodies in order to torment them. These intrusions by spirits occurred without the patient at first being aware of them; he did not notice anything until he felt the first symptoms of the illness. A priest was immediately sent for. He called upon the victim to confess, to find out whether he had violated some tabu or committed some other sacrilege. He then addressed himself to the spirit, whose replies were uttered in a strident tone, politely inviting him to remove himself. Only when the spirit proved stubborn did the priest resort to force. He jumped on the spirit if he tried to take refuge in a corner of the hut; he sprang at the walls, halted, watched for him, and went in pursuit again. The door was barricaded and, as an added precaution, the hut was sometimes covered with a net. After a hunt of varying duration, the *ivi-atua* seized the sick man's clothes, ran out of the hut, and cast spirit and clothing into the flames lit nearby. He then returned to his patient and informed him that he was finally cured. In especially serious cases the hut was set alight and the *ivi-atua* mounted guard, to hurl the spirit back into the flames if he should manage to escape.

If the patient died, the priest saved his reputation by announcing that an unknown and more powerful spirit had taken the place of the one he had driven out.

Treatment was not exclusively magico-religious in character. Magic and science were sometimes combined. One of the favourite therapeutic procedures was to make the patient sweat by laying him on a bed of banana leaves in an *umu* containing white-hot stones. The ancient Easter Islanders were also skilful masseurs. Thomson writes that during his laborious trip across the island he was much conforted by the energetic treatment of native practitioners, who rubbed his aching muscles until he dozed off.

The island's flora is too poor to have favoured the development of a pharmacopoeia of any importance. A few plants, notably vervain and the bamboos introduced last century, are held nowadays to possess medicinal properties; but the natives prefer European remedies.

The healers (*ivi-atua*) charged heavily for their services. The fees were foodstuffs or articles of carved wood. Those who failed to pay their debts exposed themselves to the medicine-man's revenge.

CHAPTER VIII

Ancestor Images

THE LITTLE wooden statuettes or *moai kavakava*, so highly prized by collectors, belong to the island's religious art, just as much as the famous statues on the mausoleums—and like them are accessories of its cult.

They represent a bearded man whose emaciated and half-decayed body shows the vertebrae, protruding ribs, and a breast-bone as hooked as the carina of a fowl. The top of the skull is sometimes decorated with a relief portraying a bird or an anthromorphic monster. There are a great number of these statuettes in museums or private collections. They are very uniform in type, and it is only in recent and already decadent specimens that the details suggestive of a corpse tend to diminish or disappear.

In addition to these *moai kavakava*, flat images of female figures —called *moai paapaa*—were also carved. These sculptures are comparatively rare, of late date, and executed in a style that has not broken completely free from that of the masculine images, which were their prototypes. The detailed treatment accorded to the sexual attributes leaves no doubt that the sculptors aimed at representing women; but they nevertheless wear the same comma-shaped pointed beard as the emaciated male figures. They also resemble this type of image in showing anatomical details characteristic of a decaying corpse, although the sculptor did not apparently wish to stress these or to suggest death.

The wooden figurines were inspired by the shape in which the ancient Easter Islanders pictured the spirits of the dead. Religious imagination and artistic creation exercised a mutual influence upon one another, and if the artist originally sought to give concrete shape to their visions, their works have imposed an entirely conventional conception of phantoms on their descendants.

A myth, of which we collected a new version, tells us how Chief Tuʻu-ko-ihu—one of the culture heroes of Easter Island—came to carve the first of these statuettes.

146

Tu'u-ko-ihu was going to his house called Hare-koka [House-of-the-cockroaches] at Hanga-hahave. As he was crossing the hill of Punapau he saw two spirits sleeping at the foot of a cliff of red stone. They were Hiti-rau and Nuku-te-mango. He caught a glimpse of their protruding ribs and hollow bellies. Another *akuaku* [spirit, spectre], who was awake, cried: 'Wake up, the noble chief has seen our protruding ribs.'

Hiti-rau and Nuku-te-mango ran after Tu'u-ko-ihu, and when they had caught up with him they asked him: 'O Chief, what did you see?' 'Nothing,' replied Tu'u-ko-ihu. The spirits asked him again: 'O Chief, are you certain you saw nothing. Perhaps you are mistaken?' 'I saw nothing,' repeated Tu'u-ko-ihu, and he went on his way.

The spirits disappeared, but a little while afterwards they met the chief again as he went on his way and asked him: 'What do you know about us?' Three times they asked him the same question, but Tu'u-ko-ihu continued to answer: 'I know nothing.' If the chief had hesitated, or if he had told them what he had seen, the two spirits would certainly have killed him.

When Tu'u-ko-ihu reached Hare-koka the people of the district were opening the ovens in which they had cooked their food. Tu'u-ko-ihu picked up two half-burnt firebrands and took them into his hut. He carved them to represent the two spirits he had seen. That night he saw in a dream some female spirits, which he reproduced next day in another piece of wood.

The news that Tu'u-ko-ihu had carved images in wood spread throughout the island. Everyone came and ordered images from him. Tu'u-ko-ihu kept his promises, but several people, in their ingratitude, made him no gift of food. Tu'u-ko-ihu refused to give them the statuettes he had made for them. One evening, when they had come to claim them, Tu'u-ko-ihu said to them: 'Come here.' They went into his hut and saw the images dancing of their own accord, by magic. They were struck with fear and paid their debts.

The function of these images in the island's religious life is obscure, but their ritual significance is well established by allusions

made to them by those who had an opportunity of living among the
Easter Islanders before their conversion. On several occasions,
Brother Eyraud saw his hosts pick up these images, execute a few
dance movements with them, and intone a brief chant in their
honour. He did not consider that these actions were worthy of
being described as 'religious' in nature.

These images were also displayed during festivals, notably at
harvest time, when the tribute of first fruits was paid. In between
times, they were kept in the huts, carefully wrapped in tapa cloth.
Their owners liked to put them on show, and they attached them to
their persons in order to dance with them. Some people wore up to
a score of them. When they were taken out of their tapa wrappings,
chants were sung and they were handled like babies. At religious
ceremonies they were given a place of honour.

Human statuettes of wood served in the rest of Polynesia as
temporary tabernacles for gods and ancestral spirits. In the Whan-
ganui district of New Zealand, each one of the little images kept in
the huts was dedicated to the spirit of one of the family's ancestors.
The latter was believed to become incarnate in the image when he
wished to converse with the living. The Tahitian *tii* were also
temporary vessels of minor deities or spirits, who were called into
them by the priests. The very realistically conceived Mangarevan
images represented gods. These comparisons give some weight to
the Easter Island tradition that their wooden images were carved
on the death of a member of the family.

These figurines were capable of being animated by a supernatural force, as the following legend testifies. A young man had
borrowed a statuette from Tu'u-ko-ihu to decorate the hut in
which he was giving a feast. The hut caught fire and everything in it
was burnt. The young man went immediately to Tu'u-ko-ihu to
tell him of the mishap and offer him compensation. As he entered
the *ariki's* hut he saw to his astonishment the statuette which he
had believed lost—intact. Tu'u-ko-ihu, who had heard a loud
clamour at the moment the fire broke out, had merely said: 'O my
brother, Little-jumping-bird, come back'; and the statue had come
back of its own accord.

Surprise has been expressed at the readiness with which the
Easter Islanders parted with these images to their visitors, and for

this reason their religious character has been doubted. Like many objects of the same order, they only became sacred when the spirits descended into them. They lost much of their sanctity outside the ceremonies or when some occurrence deprived them of their mystic aura.

These statuettes are still carved by the present-day natives, who thus continue an artistic tradition that was interrupted after the Christianization of the island, to be reborn when the Easter Islanders noticed their visitors' enthusiasm for these objects and their value as articles of barter. Today the manufacture of statuettes has become an industry. They are turned out in organized workshops by a master craftsman and his assistants. In the workshop of the most famous of these sculptors, Gabriel Beri Beri, Lavachery not only saw figurines being mass-produced, but aberrant forms made to gratify the bad taste of Chilean crews. Among these 'curios' was an image of a skeletal man wearing a naval officer's cap, others holding a second statuette in their arms, and finally some giving the military salute. Our informant Tepano sculptured figurines that differed completely from the traditional type of *moai kavakava*. They consisted of various kinds of monsters, often inspired by the shape of the piece of wood he had managed to procure. These creations, which are without parallel in the island's art, were called by their author *manu-uru*, a word that also means 'mask' in the modern dialect of the island. Tepano used an adze left him by a famous sculptor named Tomenika, to which he attributed magic powers. It was possession of this instrument that had made a sculptor of him, for before inheriting it he had not known how to carve wood. This is what Lavachery wrote about Tepano, whom we often watched at work:

The way in which the primitive craftsmen handled the adze filled us with admiration. The vigour, precision and steadiness with which Tepano struck the wood and took off a regular chip —often as long and thin as a leaf—was in no way inferior to what I have seen done by the Negro sculptors of Africa. The image gradually emerged from the block, carved in neat and equal facets. As the details appeared, the adze blows became less violent while losing nothing of their firmness. Sometimes—for example, to trace the hollow of the eyebrow arch—Tepano took the adze by the blade and used it like the point of a knife. This was also the way in which he drew the lines representing the hair or tattooing and separated the fingers of the hand. He made no use of his pocket-knife until the moment came to pierce in the centre of the eyeball a hole two centimetres deep, into which he inserted a circle of mutton bone (in the old days it would have been human bone), in the hollow centre of which he fitted a shiny knob of obsidian. Neither the bone nor the volcanic glass were held in place by any adhesive. They were so perfectly mounted one in the other and the two of them in the wood that there was no play whatever.

Finally, Tepano meticulously scraped the surface of his carving with a piece of window glass, carefully preserved for this work. He told us that in the old days a piece of obsidian was used for this purpose.

CHAPTER IX

The Great Statues

EASTER ISLAND's fame is due to its great statues. They are and will remain the very symbol of its mysterious past. Their presence on this solitary and bare islet is as much of a riddle today as at the time when Roggeveen, the first European to contemplate them, wrote in his log: 'These stone figures filled us with amazement, for we could not understand how people without solid spars and without ropes were able to raise them . . .'

Our first contact with the great statues was mingled with disappointment. Shortly after disembarking, and in the pouring rain, we went to look at those that had appeared to Cook and La Pérouse when they landed on the same shore. They lie today like ponderous hulks on the inclined surface of Koirorooa *ahu*, not far from the mole built by the Chileans with the rubble of their platforms. Their destruction was reported as long ago as 1815 by Kotzebue, who had tried to look at them from the topside of his whaler. So we did not expect to see them on their mausoleum, crowned with red hats, as they had appeared to the great eighteenth-century navigators. We had, however, supposed that even after falling to the ground these prostrate figures would have retained some majesty. Our disillusionment was perhaps comparable to the feeling which made Roggeveen and Cook imagine that these statues were an agglomerate of mud. Cut in volcanic cinder, whose grey nodules bristle all over the surface like so many warts, they show no sign of the arduous struggle of the sculptor with his material.

The majority of these statues lie face downwards, leaving nothing to be seen but the flat, narrow neck and the slightly arched back that widens out below the belt. These so-called statues are, in fact, enormous busts, monstrous legless cripples with heads too long for their massive trunks. Amidst the black rubble their yellowish hue strikes a discordant note in the colour-scheme of the landscape. The tufa of which they are made breaks up easily, and many of them seem to have disintegrated under the effects of rain and returned to the earth from which they came.

It would be unjust to deny all grandeur to these sculptures because they are no longer in position on the lofty platform of the mausoleums and because they have suffered the depradations of man and time. We became aware of a certain ponderous majesty when a tour of the island brought us to Tonga-riki *ahu*. This sanctuary was formerly surmounted by fifteen statues. Like the rest, they have all been thrown down, with the exception of the lower part of one of them, which still rests on its basalt pedestal.

The head of one statue had broken as it fell, and come to rest against a heap of rubble. Against this mound of scoriae it leans its face, pitted with two orbits as deep as those of a skull. This macabre vision is thoroughly in keeping with its surroundings in a place where everything seems to speak of death and funerals. There is nothing that does not wear an air of mourning—the plain covered with volcanic debris, the outcrops of basalt, the walls of the mausoleum, and even the sea that rolls slowly over slabs of calcined and blackened lava.

This decapitated bust, this head with its empty sockets, aid the imagination in replacing on the pedestals from which they fell the fifteen giants that have been knocked down like so many Aunt Sallies. One can imagine them as they were in better days: upright, their backs to the sea and their great orbits fixed on the tall cliff of Rano-raraku. Here the same urge is expressed as in the ancient civilizations of Asia—the overwhelming desire to combine aesthetic satisfaction with a sense of the stupendous, artistic form with staggering proportions. This mania for the colossal in a world where everything else is on a tiny scale, and among a people with limited resources, constitutes the whole miracle of Easter Island.

These rough and angular monsters must have presented a strange spectacle at sunset or on moonlight nights when their looming silhouettes were outlined against the Pacific. It has been claimed that these images were set up to defend the land against invasion by the sea. This is an absurdly romantic interpretation, for they turned their backs to the foe and invariably faced the gentle hills and stony plains of the interior. They are indifferent to the ocean's struggle with the island, but the waves are none the less bent on their destruction. They are slowly breaking up the statues they can reach with their spray and sapping the cliffs that support them. Some of the statues have already fallen victims to the surge.

A lot has been written about the disdainful sneer on these great faces. This expression is striking on the volcano statues, whose thin, pouting lips seem full of contempt. It is less evident in the images on the *ahu*. Wind and weather have doubtless brought about this softening of the features by reducing the sharpness of their contours. In our view, the Easter Island sculptors worked in a material so soft that it made for a certain laziness. They too readily accepted a single formula that they could reproduce without effort. Their first conception was bold; their mistake was to remain satisfied with it. They did not always avoid the weaknesses of mass-production.

Some of the statues were probably painted. When we entered the platform of Vinapu *ahu*, which had been emptied of its rubble and converted into a kind of vault after the fall of the statues, we discovered that the parts of the busts protected from wind and weather bore traces of red and white paint. The same was apparently true of the British Museum statue of Hoa-haka-hana-ia, which at the time of its removal, was smeared with red and white ochre.

Roggeveen, in his haste to quit these inhospitable shores, imagined that the statues wore on their heads baskets full of white stones. The oddity of this ornament made a vivid impression on the minds of all those who saw it *in situ*. Their amazement is understandable in view of the fact that these 'hats' measured up to nine feet in height and six feet and a half in diameter. One rainy day we took refuge inside one of these cylinders that had been converted into a shelter.

All the 'hats' came from Mount Punapau, a crater that rises behind Hanga-roa. Twenty-three of these cylinders have remained at their place of origin, probably dating from the time when work was discontinued on Rano-raraku. The Punapau quarry was visited by some members of Captain Cook's crew, who already noticed the abandoned cylinders. There is nothing remarkable about this modest crater, except perhaps its red colour, which causes it to gape like a bloody wound in the midst of the green pastures.

Various hypotheses have been advanced to explain the significance of these cylinders. They have been described in turn as hats, turbans, feather diadems, funerary symbols, and whitewashed hair. No one has been willing to see them for what they really are: a naive imitation of the top-knot, although—like the top-knot itself—they are called *pukao*. This headgear represents a late innovation that did not have time to become universally adopted, for a large number of the statues are without it—especially those on the volcano.

The statues that surmounted the great mausoleums numbered about three hundred. This figure is approximate, because many of them have been completely destroyed by the natives during the last few years, while others have been buried in the wreckage of their *ahu* or, in some cases, included in the material used to build new sanctuaries. The height of these statues varies between eleven and eighteen feet. Those on the south coast are generally taller and of larger bulk than those on the west coast. The largest statue on an *ahu* is that called Paro, which lies on Te Pito-te-kura *ahu*. It is thirty-three feet high and twenty-five feet eight inches in circumference, and certainly weighs more than twenty tons. It is surmounted by a cylinder that is six feet high and eight feet across.

Only a few *ahu* statues were carved in basalt: all the others came from the quarry on Rano-raraku, which lies to the east of the island, near Poike peninsula. This crater is the last in a system of volcanic cones stretching across the island from Rano-aroi. It is formed of thick layers of cinders. Its southern face, which has been eaten away by the sea, consists of a steep wall cut by a deep gash. The quarry is situated on the south-west slope and in the interior of the crater, where the tufa is most easily accessible. The entrance to these two vast sculptors' workshops is guarded by an army of statues which, unlike the rest, are not connected with any *ahu*.

If the name of Easter Island still evokes unfathomable mysteries, if the present inhabitants have been declared unworthy to be the descendants of those who carved the statues, it is because this wild spot has fired the imagination of all who saw it. Whatever their turn of mind, personal culture or sensibility, the words in which they describe Rano-raraku have always borne the stamp of sincere and profound emotion. It was the sum total of these impressions that gave birth to the legend of Easter Island as a relic of Atlantis.

During the three weeks we lived among these statues we saw them in sunshine, by moonlight, and on stormy nights. Each time we felt the same shock, the same uneasiness, as on the first day. This sense of oppression is due less to their dimensions than to their confused distribution. If they were arranged in some apparent order one could catch a glimpse of the purpose and plan of the dead; but the almost human casualness and turbulence with which this assembly of giants with huge noses and flat necks is scattered about is somehow disturbing.

All the statues have been carved on a single model, but their capricious grouping seems to endow them with a certain individuality. Some appear to have gathered for a friendly chat; others gain from their isolation a disdainful and ill-humoured air; yet others seem bowed down with care and inspire pity. All these images bore names, and some still retain them today. It is as though the natives, too, had perceived how humanly accessible these statues look.

Behind the swarms of statues standing on the grassy slope of the volcano is the army of those about to be born. Notwithstanding the fact that the workshop is abandoned and silent and the sculptors long ago dead, these rough-hewn or half-carved statues waiting to be taken down into the plain create a more living atmosphere than the finished sculptures that stand guard at the outposts of the quarry. Here everything is expressive of work and effort.

To the visitor walking round the quarry it seems as though this were a day of rest. The workmen have gone home to their villages, but tomorrow they will be back and the mountainside will ring with the blows of stone hammers; it will echo with laughter, discussions, and the rhythmic chanting of the men hauling the statues. How could they fail to come back, these sculptors who have left their tools lying at the foot of the work, where one only has to bend down to pick them up?

A few sections of the cliff have been shorn off perpendicularly and the statues carved from them have long stood on one of the island's *ahu*. In a crypt patiently hollowed out with picks, a fifty-foot colossus sleeps on a bed of stone. Another month of under-cutting and he would have been ready to leave his niche and go down into the plain. Now he will remain here for centuries, sur-rounded by ferns like an abandoned corpse. And his two com-panions, whose faces and chests only just emerge from the tufa at the threshold of the crypt, are also dead men.

To reach the neighbouring niches it is necessary to walk on bodies, to catch hold of noses, to step across blocks and outcrops of tufa transformed into statues or the embryos of statues. The visitor distinguishes one or two at first, then suddenly realizes that he is sitting on a gigantic eyebrow arch. He rises to examine it, but next to it he sees hands resting on a belly, and next to this torso another head. The contours merge so thoroughly into the grisaille of the rock that spotting the heads and bodies becomes almost a game. An enormous statue is stretched out like a sleeping giant beneath a kind of dais carved in the tufa. The water dripping from the cliff has worn its chest into a hollow.

Some of the statues are almost finished. A few blows with a hammer would have been enough to sever the long thin strip of stone holding the body to its matrix, and the statue would have been ready to slide on to the close-set, tough grass. In some cases, even, they have been chocked up with stones in preparation for the moment when they would be entirely detached from the gangue in which they were cut. A few of these unfinished statues are so pro-digious that it is questionable whether the sculptors really intended to complete and shift them. One of these colossi is sixty feet long and occupies the whole length of one ridge of the moun-tain. Perhaps it was only a huge petroglyph intended to remain as we now see it. The frenzy that impelled the Easter Islanders to carve dozens of statues simultaneously is a strange phenomenon for which we can find no explanation, not even a hypothetical one.

The statue-makers also installed themselves in the interior of the crater, where a different atmosphere reigns. The bottom of the funnel is occupied by a reed-fringed lake at which cattle drink. The horizon is bounded by verdant slopes that make of this pocket a world apart set in the island like a jewel. In this landscape the statues that rise from the shores of the lagoon towards the crest of the volcano have a more friendly and peaceful look than those that watch like sentinels on the borders of their domain.

The statues in and around the crater of Mount Rano-raraku are of a different type from those which decorate the *ahu*. The two groups are closely related, but distinguished by certain details of style whose conventional character is clearly demonstrated by their constant repetition. In the first place, the volcano statues do not show the hollow orbits that give the *ahu* statues their slightly skull-like apperance. The concave plane corresponding to the cheeks runs right up to the underside of the eyebrow arch, whose shadow creates the illusion of eyes. The back of the neck is also flatter and, as it was not intended to carry a red cylinder, the top of the head is narrower. From a purely aesthetic point of view, Rano-raraku statues are undoubtedly superior. The lines of the nose and cheek-bones are vigorous, the neck emerges more distinctly, and the overall outline is less bulky. The mausoleum statues, which rest on slabs of stone on top of a platform, are more squat and their bases broaden out to give them stability. Two of the Rano-raraku statues that have been excavated—one by Mrs Routledge, the other by our expedition—have bases ending in a peg, a detail clearly indicating that they were intended to be planted in the ground. This characteristic may well recur in other statues of this group, although the unfinished specimens do not exhibit this peculiarity and have flat bases.

Our prolonged contact with the volcano statues enabled us to observe some interesting facts. When we uncovered their bases we perceived that they were often clumsy and badly trimmed. The back was not finished until the statue was in position, and the sculptors were obliged to erect a scaffolding in order to get at it. The statues that have not undergone these finishing touches have thick, shapeless necks on which the crest that joined them to the rock is still visible. The quarry workers were generally conscientious. They polished the surfaces of their sculptures till they had rendered them almost smooth to the touch. Certain parts of the body, such as the ears and hands, were carved with meticulous care. The hands, whose fingers are as elongated as though they ended in mandarin's finger-nails, are treated in the same manner as in the wooden statuettes, with the thumb curving slightly outwards. The parallels between these two types of sculpture are important in determining the age and origin of the great statues. They also extend to other details, for instance some of the tufa statues, like some of the *moai kava-kava*, bear a sort of O and M in relief above horizontal lines. These designs must be interpreted as conventional representations of the tapa belt and its knot. A few statues bear marks on the neck, such as wavy lines, that are faithful reproductions of Easter Island tattoo patterns appropriate to this part of the body.

Landslides that have taken place at several points along the slopes of the volcano have uprooted some busts and dragged them down to the foot of the mountain. Other statues have been completely buried under the rubble. In one case only the head is visible, and in others nothing but the brow emerges from the turf.

Long before the arrival of the Whites, the natives must have visited the quarry, where they passed their time engraving designs on the walls of tufa or even on the statues themselves. They took a particular delight in portraying the frigate-bird and the god with big eyes. Their European and Chilean successors contented themselves with perpetuating their own names or those of their ships.

About four miles from Rano-raraku across the plain that occupies the centre of the island, or along the southern coast, rows of statues begin to succeed one another at more or less regular intervals. A few are broken, but the majority are simply lying on the grass. The natives say that these advance guards of the army of the volcano are statues whose magical march towards the coastal mausoleums was suddenly halted by an evil spell. A more rational explanation seems to be that these statues were left by the wayside when work at the quarry stopped. Some archaeologists have compared them to the 'tired stones' of Peru that never reached the cyclopean building-works for which they were intended. They see in their abandonment proof of a cataclysm that surprised the ancient population at the height of its creative period.

It is the isolation of these statues that has given rise to this illusion, for none of them seems to have been destined for an *ahu*. In olden times they stood at the same places where they now lie. To

prove this, there is no need of the technical arguments put forward
by Mrs Routledge. It is enough to read Captain Cook's description
of the south coast, which he had reconnoitred by members of his
crew. He notes in a region that must correspond to the bay of
Vaihu the existence of statues which—contrary to those previously
seen in the rest of the island—were planted straight in the ground.
One of them was so tall that it provided shade for the thirty men of
the expeditionary corps during a halt.

Examining the plain from Mount Toatoa at a moment when the
light was favourable, Mrs Routledge perceived that the statues,
which might have seemed scattered at random, marked sections of
roads. Traces of them, sometimes scarcely distinguishable, could
be seen to lead away from the quarry in four different directions.
These roads, which had probably been used for the transportation
of the statues, were slightly sunken and bordered by low banks.
There is no justification for the belief that they were triumphal
avenues planned to give access to the holy of holies of the quarry. If
such had been the natives' intention, the statues would have been
more symmetrically spaced out. No more orderly arrangement is
discernible than in the neighbourhood of the quarry.

The isolated statues are not all placed along more or less hypothetical avenues. There are fourteen scattered about the island in
positions where their presence is hard to explain. One of them, of
imposing dimensions, is stretched on its back, far from any habitation, on the northern slope of Mount Rano-aroi. We were surprised to discover another perched on the summit of Mount
Teatenga. One solitary statue stands a short distance from the Vaimata *ahu* in a part of the island to which its transport must have
presented immense difficulties. It may very well have been abandoned just before reaching the platform that was to serve it as a
base.

The function of these isolated statues is obscure. Some may have
formed part of mausoleums that have now vanished. Others may
have been colossal boundary posts—this, at any rate, is the rôle of
certain stone images or *tii* on Tahiti. But even if we accept the tradition based on this analogy, the small number of these boundary
statues does not accord with the inextricable network of tribal and
family frontiers.

The first interpretation that springs to mind when seeking to fathom the significance of the great statues is to regard them as images of deities worshipped by the ancient Easter Islanders. Roggeveen was so convinced of their being idols that he believed he could see traces of continued religious veneration in the islanders' attitude towards them. 'The natives,' he writes, 'squatted on their heels, bowed their heads, and alternately lowered and raised their joined palms.'

No outward sign of any religious observances was noted by other voyagers. The natives sometimes expressed vexation when visitors walked over the mausoleums, but these indiscretions never caused them any real anger.

Modern natives, questioned as to the purpose of the statues, said that they were erected merely to decorate the mausoleums. This was also the explanation given to the missionaries by Easter Islanders who had been brought up in the ancient traditions.

The great architectural enterprises of the Polynesians often contain an element of vanity and rivalry, a very keen desire to astonish and outdo the neighbours. Today this competitive spirit finds expression in an urge to produce larger wooden statues than other people. Malinowski observed in Melanesia the same need to exaggerate the size of ritual or display objects—ceremonial axes, for example. There can be no doubt that the colossal dimensions of the statues were the expression of a similar mentality.

The ease with which tufa lends itself to sculpture, together with vanity and the spirit of emulation, may explain the appearance and proportions of the statues, but not their origin and primary significance. The first question to be answered is whether these busts with the disdainful pout were really idols. The names of several of them are still known to the present generation. Captain Cook already made a list of them. None of these names are those of a Polynesian god, and many are descriptive terms—such as 'Twisted Neck', 'Tattooed One', 'Stinker', etc. . . .

Now, Polynesians have a habit of giving proper names to all the precious or remarkable objects that surround them. The statues cannot have escaped this tendency, unless their names commemorate deified ancestors. Cook was struck by the fact that many of these names were followed by the epithet *ariki*, meaning 'chief'. He deduced from it that these busts or *moai* were monuments to the dead. His supposition was only partially correct. On the Marquesas Islands, whose civilization has so many points of contact with that of Easter Island, the statues dominating the terraces of the sanctuaries represented famous chiefs or priests whose spirits had entered the ranks of the tribe's tutelary deities. It must have been the same on our island. Its monuments were erected towards the close of an evolution the main phases of which may be traced in Central Polynesia. The rectangular platforms of the Tuamotu sanctuaries, which, like those of Easter Island, are called *ahu*, are surmounted at the rear by slabs of stone which are sometimes given a vaguely anthropomorphic shape. Those with an anthropomorphic outline are called *tii*, a word employed by the Tahitians and Marquesans to designate every human image. The central stele, which is the most important, is called the *tapao ariki*, 'the sign of the chief'. Two slabs of stone planted in the forecourt of the sanctuary (*marae*) served as back-rests for the chiefs and were analogous with those on the *ahu*, against which the gods and the ancestors leaned. These stones were eventually looked upon as vessels into which the spirits entered when they were invoked by the priests. This was doubtless the part played by the Easter statues.

The sanctity of the statues was, therefore, temporary and depended on rites that caused the advent of the deities. In the ordinary way, the image was simply an ornament, a lifeless block of stone. When, for lack of worshippers, the gods and ancestors were deprived of sacrifices, the images that were no longer visited finally lost all religious significance and ceased to be the object of any cult. They became *noa*—profane.

Many people, even in scientific circles, refuse to admit that these statues are the work of the Polynesian ancestors of the present-day Easter Islanders. The most fantastic hypotheses have been advanced to explain their presence on this little island. Some writers have not hesitated to ride roughshod over geological data and invent imaginary continents, whose subsequent disappearance they attribute to terrible cataclysms. Others have sought the origin of these colossi successively in Egypt, India, Korea, and

Melanesia. Historical novels have been cooked up to describe the invasion of Easter Island and the destruction of its civilization by warrior peoples. These far-fetched parallels and this dramatic vision of the past possess such powers of attraction that no scientific proof (I fear) will dispel the enigmas of Easter Island as they appear to dreamers—whether or not they are specialists in archaeology!

There is no mystery about the relative age of the statues. They surmounted mausoleums which the Easter Islanders continued to build until the middle of last century. They cannot, therefore, be considered independently of the sepulchres, which were still in use less than a hundred years ago.

Anyone who observes the statues with an impartial eye is struck by the cleanness of the angles, the polish of the surfaces, and the precision of the details. The tempests that have flailed these colossi, the countless rains that have washed them, the winds that have lashed them, would surely have made greater changes in the surface of the tufa in which they were carved, if the action of all these atmospheric agents had gone on for as long as had been claimed.

This geological argument is amply confirmed by other observations of an archaeological nature. The stone slab supporting one of the statues on Te-peu *ahu* rests on courses of stone identical in every way with those that form the foundations of modern houses. The men who erected this *ahu* must, therefore, have lived in huts in no way different from those seen by visitors to the island prior to 1870.

The analogies of style between the stone statues and the wooden figurines testify to the fact that the two types of image were produced by one and the same people. The Easter Islanders continue to respect the traditional forms in carving the figurines, and it is impossible, on the one hand, to admit that the wooden statuettes are more or less recent, while, on the other, asserting that the tufa statues are immensely ancient.

The basalt bust now at the British Museum is without a doubt the finest example of Easter Island sculpture. It comes from the village of Orongo, where it was the object of a special cult at the time of the feast of the bird-man. Far from appearing to our informants as the relic of an unknown civilization, this statue was to their minds a god that had participated in ceremonies still celebrated by their own great-grandparents.

A descriptive, illustrated catalogue of all the statues still on the island would doubtless facilitate their classification and perhaps reveal features that would enable us to reconstruct the stages passed through by this monumental art, which appears at first sight so uniform. Travellers and scientists who visited the island, occupied by more urgent tasks, omitted to carry out this census, on which their successors could have worked at leisure. It is therefore on the basis of incomplete data that Klaus Günther has recently attacked the problem of a typology and chronology of the great statues. Like the majority of those who have dealt with this question, Günther is convinced that the bulkier, clumsier and more archaic-looking *ahu* statues are older than those on Mount Rano-raraku. Among the volcano statues, those inside the crater seem to be earlier than those spread out along the external slopes. The suggestion is that the statues were first carved to be erected on the mausoleums, then—after this practice had passed out of fashion —they were merely put up, for reasons unknown, in the vicinity of the quarry. My colleague Lavachery, who has studied the statues *in situ*, holds the opposite opinion. Simply as an hypothesis, he has put forward the following chronological schema: The first statues are those that never left their niches. They correspond to a period during which the sculptors were, so to speak, getting their hands in. Then the statues were taken down and erected on the outskirts of the quarry. Encouraged by their success, the Easter Islanders transported the first statues to Tonga-riki *ahu*, which is nearest the quarry. From then on, the practice of placing the statues on the mausoleums became general. The volcano sculptors created 'a mass-production type with a maximum height of twelve feet that could be transported in any direction'. Then came the fifth and last period, corresponding to the advent of the Europeans in the eighteenth century. For lack of orders, the sculptors did not finish the works they had begun, and as the result of the disasters that struck the island monumental sculpture disappeared.

The differences between the *ahu* statues and those of the quarry, which have been enumerated above and which consist primarily in the absence of eyes from the latter, are an important fact that must be borne in mind; but it is hard to say whether—as is commonly supposed—they have a chronological value; or whether the style of the statues simply depended upon their purpose.

Apart from differentiation between the two groups, the statues do not vary much amongst themselves. The uniformity within each series seems, of itself, to indicate that this monumental art flourished for only a short period—a few centuries at the most.

Volcanic tufa is a sort of earth bound by the presence of fragments and nodules of stone. It is friable and easily carved. The modern sculptors consider this material easier to work than wood. With nothing but an axe they cut out a large block of tufa in a day and in a few hours transform it into replicas of the great statues. Mrs Routledge possibly goes too far when she estimates the time required for a team of sculptors to carve one of the Rano-raraku statues at a fortnight. Her assessment is entirely hypothetical, but it represents a salutary reaction against those who have exaggerated the duration of this task. It must not be forgotten that the quarry workers had not only to fashion the statue, but to carve from the cliff the block to which they were going to give human shape. The depth of the crypts and caverns which they opened in the side of Mount Rano-raraku testifies to considerable effort, intensified by the primitive tools they employed. They used great mallets, vaguely reminiscent of the Chellean hand-axes, which were dressed by striking off large flakes and tapered to a point. It was with these picks that they attacked the walls of tufa, but to finish off the statues they required more delicate implements —stone gravers, about a foot long, which are found in large numbers on the surface of the island. These instruments were so easy to handle that a shaft was superfluous. While pickaxes abound in the quarry, these chisels are rarer. They were probably too valuable to leave by the statues.

Writers have repeatedly stated that the transportation of the statues was a superhuman task presupposing a population denser than the island could have supported. They have talked of weights of a hundred tons, even of five hundred tons. In dealing with this problem, the first point to establish is the real weight of the statues.

This has been greatly exaggerated, like everything to do with Easter Island. The enormous head brought back by Pierre Loti and today at the Musée de l'Homme, Paris, weighs only twenty-four hundred-weight. Taking the specific weight of the Ranoraraku tufa as a basis, we tried to determine the weight of the statues that were transported to the *ahu*: the result of the calculation was five to six tons. The volcano statues were certainly three, four, and even five times heavier; but even so, their transportation would not be beyond the limits of human capacities—especially as the distances they had to go were comparatively short. As for the unfinished monsters in the quarry, they were perhaps no more than huge petroglyphs in relief, parallels to the recumbent figures in European cathedrals. If it had been intended to transport them elsewhere, the sculptors would not have chosen almost inaccessible spots in which to carve them.

We shall never be certain of the means by which the Easter Islanders transported these bulky and crumbling masses. The problem is complicated by the fact that Easter Island has always been short of timber. One hesitates to accept the idea that the twisted trunks of the *toro-mirò* or the other shrubs that clung to the slopes of the volcano could have been turned into rollers or skids. However, the natives did not depend exclusively on the scanty local flora, but had at their disposal the driftwood brought by the sea. The pieces of wood from which they made their dance paddles and their big clubs were large enough to provide levers or the runners of the skids.

Strong ropes were needed to haul the statues. The Easter Islanders made them with the fibres of the paper mulberry, which they probably cultivated on a large scale.

If we admit that the Easter Islanders had the timber to construct skids, and ropes with which to haul the statues, the mystery is reduced to a question of labour-force and energy. Our islanders were not the only Polynesians to raise and cart heavy masses. The Marquesans incorporated in the masonry of their sanctuaries blocks weighing more than ten tons. They were dragged down sloping surfaces of earth or stones, or simply carried on stretchers by sheer muscle power. The steep slopes of the valleys rendered the task of transportation more arduous than the undulating plains of

Easter Island.

In the Tonga archipelago there is a monumental gateway, the Trilith, whose popularity rivals that of the Easter Island statues. The same pseudo-scientific fantasies surround this monument, which has also been attributed to vanished civilizations. The date at which this gateway was erected is known, however, as well as the name of the chief who supervised the work, and the technique employed in its construction. The lintel resting on the two pillars weighs fifteen tons. It was brought by boat from a neighbouring island and then pushed up a hillock until it was level with the tops of the two uprights. On reaching this height, it was dropped into the two mortices waiting to receive it.

The logs which the Maoris took from the forests to fashion their dugout canoes often weighed much more than the Easter Island statues. The explanation the Easter Islanders gave a German lieutenant of the manner in which the statues were transported along the slopes of the quarry, although unfortunately rather vague, is strikingly reminiscent of the method employed by the Maoris.

The main difficulty was not how to shift the statue, but how to avoid breaking it in the process. It was this consideration that led Captain Vandesande of the 'Mercator' to choose a basalt statue, rather than a tufa bust, for the Musée du Cinquantenaire.

Our informants believed that the statues were moved in a dream, thanks to the magic power of Tu'u-ko-ihu. This miraculous explanation doubtless expresses the secret desire of those who were harnessed to the statues and dragged them across the stony soil of their island. It would, however, be a mistake to project into the midst of the Pacific the picture with which we are familiar in connexion with the construction of the Egyptian pyramids. The statues were not put in position by gangs of slaves, but by free men, happy to take part in an enterprise carried out for the greater glory of their family or tribe. We must imagine the joyous tumult of the festivals when thinking of this effort. The heads of lineages who wished to raise a new bust on their *ahu* undoubtedly organized feasts that they prepared long beforehand. To this end, they extended the area of their fields and accumulated reserves by placing the products of land and sea under a tabu; in a word, they mobilized all their resources to pay for the anticipated aid. On the agreed day, groups of relatives and friends could be seen converging on the volcano. Fires were burning in the ovens, the feast hut was full of people. The guests harnessed themselves to the statue and strained their muscles to the sound of cries and spells recited by the priests to facilitate their task. A half-serious, half-humorous rivalry turned the undertaking into an immense pleasure party. These tufa giants were not shifted at one go: months, perhaps years, lay between the stages on their journey from the quarry to the west coast mausoleums.

It is, however, odd that the Easter Islanders should not have been able to give the missionaries information that would have dispelled the whole mystery. Why did the natives explain the transportation of the statues by myths, instead of giving us the technical details we expected from them? This is really puzzling, and one cannot help suspecting that the first missionaries were incurious and indifferent. The traditions are not entirely devoid of concrete details, however. They allude to the embankments and ramps by means of which the statues were brought to the level of the platform on which they were to be placed. One informant also spoke to us of wooden levers, crushed potatoes, and round stones which helped these heavy masses to slide along. He also showed us a hill behind the Te-pito-to-kura *ahu* that was linked to the *ahu* by an earth-bank along which the Paro statue was moved. The cylinders of red tufa were rolled down an artificial slope built up of stones and boulders. The great volcano statues were erected by a roughly similar method. Behind some of them Mrs Routledge found the mound of stones that had supported them while they were being raised into a vertical position.

If Easter Island traditions are vague and confused in respect of the transportation of the statues, the situation is the same with regard to other aspects of the ancient culture. Although their grandparents were still living in the Stone Age, none of the modern islanders will admit that the stone adze blades they find at every step could have been used to carve the wooden images. In their eagerness to adopt a new culture, they have rejected even the memory of the past.

Our thirst for plausible explanations must not cause us to lose sight of the incredible difficulties the Easter Islanders overcame in order to transport their statues. Their magical interpretations become understandable when one sees Rikiriki *ahu* perched between a steep slope and a dizzy cliff!

The presence of a soft, easily-cut tufa, with a tendency to harden when exposed to the air, certainly favoured the development of this statuary. On the other hand, the custom of raising images of the dead on the mausoleums is anterior to the discovery and colonization of the island. When the Easter Islanders immigrated to it they already possessed an artistic tradition that may have been limited to wood-carving. The absence of trees on the island on which chance had cast them compelled them to adapt their traditional techniques to a different and more easily worked material. After some tentative efforts, they succeeded in evolving a new style that became fixed shortly after its birth. It impressed itself upon them so deeply that it became part of the melancholy landscape of the island.

Quite recently an American anthropologist, Dr Sahlins, has drawn attention to social and economic factors that help us to understand the extraordinary flowering of Easter Island statuary. The Polynesians who most closely resemble the natives of Easter Island in language and culture—that is to say, the natives of New Zealand, Mangareva, the Marquesas, and the Hawaiian Islands Islands—had a strongly stratified social structure. Each of these societies comprised a whole gamut of groups and sub-groups (known scientifically as 'ramages') that were theoretically inter-related and linked by real or fictitious genealogical ties. The heads of these groups were more or less noble according to the degree of their relationship with the senior branch, the direct issue of a common ancestor from whom was descended a chief or *ariki*, a word Europeans have translated as 'king'. Corresponding to this type of society was an economic system based on exchanges and spectacular distribution of goods and food. The chiefs disposed of the production surplus, which they redistributed in the shape of feasts or payment to groups of craftsmen or gangs of labourers who, on their instructions, carried out large-scale undertakings such as the building of temples, the terracing of mountain slopes, the digging of canals, and the construction of large canoes for sailing on the high seas. Certain collective enterprises, such as fishing, were likewise organized by the chiefs on the same basis. On Hawaii thousands of men might be employed simultaneously on a common task. Some occupations were the prerogative of social groups of which the chief became the patron. Their services were paid for by gifts of food or other goods. The chief's right of distraint on a part of the production stimulated the spirit of enterprise and communal effort within these societies.

Everything we know about the social organization of Easter Island suggests that the above system existed there in an almost identical shape. The chiefs had, therefore, the means of mobilizing the members of their groups and assigning to them the tasks which they considered useful. Now, local conditions rendered these tasks much less numerous than in other islands. On Easter Island collective fishing never acquired the importance it had elsewhere, because of the absence of a reef or a lagoon that would have encouraged it; lack of timber reduced boat-building to negligible proportions; there were no forests to clear; and attempts to establish an irrigation system were fruitless. The Easter Islanders' spirit of enterprise therefore turned towards the only domain in which it was possible for them to expend their energy: the cult of the gods and the ancestors. The chiefs, who had vast resources at their disposal, employed them in maintaining and paying groups of craftsmen who carved statues to ornament the mausoleums belonging to the various lineages. Teams of considerable size could be mobilized to transport the statues and erect them on the *ahu*.

This would explain how so much effort could be concentrated on a single activity and why monumental sculpture made such strides. The latter was also favoured by the existence on the island of such an easily worked material as tufa. Nor must considerations of the prestige and glory of the chiefs and their groups be forgotten. What we do not know is the part played by the religious factor among the various motives behind the particular evolution of Polynesian art that took place on Easter Island.

One glance at the quarry leaves the impression of an abrupt cessation of work. Nearly a hundred statues have remained unfinished and others were abandoned at the moment of leaving the workshop. These signs of great activity coming to a sudden halt inevitably suggest a cataclysm or a tragedy that threw the life of the island into confusion. The natives are still vaguely conscious that some disaster paralysed the army of sculptors. Their version of events runs as follows:

The sculptors of the quarry were fed by men who went fishing for them. One day these men went to Kikirimariu, where they dived into an undersea cavity to catch a crayfish, for it was there that it dwelt with its body, its tail and its claws. The divers returned to the surface and said: 'This crayfish cannot be caught, it is much too big.' Other men dived in their turn, but they did not come back. Those who had discovered this great crayfish left it and returned to the place where they usually fish, caught some crayfish and distributed them among the sculptors. Then they set about knotting a large net for the enormous crayfish they had found.

Six men and again six men perished because of this crayfish, this crayfish with the long tail. The fishermen went back to where it was. The people they met on the way said to them: 'Six men and then another six men went in search of this crayfish and are dead.' The fishermen replied: 'Yes, but we shall kill the crayfish.' The three young men entered the sea and swam to a point above the cavity in which the crayfish dwelt. They spread their net and the youngest said: 'I shall dive first, you will follow me and drive the crayfish into the net.' The young man opened his net into which the others drove the crayfish. They took a firm grip on the net and pulled it up to the surface of the water. There were three of them, and the crayfish made four. As they landed on the beach they uttered a loud shout: '*Eeeee, ko tetu, ko te ura rarape nui!*' [Eeeee, how big it is, the crayfish with the long tail!] They took the crayfish, and everyone came to admire it. Then they slung it on their backs and carried it to the sculptors.

The sculptors called an old sorceress and said to her: 'Light the oven to cook the crayfish; how big it is, the crayfish with the long tail!' The old woman lit the fire and also put some potatoes to cook, which are good to eat with crayfish. Then she said to the men: 'When everything is cooked take the food out of the oven, but leave some for me.' 'All right,' said the sculptors.

The old sorceress went to see her brother and stayed talking to him while the crayfish was cooking in the oven. When it was ready, the sculptors opened the oven and ate it all. They thought no more about the old woman and forgot her completely. They devoured the crayfish, distributed the scraps, and went back to work. The statue they were carving was called Tokanga. They had already finished the hands, the face and the neck, and were about to detach it from its matrix in order to take it to the Matai-rai *ahu* at Vinapu.

The woman came back to the oven from which the great crayfish had been taken out. There was nothing left but the shell. She cried out: 'Where is my crayfish?' The men replied: 'There is none left, it is finished. We forgot you and that is why there is none left.' The old woman recited a spell. She said: 'Statues that are upright, fall down! It is the fault of the great crayfish, of the crayfish with the long tail of which you left nothing for me. Never again shall you steal my food. Statues, remain still for ever.' All the statues fell, for the sorceress's bosom was full of anger.

The quarry, struck by an interdict, remained under the sorceress's spell.

If, as we have every reason to suppose, manufacture of the statues was the concern of a guild of sculptors, a war of extermination or even an epidemic brought by some European ship would be enough to explain the desertion of the workshops.

Another myth explains the overthrow of the Tonga-riki *ahu* statues. A magician, who had likewise been excluded from a banquet, caused them to fall down by pushing with his foot the central beam of the hut in which he had received hospitality.

If the cause of the cessation of work in the quarry has been forgotten, the events leading to the destruction of the *ahu* statues still live in the memory of the natives. They know that most of them were thrown down during a series of inter-tribal wars waged at the end of the eighteenth or the beginning of the nineteenth centuries.

At the end of the eighteenth century the west coast *ahu* were still surmounted by their statues, but Forster—and two years later, M. de Langle of the La Pérouse expedition—observed that in the south of the island several statues had been thrown down and that the platforms on which others stood were half in ruins. The busts round Hanga-roa Bay were knocked down before 1815. The statues of the neighbouring Tahai Bay were still upright in 1837, for Admiral Dupetit—Thouars perceived as he sailed past, 'a platform on which were set four red statues, equidistant from one another, their summits covered with white stones or capitals of this colour.' In 1866, when the missionaries settled on the island, there was no longer a single statue in position on any mausoleum. What had happened during these thirty years?

The folklore texts that were dictated to me were full of the memory of inter-tribal struggles waged before the arrival of the Whites. The victor satisfied his lust for destruction and humiliated the vanquished by hurling down the statues on his ancestral mausoleum. Such profanation provoked reprisals. Every turn of fortune brought with it fresh assaults upon the great silent images. Old men who died at the beginning of the present century told their grandchildren that in the time of their fathers the island was filled with the crash of falling statues. One of them, who died in 1915, remembered that the Paro statue had been thrown to the ground when he was a child as the result of the following incident: a woman called Tupa-hotu had been killed and eaten by the Tu'u people. Her son avenged her by hunting down in a cavern thirty people belonging to the district in which the outrage had been committed. Paro was the victim of this vendetta. Ropes were passed round his neck, and a band of warriors heaved the statue over on to its face. Tepano knew the name of the individual who decapitated the Papara *ahu* and the nature of the sickness with which he was afflicted because of his sacrilege. These conflicts were known as 'the wars of the throwing down of the statues'.

Violent as was the iconoclastic fury of this period, it merely completed the work of time and preceding generations.

CHAPTER X

Feasts

The Hareauti—The feast of the boat

THE EASTER Islanders seemed to me to be conscious of the monotony of their insular existence and sometimes to suffer under it. The excitement that seizes them every time an unexpected event occurs to disturb their tranquillity is doubtless a manifestation of their secret joy at the prospect of escaping from boredom, if only for a few instants. In days gone by, inter-tribal wars gave spice to life by filling it with violent emotions. In peaceful periods frequent feasts provided the islanders with distractions of which their descendants are almost entirely deprived. They were no doubt organized by chiefs of lineages or extended families anxious to consolidate or enhance their prestige. One feast led to another, because the gifts received created an obligation to return them. The memory of these festivities, in which their ancestors competed in display and generosity, has been kept alive in the island's traditions; they are a subject about which the old men like to talk at length to those who question them.

In the Easter Island dialect, the word for a feast is *koro*. This is identical with the term employed in the old days to address one's father or a man belonging to his generation. *'O koro e,'* 'O my father,' they used to say. These words are not simply homonyms, but joined by a semantic link, for a *koro* was more specifically a feast given by a young man in honour of his father or father-in-law. It was perhaps merely by extension of its original meaning that the word *koro* came to be applied to every festival involving the distribution of food, as was notably the case when, after the harvest, a rich landowner organized celebrations for the friends and relatives who had lent him their assistance. *Koro* seem to have been especially characterized by gifts of food. Potatoes, yams and other food stuffs heaped on trestles demonstrated the wealth and generosity of the person or persons giving the feast. This practice is found in almost identical forms among the Maori of New Zealand, whose culture offers so many analogies with that of the ancient Easter Islanders.

The festival known as *paina* doubtless formed part of the cycle of mortuary ceremonies. It was organized in honour of a father, and perhaps also of a brother, a few years after their death. The dead man, whose virtues were celebrated, and whose spirit it was doubtless hoped to pacify, was represented by a sort of lay figure—a *paina* —made of a frame of sticks and reeds covered with bark-cloth. The head and limbs were constructed separately. Tufts of rushes took the place of hair; the eyes were represented by discs cut from the top of a skull, with black shells as pupils, and shaded by eyebrows of feathers. Black painting from forehead to feet reproduced male tattooing. These effigies, which were seen by González and La Pérouse in the eighteenth century, measured from nine to twelve feet. They stood behind the *ahu* on positions marked by circles of stones, which may still be observed near ancient mausoleums.

The organizer surrounded the effigy with chickens and food, which he made ready to distribute according to the rules of a cere-monial whose details have unfortunately been lost. He then climbed into the *paina* and addressed to the gathering, through the hole corresponding to the mouth, a long speech glorifying the dead man's memory and extolling his own generosity. Moved by his panegyric, the crowd burst into tears and intoned the customary funeral laments. At a given moment the orator thrust his hand out of the effigy's mouth and displayed a cock that he held at arm's length. Tradition has it that he bit its comb, but we do not know for what purpose.

One of González's lieutenants gives these effigies the name *kopeka*, a word meaning 'vengeance'. No doubt his informants wished to tell him that they were holding a ceremony in honour of a man who had been killed in battle or in some other way, and that they had simultaneously performed the rites of vengeance.

What was the significance of *koro* properly so-called, that is to say, of feasts given in honour of a relative who was still alive? Ac-cording to the statements of present-day Easter Islanders, they were a public manifestation of respect for a father, a mother, a father-in-law or a mother-in-law. The obligation to celebrate *koro* was not lost until the beginning of the century. When I asked Victoria Rapahango for details of this curious custom she burst into tears, because, as she explained to me, my enquiry had reminded her of the *koro* which her brother had celebrated some twenty years ago—in about 1915. This brother—whose memory I had voluntarily called up—had died at sea, and Victoria felt it right to pay him the tribute of her tears.

Anyone intending to hold a *koro* had to set to work well in advance in order to get together the three hundred fowls required for this ceremony. Naturally his *taina*, that is, his brothers and cousins, helped him by bringing their quota. He also had to gather together foodstuffs, either by extending his area of cultivation, or by calling on the good offices of his friends or relatives. Then he commissioned a chanter to compose chants for the occasion and have them performed by a chorus of men and women. If he accepted the commission, the choirmaster (*hatu*) received a gift of an ovenful of food, which sealed the contract.

On the day of the feast, the food that had been accumulated was heaped up on trestles, and the fowls were attached in groups of ten to a cord stretched between two stakes. The fowls provided by relatives, tied in the same way, formed a separate row, at right-angles to the first.

The organizer of the feast approached the *motuha*, that is, the beneficiary of the feast—his father or father-in-law—and gave him a chicken. The *motuha* quickly handed it to a member of his family. Then he went up to the two rows of chickens, untied them, and distributed them among certain groups of relatives. Some of the chickens were presented to the *motuha*'s brother, who threw them on his back and performed a dance. The *motuha* also handed chickens to his wife for her to distribute among her relations. Those who received a chicken immediately gave it away, so that the fowls circulated from one person to another. The obligatory nature of these exchanges was expressed in the belief that a chicken could not be eaten until it had changed hands five times.

Those who had received presents had to return them on the occasion of another *koro*, so that sooner or later the man who had ruined himself by his generosity was able to restock his farmyard with the gifts he received in return.

After these exchanges, the ovens were opened and the food taken out and distributed among the guests. The *motuha* was obliged to offer two ovenfuls of food, one to the organizer of the feast, the other to his assistants.

The feast was enlivened by songs and dances. Victoria Rapahango dictated to me the fragment of a text composed for her brother's *koro*:

I o te korongo mai nei	*Here is the feast sung*
I Moana-vera-vera-ra-tahai,	*In Moana-vera-vera-ra-tahai,*
Rima turu, turu.	*Hands raising, raising.*

The celebration of a *koro* flattered the vanity both of the organizer of the feast and its beneficiary. The latter was its hero, but the former acquired prestige by displaying his generosity and wealth. If the father was satisfied with the homage paid him, he thanked his son by reciting the following verse *ad nauseam* in a sing-song voice: 'O my son, you have given a great *koro* for your father.'

When the last potatoes had been eaten, the guests dispersed, praising the merits and filial piety of their host.

The description of a *koro* I have given here will not satisfy ethnographers anxious for more information about the rules governing these distributions. The confused recollections of modern Easter Islanders give us a glimpse of a whole system of contractual gifts analogous to those described in connexion with other Pacific cultures. We catch a hint of psychological mechanisms at work among the ancient Easter Islanders identical with those which, among their distant relatives of Western Polynesia and the Maori, associate the distribution of gifts with notions of prestige and bestow on the fact of giving and receiving the character of an obligation that is not only social, but also mystical.

The festivals called *hareauti* were held in autumn and winter. If our sources are to be believed, they were essentially profane in character, for they were organized by individuals in whom ambition or vanity inspired the wish to increase their prestige by a display of generosity.

Some time before the solemn day, a hut had to be erected in a suitable spot that served as a club, a dance hall, and a reception room. The poles that formed the skeleton of these constructions were carefully preserved after use.

The young men and girls whose dances and chants, along with a substantial banquet, constituted the principal attraction of the festivities, resided in these long houses for several weeks beforehand in order to rehearse.

We have spoken of these enjoyable periods of residence in the feast huts during our discussion of the years of adolescence. The youngsters played, sang and made their first acquaintance with the delights of love.

The intimacy was interrupted when the guests arrived on the agreed date and took their places in the house that had been prepared for them. Great importance was, of course, attached to the presence of a chief, who added lustre to the feast and gave it a religious consecration. The tabus surrounding *ariki* obliged the host and his guests to observe certain rules of ceremonial. Nothing unclean must defile the interior of the hut. A story tells of the indignation of Tu'u-ko-ihu, who, finding a child's excrement in a *koro* hut, refused to eat the bananas that had been offered him and immediately left a place where his sacred person would have been polluted.

We will let Brother Eyraud, an eye-witness, describe the rig-out of a crowd attending a *koro*.

Everyone turns up, [writes Eyraud] in all his most precious things. On this occasion the most eccentric apparel makes its appearance. . . . They wear everything they can get hold of. People paint themselves with extra care and call upon the services of a hand skilled in fixing colours and tracing capricious lines on the face. . . . On feast days an enormous roll of bark is inserted in the lobe of the ear. [The head-dresses were no less picturesque. In addition to feather diadems, the missionary lists hats decorated with buttons, calabashes, half a gourd, and even a sea-bird whose opened carcase had been more or less thoroughly cleaned out.]

On their great days, [writes Eyraud in the same letter] they dress, adorn and load themselves with everything that can somehow be attached to them. The man who has been able to get hold of a dress puts on a dress; if he has two of them, he puts on two. The woman who can lay her hands on a pair of trousers, a waistcoat or an overcoat, decks herself out in them with all possible elegance.

This grotesque display is one of the fruits of the island's decadence. Once upon a time this same crowd, draped in red and yellow painted tapa cloaks, their bodies perfumed with turmeric, must have displayed a genuine elegance.

'They get into two lines and sing.' Such is the summary description given by a witness of one of these *hareauti*.

We know just as little about the other festivals. The one called *puke* was simultaneously a game and a magical test. The children gathered handfuls of seaweed. They handed these to the adults, who threw them at the children while the latter ran away and tried to dodge them. Those who were struck by a handful of seaweed were supposedly destined for a premature death.

Kaunga is the name of a dance associated with a particular feast about which we know almost nothing. The young men and girls danced in Indian file, each girl preceded by a boy, on a narrow strip of ground paved with pebbles. The dancers held little dance paddles that they moved in time to the music as they advanced and retreated gracefully. The parents took no part in the ceremony, of which they were merely spectators. We were informed that many marriages were decided at this feast, for young men and girls made a great effort to appear at their most elegant.

The sailing ships that called at Easter Island, at long intervals, in the course of the eighteenth and nineteenth centuries, made a deep impression on the natives. This is proved by the numerous depictions of sailing vessels painted on the stone slabs of the Orongo houses and in the cave of Ana-kai-tangata.

The activities, postures and language of a ship's crew, which the natives observed during these visits, became the theme of a pantomime or ballet that was performed every year on a mound of earth (*miro-o'one*—'the earth ship'), representing the strangers' vessel. The last time this performance was given—twenty years ago—a

gang of *mataroa* (sailors) hauled on imaginary ropes while the captain, acted by the catechist Timoteo Pakarati, gave the orders,
cursing and spitting out his quid.

The following is one of the songs composed on this occasion; it
was also considered to have been an improvisation to welcome a
man by the name of To'orangi of the Eapaea lineage who came
from Chile as a sailor:

A To'orangi a Eapaea e,	*O To'orangi of Eapaea,*
A te kapu mai hiva e,	*He that comes from abroad,*
Ka hakaava ro	*They are pushing forward*
I te kaukau hakarava	*The yards*
E To'orangi a Eapaea e.	*O To'orangi of Eapaea.*
Ka hakatata haro	*They tilt*
I te kaukau hakarava	*The yards*
O To'orangi o te miro.	*Of To'orangi's ship.*
Kahu a'ava.	*The sail is inflated.*

It is uncertain whether this feast perpetuates the memory of the
visit of one of the great eighteenth-century navigators or is merely a
game inspired by more recent contacts with the whites.

First Tepano told us the feast was an historical reconstruction of
the acts of piracy committed by Poie; then he changed his mind
and assured us that it commemorated the visit of Captain Cook.
This latter interpretation, which was accepted by Mrs Routledge,
is very doubtful. Why should the natives have commemorated
Captain Cook's landing rather than that of the navigators who preceded and followed him? Perhaps this pantomime dates no farther
back than the time of the whalers.

However that may be, the game of the boat is not confined to
Easter Island. During his captivity on Penrhyn, Lemont was a
spectator at a theatrical performance in which the wreck of his own
ship was enacted.

The Feast of the Boat is no longer performed, but on the first day
of the year the Easter Islanders dress in navy uniforms and go
through actions imitating the manoeuvres of a ship's crew.

CHAPTER XI

Poetry, Music and Dancing

LIFE CANNOT have lacked charm when the tribes were at peace. Fishing and work in the fields alternated with the minor activities of everyday existence to create a calm and happy atmosphere. The Easter Islanders' ancestors, from the fortunate islands of Central Polynesia, left them a tradition of careless gaiety that has been transmitted to their hybrid descendants. These emigrants also bequeathed to them a love of music and an intense liking for the sound and savour of words. Here again, Polynesian culture has affinities with that of Ancient Greece.

The variation of syllables and their unexpected arrangement possess particular charm for the Polynesian ear. The Easter Islanders love to repeat a word whose elements seem to them to form a new and agreeable combination. This sensitiveness to phonetic nuances is sometimes expressed in unforeseen ways. Following a raid on the islet of Marotiri, the people of Tu'u brought back some twenty corpses, which they lined up on the beach and distributed as meat to their friends and relations. A chief named Ohotakatore, who had recognized among the dead an enemy called Hangamai-hi-tokerau, said: 'I want the body of this man with such a beautiful name.' When he was refused this favour, Ohotakatore betrayed his own tribe.

The smallest reefs, the slightest depressions in the ground, the most insignificant rocks, and even certain valuable objects, were individualized by a proper name. This practice allowed a story-teller to embellish his tale with long lists of names that may seem monotonous to us, but which delighted his audience. Every movement of a hero about the island afforded the opportunity for an interminable recitation of proper names, for this itinerary was described in minute detail. If the hero returned by the way he went, the list of the places he passed was repeated.

In these little shut-in Polynesian worlds, every event became significant and could provide material for a poetic composition.

180

Brother Eyraud's sheep, which were stolen soon after his arrival and cooked at the first opportunity, were celebrated in a short poem sung in all keys for months on end. The smallpox that decimated the population became the subject of a song intended to enliven banquets and set the young people dancing.

This musical and literary form has not been entirely lost. We collected a satirical improvisation that still enjoyed some popularity:

Rahi toke vie a Aru-manu-vie.	*Rahi stole the wife of Aru-manu-vie.*
Maitetu'uapai toke mai ai	*At Maiteu uapai he took*
I te vie a Aru-manu-vie.	*The wife of Aru-manu-vie.*

The crew of the Chilean ship 'Araucano' having proved less generous than that of the 'Baquedano', the natives gave vent to their resentment in the following chant:

E rakerake te Araukano,	*The* 'Araucano' *is bad,*
Te nehenehe te Pakedano.	*The* 'Baquedano' *is good.*

The ancient bards established a scholarly classification of the chanted poems, according to their character. The sacred chants were *hare-atua*; the warlike paeans, *a te haka-kakai*, that is, poems 'that incite to battle'; the songs called *ei* were generally satirical in intent and aimed chiefly at an unfaithful woman or a girl who paid no attention to the love of some man. They were composed by specialists, learned in secret by a chorus, and sung on a feast day, to the great embarrassment of the person they concerned. Lovers also improvised songs in honour of the beloved, and if the words or the tune found favour, they were incorporated into the folklore of the island. A few poetic chants—unfortunately of recent date—are still extant. With the combined assistance of our informants we were able to translate them—not always an easy matter, because of the obscure allusions they contain.

Here, first of all, is a funeral lament:

E hata tae kava	*The stinking worms*
E kaikai koe ia Tau-mahani	*Eat you, O Tau-mahani,*
I te vie honui e.	*Woman of high lineage.*

A woman of the Tupa-hotu tribe had been deserted by her

husband, who repented his action and came back at night, scratching at the door:

Tupa-hotu rakerake,	This tupa-hotu is bad,
Tae tangitangi rikiriki	I shall not shed a single tear for him.
Hove e kioe e nekuku mai nei	It is perhaps a rat that scratches
A koia o ku tata hakahou mai a.	Oh, it is he who has come back . . .

A young girl leaves her lover's arms at dawn. He sings . . .

E Miru, a ivi rari i te hupe e,	O Miru girl, you are dampened to the bones by dew,
I te hupe hau a Rano-aroi.	By the dew of the Rano-aroi.
Kae pakapaka I topa ro ai	You won't be dry when you go down to the shore
Kit te roto tatau mahute	To soak the paper mulberry
Mo te nua hute pukao.	To make the cloth for the ribbon of your top-knot.

Another love poem is supposed to be recited by a girl whose younger sister loves the same man as she does:

E Mea, a tino mamahi rua e ki te iti, ki te nui e.	O Mea, for your body the little one and the big one are fighting.
He tonga, te pua, repa hoa,	It is winter, my friend, the flower gives off its perfume,
Ka eo, ka eo, ka kava nei.	The flower is very fragrant.
He hora, te pua, repa hoa,	It is summer, the flower, my friend,
Ka mariri mai to'oku aro nei, aue, aue.	Is withered on my breast, alas, alas.
Ku mataku mai a i te vie honui e,	The older woman is afraid,
He te kotaki mo haroa o te rei, o too rei mata nei.	Here is the wreath to hang an ornament, the ornament is your face.
He tou taina, e Mea e.	O my brother, O Mea.

The following lines describe the efforts of a married woman shut up by her jealous husband and digging a way out with her hands, so that she can join her lover:

E manu e, ka pari mai toto	*O Manu, my blood oozes*
Hare keri ena aaku i te po, e	*When I dig under the house,*
Manu e.	*O Manu.*
E au tae kai i te kumara	*I do not eat the sweet potatoes*
O tau korohua nei ko, Mae-te-	*Of this old man, Maea-te-*
renga.	*renga.*

The ancient music of Easter Island has almost entirely disappeared and been replaced by tunes from Tahiti and Chile. All that remains are descriptions, such as this one from Pierre Loti's *Reflets sur la sombre route*:

> They sing, the Maoris; they all sing beating their hands as if they were making a dance rhythm. The women utter notes as soft and fluty as those of birds. The men sometimes make small falsetto voices, thin, quavering, and shrill. Sometimes, they produce cavernous sounds like the roars of enraged wild animals. Their music is made of short and jerky phrases, ending in gloomy vocalizations descending in minor tones. They seem to express the surprise of being alive and also the sadness of life. Notwithstanding, they sing in joy, in the childish joy of seeing us, in the pleasure of the small new things we bring them.

Loti is not the only one to have been moved by these songs. Other voyagers have sought to put into words the impression they made upon them. They were struck by the bass notes, by the unison, and by the range of the voices. The women knelt and accompanied the rhythm of their singing by swaying their bodies and moving their hands, as they still do in church. A chorus leader gave the key, to which all the singers tuned their voices. Thereupon, the song burst forth, pure and sonorous, and its stirring cadence set the dancers in motion. Sometimes the chorus was divided into two groups, each comprising a row of men (*pere*) and a row of women (*ihi*). They sung the verses alternately under the direction of the leader (*hatu*), who stood in the centre and juggled with a ceremonial paddle (*oa*).

There is no Polynesian society in which dancing is not the

favourite pastime. It is still so on Easter Island, but fashions have changed and no one bothers about the ancient dances. What the young people want is a good gramophone with tangos, cuecas and fox-trots. Then eyes begin to shine and the vigour of these supple bodies is awakened. If anyone insists on seeing the dances of the past, a girl or young man will execute a dance on one foot without much skill or enthusiasm. Nevertheless, this hopping really is one of the indigenous dances of the island. In 1838, when the 'Venus', commanded by Admiral Dupetit-Thouars, put in at the island, a number of natives including one woman, came aboard. They danced a sort of minuet, hopping on one foot and indulging in a highly expressive obscene dumb show. Balancing precariously on one leg, they jerked the other to the rhythm of the song.

The sacred dances were quite different in character. They were accompanied by chants celebrating the ancient heroes, the gods, work in the fields, and warlike expeditions. The rhythm was marked by a dancer who jumped up and down on a thin slab of stone covering a trench containing a calabash that acted as a sound box. This, together with sea shells, was the only musical instrument the ancient Easter Islanders possessed. The dance itself consisted of graceful, measured movements which the spectator to whom we owe this description compares with the evolutions of the geishas. There was no sudden gesture, no leaping, no extravagant pirouettes.

These dances were in the purest Polynesian tradition, a tradition derived from South-East Asia. Neither this calm, nor this grace, nor these undulating movements were, however, manifest in the religious dances performed for us by Juan Tepano. Standing with bent knees, he twirled a double-ended dance paddle, while rocking from side to side like a bear. He told us that in the absence of a ceremonial paddle the dancers brandished wooden statuettes or *moko* (lizard figures). Some put them in their mouths, others stood them on their heads, or made obscene gestures with them, placing them between their legs or pressing them against their posteriors. In the general excitement, some dancers even pretended to spit on these sacred objects.

CHAPTER XII

The Mystery of the Tablets

'No, these are nothing but the knotted cords, so wrongly
called "Origin-of-the-word", that serve only to relate what is
already known and are powerless to impart fresh knowledge . . .'

(Segalen: *Les Immémoriaux*.)

DID THE ancient inhabitants of Easter Island have hieroglyphic
script which, if deciphered, would disclose the mysteries of its
past? First to grasp the full import of this question was Monseigneur Jaussen, Bishop of Tahiti. The newly-converted natives of the
island had sent him, as proof of their devotion, a long cord plaited
from their hair and wound round an old piece of wood. The
Bishop's surprise when, upon casually examining the makeshift
reel, he perceived that it was covered with little figures all of the
same height and carefully aligned, can be imagined. Without a
doubt, these were hieroglyphs!

The existence of signs engraved on wood that might be interpreted as hieroglyphs had not entirely escaped the attention of
the missionaries who settled on the island. Brother Eyraud men-
tions in his first letter having seen tablets and staves covered with
strange signs in all the houses, but he adds that the natives attached no particular importance to them.

Two years later, while out walking, Father Zumbohm collected
a worm-eaten fragment that a little boy had found on a rock. The
following day, a native who had learned with what interest the
Father had examined the characters, sold him a large tablet in a
perfect state of preservation. Such were the circumstances accompanying the discovery of objects that were to become Easter
Island's most impenetrable mystery.

Twenty-one tablets, a staff, and three or four *rei-miro* (breast
plates) bearing a few rows of signs constitute the total body of
'hieroglyphic' texts known today. The most complete collection,

consisting of five specimens, is preserved at Braine-le-Comte, Belgium, in the Maison des Pères de Picpus. The British Museum possesses one tablet of whose antiquity, if not authenticity, I was doubtful until I had an opportunity of examining it more closely, when my scepticism was dispelled. Two fine tablets brought back by W. J. Thomson in 1886 figure among the splendid Easter Island collections on show at the National Museum, Washington. Finally, we may mention the three examples that are the property of the Bishop Museum in Honolulu. The other tablets belong to the Museums of Berlin, Vienna, Leningrad, and Santiago, Chile.

With a few exceptions the same engraved symbols recur, with numerous variations of detail, on the majority of these objects. They consist of representations of human beings, birds, fish, crustaceans, plants, ceremonial articles, and finally designs of purely geometrical character. The anthropomorphic figures are among the most numerous. All the signs, which are sttongly stylized, must be the product of a long artistic tradition. A strange and disturbing symbolism is manifest in a number of figures combining the most disparate elements: human bodies ending in geometric patterns or partially animal in form, triangles and lozenges embellished with ears, hands clinging to bars, and designs based on the vulva and other parts of the human body. All the symbols, whatever the object they represent, are the same height, so that a fish-hook or a breast-plate may be the same size as a human figure. A whole fantastic world seethes before our eyes as they run along these alternating rows of signs. From a purely technical, and even artistic, point of view we cannot but admire the quality of the incised work. In their masterly simplification, the designs have a vigour and lightness that makes one forget the heavy pressure the artist must have exerted on the wood in order to cut their grooved outlines with a shark's tooth or an obsidian graver. Graphic art has rarely reached such a level of perfection in any primitive culture.

The tablets themselves are simply flat boards, scarcely ever trimmed to a definite shape, because this would have reduced their surface area. The signs are incised on both sides of the tablets in regular longitudinal channels or flutes cut with a stone adze and separated by low ridges. The symbols, all of the same height, are spaced out regularly within these grooves, and each row runs in the opposite direction to the one above and below it (the boustrophedon system), so that the tablet has to be turned round at the end of each line in order to have the signs in their correct sequence. The tablets were 'read' from left to right, beginning with the lowest line. It is possible that some chanters, like Metoro (of whom more later), did not trouble to turn the tablet round at the end of the row but read half the lines upside down, from right to left.

These tablets are extremely valuable by virtue of their rarity, their artistic quality, and the mystery that surrounds them. Like everything else on Easter Island, they have acquired an excessive market price. The present-day natives have long sought to imitate them. A comparison between these fakes and the originals reveals the full mastery of the ancient engravers, for modern imitators have striven in vain to reproduce the regularity and elegance of their antique models. The imperfection of their handiwork has not, however, prevented them from doing profitable business with it. During the last few years the forgers have considerably improved their technique, and if they had not hit on the tiresome idea of engraving their signs on stones they might easily have duped the most wide-awake and experienced observers.

On leaving France we were commissioned to try, by all the means in our power, to obtain at least one tablet. We had no great hope of success, but nevertheless we offered a reward of 1,000 *pesos* to anyone who reported the existence of a genuine specimen; we could not foretell the price we might have to pay for the object itself. This promise caused a great stir amongst the native population. Numerous individuals began to dream of caverns and tablets. Every day some one came to tell us that the hiding-place of one or more of these articles had been supernaturally revealed to him during the night. The treasures generally lay in inaccessible grottoes where no one, however great his cupidity, would risk going to look for them. We did, however, attempt to explore one of these caves. Tepano assured us that during his youth an old man confided in him the whereabouts of a cavern in which precious objects had been hidden. Since he seemed determined to undertake the search despite our scepticism, we decided to join in. We took careful bearings and sighted the cave below Tepeu *ahu*, half-way down the cliff. The descent, down crumbling and slippery rocks, was not without danger. The black reef bristling with sharp edges lowered threateningly right below us, as we tried to reach the grotto containing the objects we coveted. The cavity was low and not very deep, and we had to crawl on all fours. There were no tablets, but we did discover some fragments of bone and fish-hooks left there by fishermen who had sheltered in the cave in days gone by. This setback did not discourage Tepano. A grotto higher up the cliff immediately became the exact spot he had been told about. The dangers of the climb increased our scepticism, and we entrusted to Tepano's son the task of dissipating his father's illusions. This was the only opportunity we had of checking the allegedly precise information concerning the whereabouts of treasure, which we received continuously. The experience was too discouraging for us to risk our men's lives in other enterprises of the same nature.

In the absence of tablets, we collected a few traditions about those who had engraved and used them. Most of their information was given us by Charlie Teao. He was not an 'ancient' and possessed no other authority than that of being the nephew of Te Haha, an old man whom Mrs Routledge had known in 1914 and who had studied in his youth at the school of the priestly caste.

Knowledge of the tablets, Teao told us, was the prerogative of a class of chanters or reciters called *tangata rongorongo*. They belonged to noble families and many of them were related to the king. They knew by heart the genealogies, the hymns and the oral traditions of the island, which they taught their pupils in special huts. They also instructed them in the engraving of the tablet signs, first on the leaves and trunks of banana palms, then on boards. Wood, being so rare, could only be entrusted to those who had acquired adequate proficiency. The system of writing was not explained until the students' memories had been perfectly trained. During their first years at school they had to learn by heart chants that they recited while making string-figures, each of which corresponded to a particular chant. These chants dealt with all the circumstances of life, love and death. A great number of them were spells that had the power to save people in danger and to multiply plants and animals. Others were panegyrics addressed to chiefs on solemn occasions.

The disciples of the *tangata rongorongo* were often their own sons or specially gifted children of wealthy families. On arriving at the school in the morning, they replied to their teacher's greeting with a joyous *ko koe a*. Then they squatted behind a flat stone that served as a desk and sharpened their styles of frigate-bird's bone. An assistant counted the children to make sure none was playing truant.

King Nga'ara took an interest in these schools. He often came to inspect them and enjoyed reciting poems himself, swaying from one side to the other. He was strict about examinations, but when children failed all the blame fell on their masters.

Every year there was a sort of open competition between the most famous *tangata rongorongo*. These bardic gatherings were the occasion for great inter-tribal feasts, the attraction of which was so great that in time of war they induced a general truce. The King organized the competition and contributed to the splendour of the feast by generous issues of food. The Miru and the tribes related to them helped the King to accumulate the necessary quantity of foodstuffs. The bards and their pupils arrived, each carrying one or two tablets. Those who were too young to take part in the competition stood in front of the King in garlands of feathers. Each bard recited in turn, and those who made mistakes were held up to ridicule by the crowd. The gibes caused some injured vanity and led to quarrels that the King was quick to pacify. The feast ended with a harangue from the King, who exhorted the *tangata rongorongo* to greater perfection and urged them to preserve the sacred hymns faithfully so as to transmit them to future generations.

Te Haha's recollections, handed on by his nephew, related to the reign of King Nga'ara, who, it seems, was a scholar and man of letters. It must not be concluded from this that all the kings took an equal interest in literature. When Nga'ara died he was borne to his last resting-place on a bier made of tablets, that were buried with him.

Many details in Charlie's account undoubtedly contain a core of truth. Its general accuracy is guaranteed by Te Haha's own story as recorded by Mrs Routledge. But it is to be feared that some of his recollections are interwoven with memories of the Mission school.

This intrusive European element must not lead us to reject these traditions entirely. The college of the *tangata rongorongo*, their

teaching, and their competitions recur among the Polynesians of
Mangareva and the Marquesas. The *tuhuna o'ono* (Marquesan possesses neither the *r* nor the *ng* sounds) were the tribe's bards and
professional chanters. Like their Easter Island colleagues, they
took part in meetings which the psalmodists of all the groups
attended in order to display the power of their memories. Those
whose memories proved to be failing lost the right to their title,
amidst the catcalls and sarcasms of their *confrères*. At Mangareva
the *tangata rongorongo* were members of a priestly caste 'charged
with the religious chants and stories'. Father Laval, who refers to
them frequently, adds that they were recruited from the country's
nobility. During religious ceremonies they formed a sort of chorus
which intoned the chants appropriate to the circumstances. One is
inevitably reminded of Easter Island on reading sentences like this
in Father Laval's chronicle: 'As they went along, the *rongorongo*
intoned chants accompanied by drumming, and one of them led
the way carrying a spear in front of him and reciting his *tao-'enua.'*
There are two striking details in this sentence: the spear carried by
the leader, which recalls the staff sometimes borne by the Easter
Island *rongorongo*, and the word *tao*, equivalent to the Easter *ta'u*,
which will be discussed shortly.

The only original element the Easter Island bards can claim to
have introduced was their tablets covered with signs. If these symbols were really the characters of a script, the Easter Islanders
would have crossed the frontier which, in many people's opinion,
divides the primitive world from the civilized. But did these tablets
in fact bear texts? In the letter already referred to, Brother Eyraud
speaks of tablets and stones covered with 'hieroglyphic signs'. The
name given to these tablets, *kohau rongorongo*, suggests that the
staves were the original form of these accessories employed by the
chanters. This word has been incorrectly translated as 'intelligent
wood', 'talking wood'; in point of fact, *kohau* does not mean 'wood',
but 'staff', 'stem' or 'stick'. The proper translation of this term is,
therefore, 'reciting staff' or 'chanters staff'. This is undoubtedly
the right name for the cylindrical rod preserved in the Santiago
Natural History Museum, Chile, which measures four feet in
length by two feet four inches in diameter and is completely
covered with signs. If the tablets were originally *kohau* or staves, the

resemblance between our Easter Island *rongorongo* and those of Mangareva and the Marquesas would be even greater, for the latter never recited their chants without their ceremonial staves, with which they beat time. But here the parallel stops, for there is no tradition of symbols having been engraved on the sticks anywhere outside Easter Island.

Te Haha and other old people asserted that there were different kinds of tablets. One type, the *kohau o te ranga*, were war charms that helped to defeat the enemy; but this name is possibly that of a particular tablet containing prayers to the god Rorai-hova.

The tablets were extremely sacred objects surrounded by tabus. Teao was convinced that the signs could kill at a distance. The magician had only to pronounce an incantation over a tablet to cause one or other of the animals depicted on it to come forth. The symbol freed from the material entered the victim and brought about his death. Something of the fear inspired by the tablets has survived. Some years ago a native named Riroko found a fragment of a tablet: from that moment on he lost all his children, one after the other, as well as other members of his family. He only escaped from the maleficent spell emanating from the tablet by burning it.

Certain tablets could become instruments of vengeance in the hands of priests assisting families of which some members had been murdered. Others ensured the fertility of the fields and were exhibited during feasts.

This sanctity did not extend to an inferior type of tablet called *ta'u*. The nature of *ta'u* is hard to discern from the scanty information we possess. Like Mrs Routledge, I was told that these tablets contained a list of exploits accomplished by an individual whose memory was celebrated by his son in a solemn feast. But apart from this, I was unable to obtain any definite facts on the subject, and it is better to admit our ignorance than repeat idle chatter.

Some tablets may contain genealogical lists of chiefs. The objections I had expressed against this view no longer appear to me entirely valid since in a recent paper two Russian scholars, N. A. Butinov and Y. V. Knorozov, have pointed out that on a tablet, now in Santiago de Chile, there is a row of signs which seems to correspond to a short genealogy.

This is about all the information we were able to obtain from our informants. It does not go far towards helping us solve the problem.

The discovery of a system of writing in an island already famous for its monuments might have been expected to arouse general curiosity. Nothing could be more surprising than the indifference of scholars in the face of this revelation. Not that they have been short of hypotheses; but the trouble of interpreting these documents with the help of the natives has been left to amateurs who had little time or training for the task. The whole question would have been completely clarified if investigators had tackled its patiently and without preconceived ideas at a time when information was still available. Despite the present difficulties, we can obtain valuable pointers from the attitude of natives who were invited to 'read' the tablets.

Efforts to extract an explanation of the tablets from the Easter Islanders were considered fruitless by the few enquirers who made them. None the less, one exceedingly important fact emerges from these abortive endeavours: the mechanism of reading seems to have been unknown to all the individuals who offered to decipher the 'script'. Placed in front of a tablet, they intoned chants without even trying to spell out the characters. The first attempt at deciphering was undertaken by Father Zumbohm. He brought together several learned islanders and questioned them on the meaning of the signs. The moment they saw the tablet they began to intone a hymn, which they continued until disagreement broke out and some exclaimed: 'No, it doesn't go like that'. Differences of opinion between the chanters were so great that the discouraged missionary abandoned all hope of learning anything from them.

Monseigneur Jaussen proved more persevering. He had learned that among the Easter Island émigrés working on the Brander plantations in Tahiti was one, named Metoro, who had studied under a famous master. One can feel in the Bishop's story the emotion that seized him when Metoro, holding the tablet in his hands, turned it this way and that and then broke into a chant. Metoro 'read' the tablet from left to right and then from right to left, not troubling to turn it round so as to have the signs in their normal position. Jaussen took down the text that was recited to him, and the manuscript was recently published. If it is translated, and each section of the sentence related to the corresponding symbols, it may be seen that what Monseigneur Jaussen took for a hymn was merely an incoherent succession of brief descriptions of the signs his informant had before his eyes. 'This is a bird, an open hand, a hunting-spear . . .' was what Metoro chanted and Monseigneur Jaussen painstakingly took down. He had got out of the difficulty by intoning a description of the symbols. Monseigneur Jaussen's attempt was conducted with patience and in a systematic spirit. It might have been successful if he, like all those after him who sought information from the natives, had not been handicapped by the preconceived idea that the tablets were the equivalent of our books.

Quarrels, harsh words and unjust treatment resulted on other occasions from this obstinate desire to have the tablets 'read' by people for whom the connexion between these objects and the island's oral literature was undoubtedly of a quite different nature. The case of Mr Croft affords a good example. This American had found among the Easter Islanders working on the Papeete plantations an individual who, he was told, was able to decipher the tablets. He immediately invited him to come along next Sunday and demonstrate his knowledge, placing in front of him a photograph of one of these tablets. The native, after glancing at the photograph, intoned a chant that Croft took down verbatim. Croft subsequently lost his sheet of paper and asked the native to run over the text again another Sunday. He obtained a new version that seemed to him different from the first, though he could not be sure; the same informant was summoned a third time for a fresh reading. Meanwhile, Croft had found the missing page and, comparing it with the other two texts, found that none of them coincided. Without hinting at this, he asked to hear the contents of the tablet once again. His doubts were confirmed: the new text bore no resemblance to the preceding ones. This was too much for Mr Croft's patience. He pointed out to the poor Easter Islander that identical symbols could not change their meaning according to the Sunday. He was so convinced of this that he sent his informant packing.

Thomson, the paymaster on an American man-of-war, was a man of alert and curious mind, but he evinced the same lack of discernment. During his visit to Easter Island in 1886, he met an old man named Ure Vaeiko who had studied the tablet signs in his youth and was acquainted with the oral traditions of his ancestors. Thomson purchased two new tablets and was extremely anxious to have them interpreted. Unfortunately, Ure Vaeiko, who had become a good Catholic, did not want to endanger his eternal salvation by this momentary return to paganism. Fearing he might succumb to the tempting offers made to him, he decamped. Thomson took advantage of a stormy night to run him to ground in the hut where he had taken refuge. There he flattered his vanity and made him recount ancient legends, while plying him with little glasses of spirits. Feeling at the top of his form, Ure Vaeiko lost his fears concerning the next world and made no difficulty about 'reading', not the tablets themselves—that would have been a mortal sin—but the photographs of them belonging to the good Bishop of Tahiti, Monseigneur Jaussen. He recognized them by certain details and reeled off the contents from one end to the other without the slightest hesitation. Those who were watching observed that he paid no heed to the number of symbols in each line. Worse still, he did not even notice when the photograph he was supposed to be 'reading' was removed and replaced by another. He was still going strong, reciting hymns and legends, when he was brutally accused of fraud. Sadly out of countenance, he launched into explanations that Thomson does not seem to have properly understood.

There is something pathetic about these misunderstandings arising from the encounter of two mentalities operating on different planes. It would be ludicrous to believe, like these enquirers, that the natives intended systematically to deceive them. They were not ignorant people, as the few facts we know about them show. The responsibility for these lost opportunities lies entirely with the Europeans.

In 1914, when Mrs Routledge made a last attempt to consult oral tradition, it was too late. Old Tomenika, who could have enlightened her, died in the leper-colony a fortnight after a conversation in the course of which he had murmured the last verses of a chant and drawn a few symbols with a tembling hand. This inquiry conducted *in extremis* nevertheless resulted in a gain for science. Like all the other Easter Islanders who had been subjected to

the test of reading, old Tomenika was invited to give a demonstration of his knowledge. He drew noughts and ticks on a piece of
paper and recited a chant. He was given some sheets of paper on
which he drew symbols, some of which were signs from the tablets.
When he was asked to read them, he repeated part of the same
chant as the previous day, the signs having taken the place of the
ticks. Groups of four or five words corresponded to each symbol.
From this Mrs Routledge rightly concluded that 'the signs were
not to him, now at any rate, connected with particular words'.
Thus our last hope of learning the real meaning of the tablets vanished for ever. The glorious sunset Mrs Routledge tells us she
admired after leaving Tomenika announced the deep night that
was falling on the island's past.

In 1932 the question of the existence of an Easter Island script
took an unexpected and sensational turn. No new key had been
found for the deciphering of the tablets, but it seemed as though the
mystery surrounding their origin had been finally dispelled and
that light had been cast on the distant affinities of Asiatic civilizations with the cultures of Polynesia. In a communication presented
to the Académie des Inscriptions et Belles-Lettres, a Hungarian
linguist, Guillaume de Hévesy, drew the attention of the learned
world to remarkable similarities between the signs on the Easter
Island tablets and those of a still undeciphered script recently discovered in the Indus Valley at Harappa and Mohenjodaro. With a
few exceptions, the concordance between a hundred hieroglyphs
or pictograms taken from the Indus seals and a hundred symbols
from the Easter Island tablets appeared complete and undeniable.
Only the logical conclusions implied by this correlation came up
against serious difficulties that had to be eliminated before the relationship between the two scripts could be accepted as a scientific
fact.

The following, in brief, are the main objections that immediately
spring to mind when we consider the implications of de Hévesy's
discovery. The Indus civilization, contemporary with that of
Sumer, reached its height between the end of the fourth and the
middle of the third millennium B.C. The civilization of Easter
Island began its decline at the middle of last century and has
drawn out its agony to the present day. Some 13,000 miles separate

the volcanoes of Easter Island from the muddy banks of the Indus. Between them stretches the mass of the Indian sub-continent, the islands of Indonesia, and vast expanses of ocean. Furthermore, the two civilizations have almost nothing in common: the people of the Indus lived in great rationally planned cities with the earliest known sewerage system. They knew how to weave, were acquainted with metallurgy, and were first-rate potters. They possessed numerous domestic animals, travelled in carts, and entertained commercial relations with the towns of Mesopotamia. The citizens of Mohenjo-daro, proud of their city, their buildings, their arts, and their many techniques, would have treated as savages the Easter Islanders who, only yesterday, were living in the Stone Age, carving statues of a monotonous uniformity in the tufa of their volcanoes, dwelling in wretched reed huts and—worst of all —indulging in cannibalism. In spite of all these differences, the sophisticated peoples of the Indus and the 'primitive' natives of the Polynesian Ultima Thule are supposed to have shared that marvellous instrument which appeared so late in the history of civilization —a system of writing.

A new mystery was therefore born from the sum of all these contradictions. To diminish the distance in time and space separating the two scripts, de Hévesy put forward the hypothesis that the Easter tablets were perhaps relics thousands of years old, which the islanders' ancestors brought to the island. In support of this supposition he cites a vague tradition, collected by Thomson, to the effect that Hotu-matu'a, the discoverer of the island, brought with him sixty-seven tablets. According to this view, the tablets that have come down to us and are now owned by several museums might have been part of this original collection. If this were so, they would have been just as mystifying to the Easter Islanders of last century as they are to us. I shall take the opportunity later of giving my opinion as to the credibility of the details of the tales and legends that constitute the island's folklore. If we are to accept every element of the Hotu-matu'a legend as an article of faith I shall claim equal rights for the version that speaks of 'paper books' allegedly contained in Hotu-matu'a's luggage. From this it appears that the ancient Easter Islanders did not have recourse to wooden tablets to write the texts of their traditions until later, when they had run out of paper. Let us recall here that Hotu-matuʻa plays in the island's legendary history the rôle of a culture hero, and that he is credited not only with the introduction of cultivated plants —which is doubtless perfectly true—but also with the foundation of most of its institutions. It is therefore natural that storytellers should accord him the honour of having brought the first tablets with him. There is a wide gulf between this vague mythical tradition and the possibility that the wooden tablets could have been preserved for countless centuries, in the course of which their possessors ploughed the seas and engaged in savage battles. How many tablets must have been burnt in the huts that were set on fire during the wars between tribes and lineages! In point of fact, all those extant were engraved on Easter Island at a comparatively recent date. Proof of this has been furnished by de Hévesy himself. He had hoped that a microscopic analysis of the tablets' wood, by enabling the tree from which it was taken to be identified, would furnish a valuable pointer to the origin of these objects. The results of this investigation were disappointing. Among the tablets whose authenticity is beyond question, three were cut in wood that is foreign to the island—*Fraxinus excelsior* (ash) and *Podocarpus latifolia*. One large tablet in the Braine-le-Comte collection, measuring thirty-seven by four inches, is called the 'Oar' because it is actually engraved on a European ashwood oar. It cannot, therefore, date from before 1722. For other tablets the natives have used the indigenous *toro-miro*.

To dissociate the tablets and the signs that cover them from the totality of Easter Island culture, to see in them anything but the products of a local art, one must be blind to the lessons of style and deaf to the testimony of the natives themselves. The Easter Islanders have never ceased to assert—and the first statements were made by those who were still acquainted with their ancient traditions—that the tablets were engraved and used by bards, the *rongorongo* or *tangata rongorongo*. The last of these lived in the nineteenth century and the names of some of them are still known today. The symbols themselves reflect the agricultural and geographical environment of the island, depicting animals and plants belonging to the local fauna and flora. They portray the slightly stylized outline of adzes, dance paddles, pectorals (*rei-miro*), wooden pendants (*tahonga*), fish-hooks and other objects of which specimens have been collected at a recent period and which may be admired in the show-cases of numerous museums. At one point, Hévesy believed he had identified among these signs representations of elephants and monkeys. These samples of the Indian fauna are, in fact, only a badly drawn bird with a long beak and a bird-man. If any doubt remains that the tablets were incised by Easter Island hands, it should be dispelled by the fact that the British Museum possesses a wooden *rei-miro*—one of the most typical ornaments in the Easter culture—which bears a long 'inscription' in characters identical in every way with those of the tablets.

Finally—the last argument—the petroglyphs discovered by our expedition and published by Lavachery bore drawings which, in style and subject-matter, are related to the 'hieroglyphs' and testify to the existence on the island of a graphic art that reached its highest level on the tablets.

The relationship between the graphic system of the Indus and that of Easter Island has been accepted as irrefutable by several scholars, including Professors Langdon and Rivet. Others have reserved judgment or been openly sceptical. The most meritorious effort finally to solve the problem of the origin of the Easter script is contained in a monograph, *Die Osterinselschrift*, published in 1938 by the Viennese scholar Robert von Heine-Geldern, who has brought to bear on this problem all the resources of an incomparable erudition and an ingenious mind.

Heine-Geldern considers any direct filiation between the two scripts extremely doubtful, for the number of signs that are different is much greater than the number of those that resemble one another. The similarities between the two systems represent, in his opinion, survivals from an earlier stage of this script.

Heine-Geldern's archaeological researches had led him to place the origin of Polynesian civilization in China. It was therefore very natural that he should ask himself whether a knowledge of writing might not have reached the Polynesians from this source. On comparing the Indus and Easter Island symbols with those of the ancient Chinese civilization known to us from inscriptions on shells and bones and going back to the second millennium B.C., he found that these three scripts did indeed share certain signs in common

—notably ten anthropomorphic Chinese signs, which he believed he could also identify in the other two systems (see Fig. 4). These resemblances, according to Heine-Geldern, also extend to the meaning of the symbols in so far as they are known to us. Thus three wavy parallel lines that meant 'water' in ancient China signi- fied 'rain' or 'wave' on Easter Island. The Chinese expressed the idea of 'circle' or 'encircle' by a symbol shaped like the figure eight, which suggested to the Easter Islanders 'enclosure' and 'enclose'. The Easter sign for 'earth' is very similar to, if not identical with, a variant of the Chinese symbol for 'mountain'. It is a pity that Heine-Geldern confined himself to these three examples. A more extensive list of parallels on these lines would have greatly streng- thened his thesis, if the interpretations of the Easter signs, which rest on the authority of Metoro, are correct.

Despite these correlations, Heine-Geldern does not claim a direct filiation between the Chinese script and that of Easter Island, but derives the latter from a Southern Chinese script related to that used in China proper during the Shang-yin dynasty and no doubt dating from the same period. Heine-Geldern goes on to suppose that there existed in Central Asia or Iran a system of writing that was the parent of those we know by the Indus Valley seals, the Honan shells and bone fragments, and the Easter Island tablets.

Heine-Geldern explains the diffusion of this script over such great distances by the migration of a people who, about one thou- sand years before our era, set out to settle the Pacific islands and introduced into them skills and an art of which certain vestiges have survived down to the present day. Among these he singles out the Easter script, the peculiar artistic style of the Marquesas, cer- tain types of axe, and the system of reckoning time by decades that seems to have existed on Easter Island, if we can believe the state- ments of Mrs Routledge's informant on this point. Heine-Geldern is the first to admit that these survivals—important as they are in his eyes—are not very numerous. If the ancient civilization borne by the first emigrants from the Asian continent is not better pre- served, this is because it was submerged by the invasion of the Polynesians properly so-called, who must have occupied the Paci- fic islands in about 1000 A.D. The destruction of the aristocracy and the priestly caste, which alone possessed the secret of the script, would explain the latter's disappearance everywhere in Polynesia except Easter Island, where it was saved by a fortunate chance. The catastrophes that descended on the Easter Islanders last century give us an idea of the way in which an art or science that is the prerogative of a restricted class or guild may disappear in a few years.

Heine-Geldern has not confined his investigations to the continent of Asia. Boldly taking up a suggestion made by Professor Hornbostel, he demonstrated parallels between the Easter Island signs and those of a pictography still in use among the Cuna Indians of the Panama Isthmus. Its existence has been revealed to the learned world by Erland Nordenskiöld, who has published fine specimens of the picture-writing employed by medicine-men to memorize incantations. Each medicine-man has his own pictography, but there is none the less sufficient resemblance between the designs they draw to allow us to speak of a system and a stylistic tradition. Hornbostel was struck, above all, by the likeness between many of these pictograms and the ideograms of the ancient Chinese script. Heine-Geldern's attention was caught primarily by the affinities of the Cuna drawings with the Easter signs. It cannot be denied that the presence in Panama of a three-thousand-year-old system of picture-writing, whose place of origin is across the ocean in China, would set a problem the solution of which would not be easy even for the most audacious diffusionist. Heine-Geldern advances the hypothesis that the relationship between these three scripts is due either to an influence exercised by East Polynesian culture on Central America, or to the three scripts having a common origin, which could only lie in China.

Among the many attempts to trace the origin of the Easter Island 'glyphs' an important place must be reserved for a study by Professor G. H. R. von Koenigswald, whose sensational discoveries of fossil men have rendered him justly famous.

Convinced that Indonesia has too often been neglected in Polynesian research, he published a series of patterns embroidered on cloth from Sumatra that showed the closest possible analogy with the Easter signs. Basing his hypothesis on this and other parallels, the learned prehistorian suggests the possibility of a migration which, starting from Sumatra and passing through Java, reached Hawaii on the one hand and Easter Island on the other.

An Argentinian, Professor José Imbelloni, has recently published a study of the Easter Island tablets that contributes few original elements to the solution of the problem, with the exception of a new parallel he draws between a dozen Easter Island symbols and characters belonging to a Brahmi script (third century B.C.) that occurs on inscriptions found in the caves of Ceylon. He also points out the resemblance between the symbols on the tablets and certain signs in the script of the Lolo of Szechuen, and draws attention to the characters of the syllabary used on Woleai—an island in the Caroline Archipelago—whose origins are obscure and which may very well be merely a script invented on the spot under the influence of Malay, Indian, or even European writing. On the basis of these rather vague comparisons Imbelloni claims to be able to demonstrate the phases of an 'Indo-Pacific graphic system'.

One of the most striking differences between te Indus Valley and Chinese signs on the one hand, and those of Easter Island on the other, lies in the way they are drawn. While the former are linear and schematic, the latter are formed by a double line bounding a silhouette. In other words, the Easter symbols are more realistic than those of the other scripts. From this it has been deduced that they represent an earlier system of writing than that disclosed by the Indus seals. Imbelloni does not take this view. He gets round the difficulty by the hypothesis of a 'rejuvenation of the Easter Island script, which was originally linear but which, after penetrating the Oceanic world, underwent a plastic interpretation dominated by the bird myth'. In other words, this stylistic transformation was due to the bird cult in Oceania. Such methods of interpretation are, to say the least, puzzling.

These, in broad outline, are the explanations put forward by the adherents of diffusionism. A book addressed to the general reader is no place for long scientific discussions, and I must therefore confine myself to general objections rather than an examination of details. Moreover, I could not follow Heine-Geldern into the domain of Asian archaeology, which is not my field of work, and I leave it to others to say whether his hypotheses concerning the origin of the Indus Valley and Chinese scripts is in line with present knowledge.

To begin with a general comment: the subjective element in these comparisons must not be overlooked. The correlations that struck Heine-Geldern would certainly not have caught my attention, but I repeat that we are dealing here with a personal factor that eludes the scientific yardstick. Furthermore, the problem set by the identity that seems to exist between the symbols of these different systems of writing does not appear to me insuperable. It has been claimed that the important thing is the fact of the similarity, not its explanation. Alas, I am not so sure. If we suppose, with Heine-Geldern, that these three scripts are derived from a common source, after which each one evolved in a distinct direction, it is difficult to understand why certain composite or simple signs remained unchanged for five to six thousand years while so many others were modified or lost. Even admitting the force of habit, such a stability in an ideographic or even pictographic script would be a strange phenomenon demanding an explanation. It is not for us to provide it.

My disagreement with Hévesy and Heine-Geldern is based, above all, on a question of method and also on a different conception of the nature and development of cultures. Thus I should have wished, before undertaking a comparison between the Easter Island signs and those of other scripts, to classify all the symbols occurring on the tablets. Anyone who examines the available documents on the Easter Island script attentively will see that the same signs are by no means always drawn in the same way and that they are far from showing the uniformity of our printed characters. It is hard to believe that any particular change of meaning was expressed by the presence of an arm or leg, the position of the head, or the shape of a hand. If the same variations occurred with some frequency, of course, we could consider them separate pictograms or ideograms, but can we say that this is the case? Different signs are frequently joined together, perhaps without any alteration in the meaning of the individual symbols so combined. Comparisons between anthropomorphic symbols are not without danger. There is always the risk that more or less stylized representations of the human figure may create the illusion of a similarity between pictographic systems that have nothing to do with one another. Correlations of this sort are foolhardy even when the figure is depicted holding something in its hand, especially if we do not know what this object is. The fact that there are men holding sticks, weapons, or other instruments on both the Indus Valley seals and the Easter Island tablets does not seem to me a very decisive piece of evidence on which to assert a link, even if indirect, between two cultures that are utterly different from so many points of view.

My doubts are based on the resemblances I have noted between the Easter signs and the geometric motifs and anthropomorphic or zoomorphic figures that abound in numerous ancient and modern pictographies. It is not only the Cuna Indians who draw symbols resembling those of Easter Island, but also the Quechua and Aymara Indians of the Andes, who have adopted a picture-writing that helps them memorize Catholic prayers. Is one to conform to the comparative method described above and trace a link between Easter Island and the Andean Indians, simply because it occurred to them in the last century, to invent images to correspond to the words of the Catholic prayers? What are we to say of the ideographic or syllabic scripts devised by several tribes—Eskimoes, Bamum Negroes, Vai, for example—which also employ symbols whose equivalents are to be found on the tablets? We know that these scripts were created by men who, unable to read and write themselves, knew that other peoples transmitted words by means of signs.

The scientist's whole attitude towards the affinity of cultures separated by space and time depends in the last analysis on his conception of culture and man's inventive faculty. Since I myself belong to that group of anthropologists which is devoted to the study of the reciprocal influences cultures exercise upon one another, I think I am in a position to grasp the significance of the investigations carried out by the 'historical school' and I know the part it has played in twentieth century anthropology; but I believe it has sometimes exceeded the bounds of prudence and forgotten that a culture is not composed exclusively of features that combine and disperse pretty well at random. Every element a culture borrows is integrated into a structure that modifies it and is modified by it. Institutions that are pure survivals without functional value are an exception. Primitive man, like modern man, though he also depends on external stimuli to transform his culture, is not incapable of innovating. Cultures sometimes change rapidly and develop a great creative force in domains that suddenly assume particular importance in the eyes of a group. We know the part played by sacred chants, magical incantations and genealogies in most, if not all, Polynesian societies. Voyagers and missionaries have reported the value the priests attached to exactitude in recitation, lest the slightest mistake might destroy all the efficacy of a long ceremony. In many islands the priests or the chanters, who were the depositaries of this oral literature, have utilized mnemotechnical methods that we shall enumerate farther on. Was it beyond the creative genius of the Easter Islanders to invent a pictography that does not seem to have differed essentially from systems devised by other groups at approximately the same cultural level as the Polynesians?

To my way of thinking, it is impossible to consider the problem of the origin of the tablets as solved. It seems to me that other proofs, obtained by a more rigorously scientific method, are necessary before a verdict can be pronounced in favour of Hévesy's and Heine-Geldern's conclusions, attractive though they are.

Must we then, after so many setbacks, abandon all hope of getting to know more about the tablets? Not at all, though it must be admitted that the data on which we can draw for a solution of the problem are scanty.

Polynesian dialects make extensive use of the duplication of words to add intensity to the expression of an idea or to indicate plurality. The famous chants recited by the *rongorongo* are generally interminable poems abounding in repetitions and enumerations. In addition, every sentence in the Polynesian dialects contains a large number of particles indicating movement, position and other relationships. If the signs correspond to a syllabic or alphabetic system we ought to find the same sequences of symbols continually recurring wherever the same words or sounds were repeated in the text. The decipherer's first task is therefore to extract these groups of identical signs. An analysis of two tablets which I undertook was not encouraging though I was able to find a few rows of identical symbols.

I do agree with Heine-Geldern on one important point. The signs on the tablets are too uniform and too conventionalized to be entirely comparable with the designs that occur in the pictographs of other peoples. The Ojibway or Cuna Indians, who draw figures to evoke a sentence or passage in an incantation, enjoy greater freedom of expression than the Easter Island scribe.

When we are endeavouring to decipher an unknown script, the first thing to do is to classify and count the signs. This I have tried to do with the tablet known as Aruku-kurenga. Out of a total of 960 symbols the image of the sooty tern—symbolizing the god Makemake—is repeated 183 times. Nearly a fifth of the tablet is,

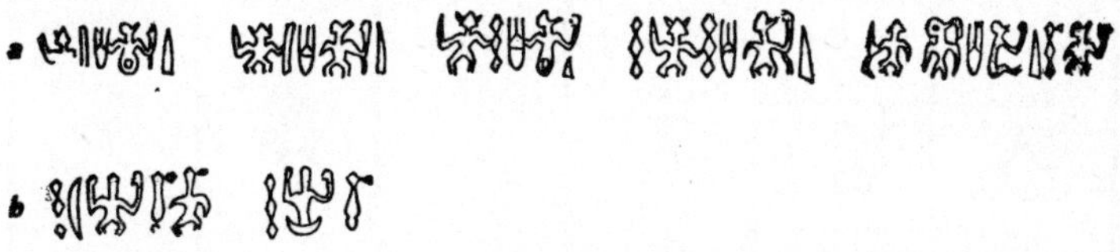

Fig. 4. Similar symbols in the Indus script: (a) on the Easter Island tablets; (b) in the most ancient forms of Chinese writing according to Heine-Geldern. *Die Osterinselschrift*, Anthropos, Vol. 33, page 873.

therefore, covered by a single sign. An individual with a lozenge for a head is reproduced ninety-four times. Depictions of human beings and birds represent about one-third of the symbols. This proportion does not seem to favour the hypothesis of a syllabic or alphabetic script.

Despite the conventional character of the signs, the Easter Island script none the less bears an affinity to primitive pictographies by virtue of the number of realistic representations, such as human figures, birds, turtles, crabs, artifacts and so on. The symbols we designate geometric may possibly depict objects we can no longer identify. There is no reason, *a priori*, why each character in this system of writing should not be associated with a line of poetry or even a whole verse. To read the tablet the bard would have to know the text of the chant by heart, and the sole purpose of the signs would be to save him from lapses of memory that

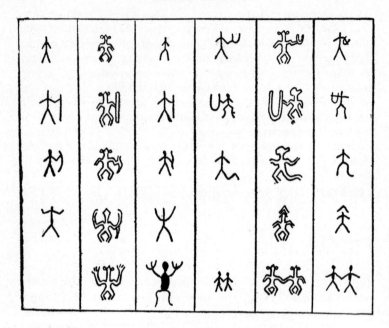

Fig. 5. Sequences of identical signs in row 1 of tablet
Aruku-kurenga.

would be considered very bad omens. In this case, the Easter
Island tablets may be regarded as a mnemotechnic instrument for
the use of the *rongorongo*, the Polynesian bards. Analogies with
other civilizations support this interpretation. The Ojibway
Indians, for example, draw figures and symbols on strips of bark,
the sight of which arouse associations with the sentences or verses
of the spells they are reciting. Picture writing is not always simply
an aid to memory, however: it also possesses an intrinsic magic
power calculated to enhance the efficacy of the words.

There is one fact which has not sufficiently struck those who
have studied the tablets and of which great account should be
taken in interpreting them. Whatever the shape and size of these
pieces of wood, they are invariably covered with signs on both

sides, without the slightest space being wasted. The tablets are of various and largely fortuitous shapes. If the sum total of the signs corresponded to a text of predetermined length, they would not invariably extend over both sides, not excepting the bevelled edges. Are we to credit the scribe with a miraculous instinct that led him always to choose a piece of wood whose dimensions exactly coincide with the length of his text? When the symbols are incised in a cylindrical staff, they run all round the circumference without anything to show where the inscription begins or ends. It is as if the scribe had been determined to engrave as many signs on the wood as possible. Such an aim is hard to reconcile with the hypothesis that these signs are the characters of a script.

The number of symbols on the large tablets far exceeds the length of ordinary Polynesian chants, if we accept the idea that each sign corresponds to a verse or a bar. It may be objected that each tablet contains several chants; but, in that case, why are they not separated by a space or a conventional sign? Why does the text appear so continuous that even faults in the wood have been covered with signs? This creates an added difficulty for the script hypothesis. All the same, unless we deny the authority and unanimity of traditions, the tablets were associated with literary pieces. What was the nature of this link between the chants and the tablets?

The Maori orators and reciters added emphasis to their words by the manipulation of a finely engraved club held in the hands. The genealogists made use of a staff marked with notches representing the ancestors. This aid to memory was really a useless accessory, because the reciter knew his list of ancestors off by heart; but the staff enabled him to give the audience a concrete image of the generations of ancestors. The priests of Tahiti and the Tuamotus symbolized the liturgical poems by a staff or an object of plaited straw, which they deposited on the altar after finishing the chant it represented. These few examples reveal a tendency to create concrete representations of sacred poems and other literary pieces. The Marquesan bards (*ono'ono*) used to associate their liturgical poems with objects which, although very different to look at, were of the same order as the rest: these were little bags of plaited coconut fibre from which hung knotted cords. The exact significance of the bags is not clear, but the knots are said to have fulfilled the same function as the notches on the Maori staves and to have been aids to the memories of the reciters of genealogies. The recitation of a list of ancestors was generally preceded by a lengthy enumeration of abstract notions, gods and natural elements which, by uniting, produced the world and ultimately the first humans. This part of the genealogy—the *rumu*, or root—was symbolically represented by the fibre 'bundle' or bag. There would have been nothing mysterious about these bundles if they had been solely aids to memory; but they were material representations of the chants relating to the genealogies. Of what use can these strange balls of string have been to the bard? Some informants gave us to understand that each verse of the poems corresponded to a knot, but this is far from having been the case with all bundles. One of them was described as a 'receptacle' containing the chants. The bard held it in his hand and asked his auditors which hymn they wished to hear. He then intoned the chant requested, without letting go of the bundle. These objects so fully represented the concrete form of the chants that they were solemnly presented to the young men after their initiation into tribal folklore. Thus the Marquesas, whose culture offers so many analogies with that of Easter Island, furnishes a complex of facts and ideas that perhaps provides the key to the riddle of the tablets.

I therefore advance the following provisional interpretation of the mystery of the tablets: The *rongorongo* or Easter Island bards used staves (*kohau*) to augment the effects of their recitations. On these staves they engraved sacred symbols. These symbols, like the notches on the staves of the Maori orators, may originally have been aids to memory; later the decorative or mystic aspect of the symbols gained over their pictographic significance. The tendency arose to multiply them haphazard on the staves or tablets carried by the bards. We may suppose that the signs were arbitrarily associated with the chants, each symbol representing a significant word, a phrase, a sentence, or even a verse. The custom of chanting a poem while looking at a figure has not entirely disappeared from Easter Island. After producing a cat's-cradle, the player recites a poem that is often interpolated in a story. The solution to the problem is possibly suggested by the remark of one informant: 'Our ancestors recited poems for tablets covered with images; we, in our ignorance, recite them for the string-figures.'

I have given my own interpretation of the significance of the tablets. It will certainly have to be revised when Dr Th. S. Barthel publishes his book *Grundlagen zur Entzifferung der Osterinselschrift*. In a letter which I received just before sending this book to the press, Dr Barthel informed me that he had arrived at conclusions which differ in many respects from mine. One must await the publication of his book before passing any judgement on these, but Dr Barthel's hypotheses concerning the nature of the Easter Island script are certainly of great interest and may be the key to the riddle.

I am most grateful to Dr Barthel for permission to summarize the result of his painstaking investigations. Dr Barthel thinks that Easter Island writing can be defined as a conventional system of recording communicable traditions. It uses a limited fund of graphic elements which can be increased remarkably by means of further combinations following strict rules. The Easter Island script is more evolved than mere pictography and contains ideograms with fixed and variable meanings, different levels of symbolization and word-signs which can be used for noting names, in rebus-fashion for homonyms. This system cannot render a spoken sentence completely with all its grammatical particles, but it may be defined as 'embryo writing'. The scribe had to choose the main ideas before expressing them in a sort of telegraphic style. Thus the tablets consisted of different groups of 'catch-words' which conveyed a clear and definite meaning. Such 'condensed texts' accomplished a mnemonic function, but the system itself cannot be equated with other mnemonic devices. The principles of text-condensation and partial phonetic indications made understanding difficult, but not impossible.

There are often strange coincidences in discoveries. In recent years Russian scientists (B. Kudriatsev, A. Olderogge, N. A. Butinov and Y. V. Knorozov) have also endeavoured to unravel the secret of the tablets. They have now arrived at important conclusions which were brought to my attention a few weeks after I became acquainted with Dr Barthel's research. The Russian scholars have discovered that several rows of signs in different tablets were identical, and they have listed many recurrent combinations of two or more signs which seem to correspond to words or sentences. Professor Olderogge believes that the Easter Island script had already reached a stage of development comparable to early Egyptian hieroglyphics. Some signs seem to be ideograms, accompanied by a key sig, while others appear to have a phonetic value which is also determined by a key sign.

CHAPTER XIII

Easter Island Myths and Legends

DURING OUR stay at Anakena, Tepano dictated to us the legend-ary history of his people. He felt inspired by the royal mausoleums and he enjoyed having only to stretch out his arm to show us the spot where the events in his story actually happened. His memory was not always reliable. He hesitated over some proper names and forgot a few details; but he had a surprisingly clear recollection of the main facts. He apologized for his lapses and in the evening, when our sessions of inquiry were over, he used to walk away thoughtful and downcast at having left us only an imperfect picture of his ancestors' exploits. Tepano loved these legendary tales; he believed in them and nothing seemed to him too miraculous or exaggerated. Forestalling our scepticism, he exclaimed frequently: 'The people of the old days knew more than we and they had much more *mana*.'

I hope this English translation may have retained something of the simple pungency of the original text, stripped of its tedious rep-etitions. The reader must visualize great fields of stones, a fire-blackened shore, green hills in the distance, and the sea, that old friend of the Polynesians, whose winds and waves carried the first men to the strand on which we were listening to their story. Here it is:

The land of our fathers was a great island to the west called Marae-renga. The climate was warm and many trees grew there, of which our ancestors made large boats or gathered together to build them-selves houses. In spite of the shade, people were sometimes killed by the heat.

Hotu-matu'a was a chief of this island, but he was forced to leave it after a quarrel with his brother Te Ira-ka-tea. We do not know the cause of this dispute, which provoked a war between the two chiefs. Another story is also told. Hotu-matu'a's brother was in love with a woman whom the *ariki* Oroi wished to marry. The young woman, hesitating between the two, promised Oroi she would be his if he walked round the island without stopping to rest or sleep. Oroi submitted to this test, but meanwhile the girl ran away with Hotu-matu'a's brother. There was war between the tribe of Oroi and the tribe of Hotu-matu'a. Oroi being the stronger, Hotu-matu'a was obliged to set out in search of new lands in order to escape death or dishonour.

There was in the island a certain Hau-maka, who had tattooed King Hotu-matu'a. Hau-maka had a dream: his soul journeyed across the sea to an island where there were holes [craters] and fine beaches. Six men had landed there at the same time.

Hotu-matu'a understood that Hau-maka's dream was a promise. He chose six men, gave them a canoe, and told them to sail straight ahead until they reached the land Hau-maka's soul had seen. As they moved away from the shore the King called after them: 'Go and look for a fine beach where the King can settle.'

The crossing was quick and fair. The six men came in sight of Easter Island and when they saw the crater of the Rano-raraku they cried out: 'There is Hau-maka's hole.' This was the first name of the volcano. They sailed round the island looking for the beach the King had told them to find.

Our beaches are small and littered with rocks; nevertheless, every time they caught sight of a beach, one of the six men called out: 'Let us stop here. There is the beach for King Hotu-matu'a'; but the pilot said: 'No, this beach is not worthy of a king.' They doubled Poike headland and came to Anakena, where we are now. When they saw this fine stretch of sand in front of them, and this calm green water, they all stood up and said: 'Here is the beach of which Hau-maka dreamed and where our King will live.' They turned the prow of their canoe towards it and disembarked.

A large turtle lay asleep on the beach. They wanted to turn it over on its back, but it seriously injured one of the young men with one of its feet. His companions picked him up and carried him into the Ihu-arero cave. They remained there three days caring for him. Then they remembered Hotu-matu'a's order and wished to go to the west coast of the island to meet him. They did not know what to do with the injured man, but were ashamed to leave him all by himself. They piled up five heaps of stones in front of the cave and ordered them to speak on their behalf every time their companion called them. Then they left.

No sooner had they reached Mataveri than they saw Hotu-matu'a's double canoe approaching the shore. The King shouted to them: 'What is this country like?' 'It is a bad country,' replied the young men, 'the taros are smothered by weeds, and it's no good pulling them up, they grow again.' Then Hotu-matu'a uttered a curse: 'Bad country, you shall be good at low tide, but the high tide shall kill all of you.' We do not know what Hotu-matu'a meant by these words. Some think that this malediction was addressed to Marae-renga, which vanished beneath the sea. In any case, the young man, frightened by these words, cried out: 'Why did you say these things, Hotu-Matu'a, are you not afraid that your words may bring us bad luck?'

Then Hotu-matu'a cut the ropes joining the two boats. He told Tu'u-ko-ihu to sail along the northern coast and he himself set off towards the south. The two boats reached Anakena at the same time. Seeing that Tu'u-ko-ihu's boat was gaining on him, Hotu-matu'a stood up in the prow of his canoe and cried: 'Paddles, do not thrust.' Such was the power of his *mana* that Tu'u-ko-ihu's boat halted and Hotu-matu'a was the first to land on the sands of Anakena. At that moment he heard a moan: his wife had been seized with the pains of childbirth. He immediately called Chief Tu'u-ko-ihu, who came and received a male child whose navel cord he cut according to the rites and for whom he recited a charm: the charm glorifying the power of young chiefs when they come into the world to carry on the lineage of the gods. While Tu'u-ko-ihu was receiving the young prince, his own wife brought into the world a daughter, Princess Avareipua.

The same day, all the people who had come in the canoes disembarked. They unloaded the plants and animals they had with them. These plants were taros, yams, sugar-canes, bananas, *ti* and then all the trees that have disappeared—such as hibiscus and *toromiro*. As for the animals, only the chickens and rats had survived. Hotu-matu'a had set out with several other species, but these did not come to the island until the white men brought them later.

Oroi—the same who had made war on Hotu-matu'a—was among those who landed. He left the boat at night, for he had voyaged secretly to take his revenge. For a long time Oroi wandered about the island until the day when he saw Hotu-matu'a's sons resting in the sun lying on their bellies. As they had swum a great deal for their pleasure, they were sleeping. Oroi went up to them and killed them by sticking a crayfish's tail into their behinds.

In the evening, Hotu-matu'a, seeing that his sons did not return, went to look for them. He found their bodies on the beach. He examined them closely and said: 'O Oroi, you have crossed the seas to continue your war, for I recognize your hand!' And the King wept bitterly over his children.

A year passed. Hotu-matu'a had travelled over the whole island, inspecting the new villages, taking part in the feasts, and teaching the people the sacred chants of their ancestors. Oroi followed him everywhere, seeking an opportunity of killing him. He had plaited a rope and stretched it across the King's path, but the King saw it and stepped over it. Oroi pulled the rope, but he could not make the King fall. Hotu-matu'a said to himself: 'O Oroi, the day will come when you will die by my hand!'

When Hotu-matu'a was passing Hanga-te-tenga, Oroi stretched his rope across the path as usual. The King pretended to be caught and fell in the grass. Oroi leapt upon him to kill him, but as he leant forward Hotu-matu'a sprang up and split his skull with his club. This was how Oroi perished, who had been a chief on Maraerenga. His body was placed in an oven, but his flesh, being a chief's, could not be cooked. It was taken to an *ahu* that still bears his name.

When he was old, Hotu-matu'a divided the island among his children. Each of them became the ancestor of a tribe. After carrying out this partition, Hotu-matu'a went to the Rano-kao volcano. He ascended to the summit of the crater and sat down on the rocks facing the west, looking towards his fatherland, Marae-renga. He called upon four gods that lived in the land of his birth: 'Kuihi, Kuaha, Tongau, Opapaku,' he said, 'the time has come to make the cock crow.' The cock of Marae-renga crowed and his crowing was heard across the sea. The hour of his death had come. Hotu-matu'a turned to his sons and said: 'Take me back.' They carried him into his hut, where he passed away. His body was buried in an *ahu* at Akahanga.

THE WAR OF THE LONG-EARS AND THE LITTLE-EARS

Many years passed. The island was ruled by people with long, pendulous ears. They were intelligent; and it was they who built all the *ahu* on the coast. The work was done by the people with little ears, whom they had reduced to slavery.

One day, the Big-Ears said to the Little-Ears: 'Go and throw into the sea all these stones that clutter up the ground.' The Little-Ears replied: 'We shall do nothing of the sort, for we need these stones for our food. We need them to cook with and also to make the potatoes, the sugar-canes and the taros "suffer". For when these plants suffer, they grow and become stronger and larger.' The Big-Ears were angry at this disobedience and plotted the destruction of the Little-Ears.

At the foot of the Poike promontory they dug a pit extending from the north coast to the south coast. They filled it with branches and grass, for it was their intention to roast the Little-Ears in it. Now, it happened that a Little-Ear woman lived at Potu-te-rangi, where she was married to a Long-Ear man. Her relatives and friends of the Little-Ear tribe did not know why such a large pit had been dug and they wondered what the wood and grass heaped up in it were for. The Little-Ear woman pestered her husband with her questions until he told her the pit was an oven to cook the Little-Ears in. The same night, this woman passed on the news to her relatives: 'Watch my house,' she said, 'and when the Big-Ears are lighting their oven come up behind them and push them into the fire. And instead of a feast of Little-Ears there will be a feast of Big-Ears.'

The woman went back into her house and said: 'Now act quickly.' She stood in front of the door of her hut with a basket she pretended to be weaving, but really it was to warn her tribe of the danger. When she saw the Big-Ears preparing to attack, she gave a signal, and the Little-Ears advanced on the house and fell upon the Big-Ears, who had just lit the wood and leaves at the bottom of the great pit. Surprised by this sudden attack, they offered no resistance, but fled straight in front of them. Where could they go? They fell into the fire, where all of them—men, women and children

—perished, with the exception of two warriors, who succeeded in crossing the obstacle by walking over the corpses. They ran towards Anakena and took refuge in the cavern of Ana-vai. The Little-Ears followed them and poked them with pointed sticks to make them come out. The two men ran from one end of the cave to the other, making a strange noise, the sound of which has always made us laugh: 'Ororoin'. Finally, a *matato'a* approached the troop of Little-Ears who were tormenting the two men, and said: 'Warriors, let us spare these men. Why should we kill them? Let them go free.' The Little-Ears returned to the pit in which the Long-Ears were just burning up. They filled it in and went home—henceforth sole masters of the island.

The two Long-Ears were adopted by the Little-Ears and I know their sons: one lives at Hanga-roa and the other is in the leper settlement.

THE GREAT WAR OF THE TU'U CONFEDERATION AGAINST THE CONFEDERATION OF HOTU-ITI

The people of Hotu-iti never liked those of the west. There were many wars between them in which sometimes one and sometimes the other group emerged victorious.

I shall tell you about the cruellest of these wars. I cannot tell you when it took place. I do not know whether it was a long time after Hotu-matu'a or only a few years before Captain Cook. Many people perished and if you walk about the island you can see their bones scattered among the stones.

The war started like this: Two young men, Makita and Rokehaua, had come to Hotu-iti to pay a visit to Kainga. The latter was a great warrior who had a fine hut and was generous to his visitors. He said to them: 'Young men, come into my hut.' When they had crossed the threshold he rubbed noses with them as a token of friendship. Kainga roasted a fowl for them and sent an adopted child to bring them the giblets he had grilled on the stones of the oven. When the little boy entered and offered him this choice dish, Rokehaua asked: 'What's that you are bringing me?' 'These are chicken's giblets,' replied the child. Rokehaua thrust them aside, saying: 'Chicken's giblets . . . Know that I do not want any, for I am used to feeding on human entrails.'

The child repeated these words to Kainga. 'They want human entrails, do they?' said Kainga. 'All right, they shall have them.' He called the child and ordered him to lie down on the ground. The little orphan understood what awaited him. He wept and sung a song: *Alas, alas, farewell country where I have lived.* . . . Kainga slit his throat, opened his belly, and took out the entrails, which he grilled on the stones of the oven. He took them to his guests himself. When Rokehaua saw the dish that was being offered to him, he woke Makita and said to him: 'Look, here are human entrails.' Makita, who had not heard his friend's imprudent words, realized that they would not have long to wait for Kainga's revenge. He fled from the house through a hole in the wall, and Rokehaua followed him. They fled because they had caused the death of Kainga's adopted son by their words. From afar Kainga shouted after them: 'You have rejected the food your host Kainga offered to you. There will soon be a boat whose keel will be at Pepe and whose caulking will be on Rano-aroi.'

Kainga called together his people and told them to collect timber to build a great boat. He sent gangs of workmen to Rano-aroi to fetch moss to caulk the planks.

SECOND EPISODE OF THE WAR

Long ago—but how long ago I cannot say—the Tupa-hotu and the Miru were at war. It was a long war. This is how it began. Kainga, the Tupa-hotu chief of the western tribes, quarrelled with Toari, a warrior of the eastern tribes. In all the battles in which he had met him he had not been able to kill him.

Kainga had a son, Uri-avai, who was still a child. This son had a dream: his soul had left his body and, after wandering in the plain, found itself facing a cock. The soul took a stone and threw it at the cock, which fell dead. When Kainga heard the story of the dream he was overcome with joy: the dream foretold the death of the cock of the Tu'u, the warrior Toari.

He gathered his warriors, took the child with him, and marched against Toari's bands. When they were in the enemy's presence, he gave two javelins to his son and told him to throw them at Toari. His son's dream had not been in vain: Toari fell dead, like the cock. His desire for vengeance satisfied, Kainga left the battlefield; but the people of Tu'u, infuriated by the death of their chief, charged the Tupa-hotu, who fled in all directions. Among the fugitives was another son of Kainga, Rau-hiva-aringa-erua [Rau-hiva-of-the-double-face]. The face he had at the back said to him: 'I see Pau-aure-vere coming, he has a javelin in his hand, he is going to kill me. Face that is in front, look!' But the front face replied: 'What do I care, back face, I don't want to see.' While the two faces were arguing, Rau-hiva was killed. He died because of his two faces and their argument.

The defeated Tupa-hotu took refuge, some on the islet of Maro-tiri, some in the cave of Ana-te-ava-nui, in the face of the Poike cliff.

The Miru sent canoes to the island of Marotiri to kill all the enemy within reach. They came back laden with dead, whom they put down in rows on the beach and distributed among the warriors of the tribe for their evening meal. Every day the Miru canoes returned to Marotiri and brought back fresh human flesh.

A Miru warrior, named Oho-taka-tore, came from his village to the bay of Ana-havea, where the bodies were handed out every day. He came to the beach just as the canoes back from Marotiri were unloading the enemies killed during the day. Among the dead, Oho-taka-tore recognized a Tupa hotu warrior called Hanga-maihi-tokerau. Turning to the troop of Miru warriors, he said to them: 'Comrades, give me the body of the warrior with such a splendid name. I should like to eat him, because his name is sweet in my ears.' Poie, the leader of one of the canoe teams, said to him: 'Oho-taka-tore, the body of the warrior with the beautiful name shall not be yours. Why did you come when evening was falling?' Without a word, Oho-taka-tore took off his feather diadem, put it on upside down, and went away. The people said: "Oho-taka-tore is certainly angry. What is he going to do?'

Oho-taka-tore had a daughter married to a Tupa-hotu man named Moa. He sent for her and asked her: 'Does your husband still think of the Tupa-hotu people?' 'Father, why do you ask me such questions?—you know very well. Do you think your son-in-law shares with me his thoughts about his people?' 'Go and fetch him, my daughter, and tell him to think of his tribe, which is hard pressed by the Miru.' And he revealed to his daughter a plan that was going to do great harm to the Miru and bring joy and life to the

Tupa-hotu.

This is what happened on the island of Marotiri that same night. A Miru warrior was keeping watch there, killing every Tupa-hotu who ventured to the foot of the rock. Kainga, a Tupa-hotu warrior, observed him from the summit of the islet. Now, Kainga's son, Uri-avai, had taken advantage of the moonless night to swim to the islet, where his father was waiting for him. He came ashore unsuspecting. Vaha, who had heard him swimming, asked him: 'Who are you?' 'Uri-avai,' he replied, 'I am Uri-avai.' 'And I am Uri-avai's enemy,' retorted Vaha. So saying, he thrust his obsidian javelin into his throat. Kainga had recognized his son's voice and had heard his body fall. Vaha swam towards the main island, dragging the corpse along with him. Kainga followed him. He saw him walking along the beach. 'If he manages to get into the interior of the island he will be safe, but if he passes close to me, woe betide him.' At that moment, Vaha drew close to him and Kainga called out to him: 'Who are you?' 'Vaha, the enemy of Uri-avai,' came the reply. 'I am Kainga, the enemy of Vaha,' said Kainga, transfixing him with his javelin. Kainga took his child on his shoulder, wept his death, and buried him in a little *ahu* called Ainini. Then he swam back to the islet of Marotiri, dragging Vaha's corpse behind him. The Tupa-hotu who had stayed there were dying of hunger. Great was their joy, therefore, when they saw the corpse of Vaha. Alas, they had no fire! To eat it, they warmed his human flesh under their armpits and between their legs. They devoured it with relish.

Oho-taka-tore's daughter had given Moa her father's message. Moa said nothing, but went and fetched potatoes from a field. He cooked them and put them in a fishing net. That night he left the house very secretly and went to Poike, where the Ana-te-ava-nui cave is. The Tupa-hotu who had taken refuge there were in great danger of extermination. The enemy had lowered a net from the top of the cliff containing warriors, who hurled javelins into the cave, killing those who were near the entrance. In order to hold out longer, the warriors in the cavern had placed the women and children and all those of no use in the war in front. When these had all been killed by the javelins, thirty warriors who refused to surrender were left in the grotto. Moa did not climb down the cliff at once. He stopped by a *niu* tree, from which he cut eight branches and added them to the load he carried on his shoulders. Then he walked along the crest of the cliff and observed that the Miru had dug holes in which they were sleeping. He went down the face of the cliff and came to the entrance of the cave. The sentinels asked: 'Who are you?' He replied: 'I am Moa.' Then they wept, saying: 'Alas, young man, come here.' But Moa told them to cease weeping and take his load before dawn came. Moa distributed the provisions he had brought with him and made them eat the food to recover their strength. Then he asked them: 'Where are the bones of Pere-roki-roki?' They showed him at the foot of the cliff a heap of bones from which the flesh had just rotted away. He commanded that they should be fetched. With the bones he made hooks, which he fixed to the ends of the eight branches. Then he explained to the warriors in the cavern the plan he had in his head: 'When the enemy lower the nets with the warriors to throw javelins into the cave, catch the net with these hooks; kill those who are inside it; put yourself in their place; and have yourselves hoisted to the top of the cliff. There fall upon the enemy and wipe out the Miru, but spare the members of my family.' At these words Moa began to weep for the sufferings of his people. 'Farewell,' he said, 'I shall come back, unless the enemy take me prisoner.'

Moa managed to reach the top of the cliff without being seen. He dipped his net in the sea, covered it with seaweed and other detritus, and returned to his wife's village as though he had simply been out fishing. At dawn, the Miru, as usual, let down a net containing two warriors. It was caught by the eight grapnels and pulled into the cave, where the two Miru entangled in its meshes were put to death. With the help of the ropes and the net, the Tupa-hotu reached the top of the cliff and killed the warriors who were on guard. The Miru, taken by surprise, fled, and the Tupa-hotu went in pursuit, killing everyone and sparing only the young women, encouraging one another with the words: 'Choose your women, I'm not shy.' The only people to be spared were the relatives of Moa. They fled like the rest, but the Tupa-hotu called after them: 'Do not tire your knees so. Stay where you are, no harm will be done to you.'

The thirty Tupa-hotu came level with the island of Marotiri.

There was great rejoicing on the island. 'We have covered our ovens with the leaves of the mountain,' they shouted derisively, meaning by these words that they had eaten raw flesh warmed under their arms and between their legs. They dived into the water, attacked the Miru on the shore, joined forces with the others, and shared in the great massacre. Only the pretty women were spared.

Kainga pursued Poie fiercely, chasing him across the whole island. But just as the Tupa-hotu were going to seize the vanquished chief, Kainga called to them: 'No, leave him, so that this game can go on.'

The Tupa-hotu men begot children with the Miru women. The Miru also had children. The years passed, the children of yesterday had become young men skilled in handling the javelin, when war broke out again.

The young Tupa-hotu went to the house of Poie, who had been spared in the other war. They wanted to kill him. Poie was not at home, but fishing at sea. His father-in-law was a bad man without honour. He said to the Tupa-hotu: 'If I am out of doors with my bald head exposed to the sun, it means that Poie is at sea; but if I stay indoors, come, for it will be a sign that Poie is at home.'

His daughter, Poie's wife, heard these words and ran to the shore. When she saw her husband, she cried to him: 'O Poie-nui-nui-a-tuki, the enemy are here. They are many, and your father-in-law is a man without honour.' Poie fled, but his enemies hastened in pursuit and gave him no time to hide. He threw himself into the sea, to make for one of the off-shore islands; the enemy band swam after him. Poie's brothers had joined him, but they were taken and their throats cut. Poie, seeing his brothers' blood flowing, cried: 'The blood of my four brothers has mingled in a single sheet.' Poie was taken to Orongo. A young boy who was there said: 'Let this man be given to me.' Kainga handed Poie over to him. Bundles of dry sugar-canes were tied round him and set on fire. The flames crackled, and Poie died in fearful agony. When Poie was dead, the Tupa-hotu again ran through the country of the Miru, killing everyone they met.

THE ORIGIN OF TATTOOING

The Lizard Woman and the Gannet Woman came from their house at Hakarava and went to the bay of Hanga-takaure. The Lizard Woman asked: 'What is the name of this *ahu?*' 'It is Hanga-takaure, the name of this land,' answered the Gannet Woman. 'What is Hanga-takaure to myself and to two beautiful women, the Lizard Woman and the Gannet Woman?' They continued along the south coast and at each settlement the elder sister, the Lizard Woman, asked her younger sister, the Gannet Woman, for the name of the place. When she had been told she always replied: 'What is this place to myself, and to two beautiful girls, the Lizard Woman and the Gannet Woman?'

The two sisters dived into the water and swam to Motu-nui. They stayed there and slept with the young men Heru and Patu. They became pregnant, gave birth to children, and reared them until they were grown. These two women were tattooed on the thighs, the cheek bones, the throat, the lips, the forearms, the jaws, and marked with circles on the buttocks.

The husbands went to Poike on the main island and slept with two other women who became pregnant and gave birth to children. The husbands returned to Motu-nui.

The children of the Lizard Woman and the Gannet Woman had been tattooed on the legs and jaws. They went to the main island and arrived at Orongo. The older one jumped on a stone of unusual size and shouted: 'Look at me, brother, as the red new moon.' The younger one sprang on a small stone and said: 'Look at me like the round moon.' They went to Vinapu, to Maherenga, and to Papa-tangaroa-hiro in search of surf-riding. Finally at Otuu they saw men, women, and children watching the surf-riders and the breaking waves. The young men asked the people for surf boards and went out to where the waves were breaking. A big wave reached its peak, then came a flat wave; the young men were carried on the waves and landed on shore. The people shouted: 'The surf-riders have landed!' the young men returned the boards to their owners. They went away and bathed in fresh water, then sat by a rock.

Two boys went to a well and drew water. The young men, sons

of the Lizard Woman and the Gannet Woman, made a spell and broke their calabashes. 'Why have you broken our calabashes?' asked the boys. 'We don't know. Who are you?' asked the young men. 'We are the sons of Heru and Patu,' replied the young men. 'How could you be sons of Heru and Patu, you are crabs, crayfish and octopuses.' The two men told their father what the young men had said, and the father said: 'Go and fetch these young men.' The two ugly men went to get the young men and together they went to the house of the father. The two young men went into another house where there were two girls. They stayed there and were fed with chicken, sweet potatoes, and fish by the father. They seized the girls to sleep with them but the girls did not want that. In the morning the girls saw how beautiful the two young men were and fell in love with them. They seized them and pulled them about, but the young men did not want them. So the young men left and went toward Hanga-nui. The girls followed them to Orohie, to Maio, to Papa-haka-heruru. The young men arrived at Vaika-ranga and entered a long feast-house for boys and girls. Inside were two ugly girls called Angu, who were jealous when they saw the good-looking girls called Hangu-arai, and decided to deceive them. All the girls went to the shore to bathe. The ugly Angu said: 'Let us go to the rocks and jump.' The Hangu-arai girls replied: 'You jump first and we will jump after you.' One of the Angu jumped. 'May she sleep on the rock,' said the Hangu-arai. The other ugly Angu said: 'She is dead.' 'No she is just asleep,' said the Hangu-arai, 'you jump and be finished.' The other Angu jumped and died. The Hangu-arai then returned to their husbands, Heru and Platu.

The two mothers stayed on the island. One day the elder went to a heap of rock called Rangi-manu and shouted to the sea: 'You Vivivivi and Vaovao come and tear me to pieces.' They came and lacerated her and she died. Then the younger sister did the same thing.

CHAPTER XIV

The Origins of Easter Island Civilization

MOST ATTEMPTS to explain the 'mysteries' of Easter Island presuppose that the natives living there at the time of its discovery were not the authors of the civilization whose remains inspire our wonder. These are commonly attributed to a powerful people possessing resources and technical means superior to those of the Easter Islanders of the historical period. The sudden end of this civilization is explained as the effect of a natural cataclysm or invasion by a race of barbarians.

It has now been proved that the surface of the island was virtually the same when it was first occupied by man as it is today. Nowhere have geologists found any trace of a recent volcanic eruption which—according to the hypothesis advanced by Forster, the naturalist with Captain Cook's expedition—put an end to the island's prosperity and left behind an impoverished and decadent population. Modern geographers refuse to see in this volcanic island the fragment of a continent that has been swallowed up by the Pacific.

The latest theory regarding the origin of the Polynesians, and hence of the inhabitants of Easter Island, is that put forward by Thor Heyerdahl, who braved the waters of the Pacific on his raft, the 'Kon-Tiki', to prove its truth. It is not without some hesitation that I question the links he establishes between Easter Island and Peru. In the first place, it is hardly fair to dissociate his ideas on Easter Island from the sum total of his work and conclusions. I do not intend to embark on a discussion of the peopling of Polynesia as a whole, however, and am therefore compelled to limit the debate to questions of detail which, important as they are, are nevertheless only isolated elements in a great mosaic. There are times when I find it impossible to accept Heyerdahl's method or to support his conclusions, in spite of the admiration I feel for his vast erudition and the cogency with which he presents his arguments. He has such confidence in his views that one feels sincere regret at not being able to share them.

At the present time, Heyerdahl is on the soil of Easter Island seeking to wrest from this much-explored piece of land its ultimate secret. Fortune, which has so often befriended him, may perhaps have reserved for him discoveries that will enable him to close the debate. If I enter this discussion here it is with the aim of putting before the reader a brief outline of Heyerdahl's hypotheses and acquainting him with some of the objections they have raised; but the question cannot be finally settled until we know the results of his expedition.

In his monumental work, *American Indians in the Pacific. The Theory behind the Kon-Tiki Expedition*, Thor Heyerdahl set out to show, by drawing numerous parallels of an archaeological and ethnographic nature, that the islands of Polynesia were peopled by settlers from America. These maritime migrations, he says, were made in two stages. The first left Peru towards the middle of the first millennium A.D. and carried into the Pacific a megalithic type of civilization, of which Easter Island has preserved the finest examples. The first inhabitants of Polynesia, after some centuries of isolation, were suddenly submerged and partially annihilated by a new wave of emigrants, this time from the north-west coast of North America, where they had evolved a culture closely resembling that of the Kwakliut and the Haida of British Columbia. This new colonization of the Pacific islands took place between 1000 and 1300 A.D. The invaders spoke a language from which the modern Polynesian dialects are derived. These newcomers mingled with their predecessors who, curiously enough, belonged very largely to the white race. Heyerdahl is actually convinced that a people, or more exactly a group of men, with fair skin, aquiline noses and bushy beards exercised a decisive influence on the development of the American civilizations, and in particular on those that flourished in the Andes, in ancient Peru. It was these mysterious civilizers who, having already assumed the white man's burden, set out on rafts in quest of new lands, once their mission had been accomplished in Peru. The many bearded and fair-skinned Polynesians described by the first voyagers were, according to this theory, the descendants of the white men who followed Kon-Tiki-Viracocha in his conquest of the Polynesian islands. In his reconstruction of the past of the American continent Heyerdahl proceeds rather in the manner of Herodotus, who faithfully collected the myths of the peoples he visited in order to reconstruct their history and link it up with the traditions of Greece.

To my way of thinking, Heyerdahl's thesis collides with two sets of facts that cannot be disposed of so easily. Firstly, the affinity between the dialects of Polynesia and the other languages of the Austronesian group is much closer than he supposes, and linguists are struck by the similarities of the Polynesian and Indonesian languages rather than by their differences. Secondly, the presence of numerous cultivated plants of Asian origin on the most distant islands of Polynesia is easily explained if we accept, as we have done up to the present, that they were brought by the Polynesians. But they raise a difficult problem if we take Heyerdahl's view. We may suppose that, once established in Polynesia, the Indians entered into contact with the Melanesians or even the Indonesians, and brought back to their islands plants and skills they did not possess in America. But this presupposes that they were able to sail from west to east, against the winds and currents, which is expressly denied by Heyerdahl in formulating his basic premises. His conviction that it was difficult, if not almost impossible, for primitive peoples to sail against wind and currents is a cornerstone of the theory that led him to undertake his daring voyage.

Heyerdahl is on firmer ground when he compares the great Easter Island statues with those of the Andean zone. It so happens that I am writing these lines a few weeks after returning from Tiahuanaco, on the banks of Lake Titicaca, where I re-examined the few monoliths that rise among the ruins of this famous site. I sought in vain to discern the slightest stylistic resemblance between them and the Easter Island *moai*. In fact it would be difficult to imagine a more dissimilar artistic tradition. The great images at San Agustín in Colombia are only known to me from photographs, but I doubt whether they have much in common with the great busts of Mount Rano-raraku.

Of all the points of resemblance Heyerdahl perceives between Easter Island and ancient Peru, the most valid is that which has been pointed out so often before between the seaward-facing façade of the famous Vinapu *ahu* and the walls of several buildings at Cuzco dating from pre-Inca times. The latter were constructed, without mortar, of splendidly polished blocks of stone, some of which fit together with astonishingly neat tenon and mortise joints. Now, this type of masonry, which occurs in three mausoleums on Easter Island—those of Vinapu, Ahu-te-peu and Hanga-paukura —is far from being typical of the island's architecture. The resemblance between the two building techniques is deceptive, because the Easter Islanders have used relatively thin slabs to face coarse rubble walls, while the Cuzco masons boldly squared solid blocks of stone. If Indians experienced in stone-masonry had imported their art into Easter Island, it is hardly likely that they would have applied it to a type of building of which they had no equivalent in their homeland and would have failed to erect temples on the model of those at Tiahuanaco, Pucara, Cuzco and other famous sites in Peru and Bolivia.

To continue our critical scrutiny of the parallels between Easter Island and Peru or South America: a whole chapter of Heyerdahl's book is devoted to the problem of the Easter tablets and script. While he sides with me in the controversy concerning the Asian origin of the latter, he is quite ready to accept the analogies between the Easter signs and the picture-writing of the Cuna Indians pointed out by Heine-Geldern. He doubts whether there was any direct connexion between the Easter Islanders and the Cuna Indians, however: in his opinion the Easter script must have been introduced into the island by Hotu-matu'a, that is, by the Peruvian chief who, in his opinion, led the first settlers from America. But this would imply that the ancient Peruvians had a script. Heyerdahl does his best to prove this by invoking the very questionable and much-disputed authority of Montesinos. It is perfectly possible that the Incas or the peoples who preceded them represented mythical episodes, and even historical events, on planks of wood; but there is nothing to suggest that they possessed a script properly so-called. Archaeology is silent on this point. Under these circumstances, how can a Peruvian origin be postulated for the Easter Island tablets? Foreseeing this objection, Heyerdahl replies that two symbols from the tablets seem to derive from Peruvian art and to portray animals foreign to the island's fauna. He interprets a bird with a long beak as the condor and a very schematic anthropomorphic or zoomorphic sign as the extremely stylized outline of a puma.

The other parallels drawn between Easter Island and Peru seem to me too vague to consider at any length. The floats made of conical bundles of reeds employed by Easter Island swimmers resemble reed floats used on the coast of Peru. A type of Easter Island feather head-dress does indeed recall the feather diadems of the South American Indians, but all feather diadems look very much alike the world over. The Easter Islanders deformed the lobe of the ear and inserted heavy ornaments, like the Incas of Peru and countless South American tribes. But these peoples are not the only ones to merit the name of 'Long-Ears'. Easter Island stone fish-hooks are indistinguishable from Californian fish-hooks—but California is not Peru.

What surprises me is that Easter Island culture does not present more analogies with the various civilizations of ancient Peru, for the common elements that have been pointed out are unimportant and do not provide a very firm basis for Heyerdahl's thesis. I have often wondered why the Peruvian Indians did not preserve in the Pacific the two arts in which they excelled—pottery and weaving. Since they are supposed to have introduced cotton, why did they not make use of it to weave the splendid garments obtained in such large numbers from the burial grounds on the Peruvian seaboard? The list of objects and techniques the Peruvians are said to have spread in the Pacific seems to me very scanty in comparison with the refinement of the Peruvian civilizations disclosed to us by archaeology.

Faithful to his tendency to see myths as texts possessing strict historical validity, Heyerdahl has submitted Easter Island folklore to a microscopic examination. According to Easter tradition, the island was, if not discovered, at least colonized by a great chief named Hotu-matu'a, who is credited with having introduced all the plants cultivated prior to the advent of the Europeans and with having, *inter alia*, created most of Easter Island institutions. In Heyerdahl's view this semi-mythical account refers to the arrival of a Peruvian chief who, accompanied by his retinue, discovered

Easter Island and settled there round about the fifth century A.D. This hypothesis rests entirely on a passage in the version published by Thomson, where it says that Hotu-matu'a came 'from a group of islands lying towards the rising sun, and the name of the land was Marae-toe-hau, the literal meaning of which is the "burial place". In this land, the climate was so intensely hot that the people sometimes died from the effects of the heat and at certain seasons plants and growing things were scorched and shrivelled up by the burning sun.' As a description of Peru this is rather vague. But is this text authoritative at all? Can it be considered a venerable tradition that the Easter Islanders have handed down from father to son for 1,400 years? Unfortunately we have proof that this tradition is extremely questionable and undoubtedly of very recent date. Thomson's principal source on Easter Island was a Tahitan named Salmon who had settled there in 1877. This Salmon had made himself the cicerone of all visitors to the island. Now, in 1882—four years before Thomson's visit—he told Geiseler that the Easter Islanders came from the west, from one of the Tuamotu, but he added that some of them identified Marae-renga, Hotu-matu'a's homeland, with the Galapagos. Those who held this opinion had no doubt learnt of the existence of this archipelago either from the whalers, who visited it frequently, or from their countrymen repatriated from Peru, or from Salmon himself. However they heard of it, we can spot in this belief the origin of the tradition echoed by Thomson a few years later. It remains to be added that the confusion between Maraerenga and the Galapagos has not been perpetuated. Those who doubt my testimony can read what Father Englert has to say on tthe subject. In the very detailed version he gives us of the Hotu-matu'a myth there is a passage worth quoting. It concerns a companion of the leader of the migration who has left his wife in their homeland: 'The wife of Nuku-kehu had remained in Hiva [the mythical country of Hotu-matu'a]. Nuku-kehu suffered every time he saw the sun set in the direction of Hiva, where lived Maramakai.'

Since we are discussing every detail of a myth as if we were analysing an historical document, I must say I am surprised how little note Heyerdahl takes of the tradition that Hotu-matu'a and his scouts sailed in canoes and not on rafts, although he is convinced that the Pacific was peopled by sailors using the latter type of craft.

Heyerdahl does not question the veracity of mythical tradition when it concerns sweet potatoes and tobacco, but he distrusts it when the text speaks of bananas, taros and sugar-canes, which are recognized as having been formerly unknown in the New World. He states quite rightly that modern Easter Islanders believe their first king brought everything that grows on their island in his ship's hold. But one cannot simultaneously employ a myth to prove a thesis and use the thesis to test the veracity of the same myth.

The celebrated Norwegian seafarer uncritically accepts the list of Easter Island's fifty-seven kings which figures in Thomson's account and the errors in which have been frequently pointed out. This enables him to place Hotu-matu'a's arrival at about the end of the fifth century A.D., a date that corresponds to the period at which the mysterious white men left Peru on rafts in search of new lands. In his eagerness to prove his thesis, he does not even bother to compare this list with those we owe to other authors, with the aid of which Thomson's numerous errors can be corrected by cross-checking. Also basing his opinion on the king-lists, Father Englert, who has studied Easter Island genealogies closely, came to the conclusion that the island was discovered and colonized in the six-teenth century. There is a difference of a thousand years between his estimate and Heyerdahl's. Which of them is right, Heyerdahl or Father Englert? Undoubtedly neither of them, though Father Englert's estimate is probably nearer the truth.

The war between the 'long-eared people' (hanau-eepe) and the 'short-eared people' (hanau-momoko) forms the theme of a legend full of sensational incidents and still popular among the natives of the island. Numerous versions exist, of unequal value. The one dic-tated to me by Tepano is reproduced, slightly abridged, in Chapter Thirteen. This myth, legend, or story—one is not quite sure how best to define it—is considered by some scholars to be a strictly his-torical document preserving under a slightly fabulous veneer the recollection of real events that took place on the island in the course of the seventeenth century—only a few years before the advent of the whites. To Heyerdahl's mind the 'Big-Ears' cannot be anyone else than the Indians from Peru, who must have landed on Easter around 475 A.D. Their 'long ears', the tradition of which has come down to us, immediately suggest the deformation of the lobe of the ear that earned the Incas of Peru the Spanish nickname of *Orejones*, 'Big Ears'. The 'men with short ears' are to be identified with the Polynesians proper who, after leaving the north-west coast of North America, scattered over the Pacific, where they finally reached and conquered Easter Island. Englert supposes that the 'people with the big ears' were Melanesians who came in about 1610 from an island he does not identify. Bórmida, who considers the Melanesian hypothesis absurd, nevertheless accepts the date, but regards the 'Long-Ears' as Polynesians from some unspecified island. The historical conclusions drawn from this tale are disconcerting when we recall that the 'Long-Ears', so brutally exterminated by their rivals in the seventeenth century, were seen and described by voyagers in the eighteenth and nineteenth centuries. For at this time all the Easter Islanders had long ears, if by this is meant that they deformed the lobe of the ear so as to insert heavy ornaments. Even without this exact evidence, the ears of the tufa statues and wooden figurines, which are all elongated, would have told us that this fashion, if not universal, was at least widespread in those days. The last 'long-eared' Easter Islanders died in the second half of the nineteenth century. Tepano claimed to have known some and pointed out their descendants.

The legend of the war between the two groups who differed by the shape of their ears contains episodes that are only intelligible if interpreted as popular explanations of certain natural peculiarities of the Easter landscape. Several versions of the story give the cause of the conflict as the refusal of the Short-Ears to comply with the Long-Ears' order to throw the stones that littered the soil of the island into the sea. In the district attributed to the Big Ears there is a tract of land which, for some geoloical reason, is not strewn with the blocks of disintegrated lava that render walking so tiresome everywhere else. This anomaly must have struck the natives. They explained it by supposing that a tribe once attempted to tidy up the island, but was forced to abandon this arduous undertaking. The pit into which the Short-Ears pushed their enemies and roasted them corresponds to 'a gully running from north to south across the island, with the snout of the lava flow on one side and the much higher sea-cut cliffs on the other'.

This natural pit suggests a manmade trench. It was natural for the natives to believe that it was dug by man and to invent a story to explain its origin.

If the two hostile groups had not been distinguished by the shape of their ears, this tale would never have caught the attention of scholars. In my opinion, this anatomical detail is a re-interpretation of an old tale that was made at a relatively recent period, when the progressive abandonment of the deformation of the lobe of the ear led to the belief that this fashion once corresponded to an ethnic difference.

But what point is there in devoting so much thought to the ex-egesis of a story, when we know now that the famous *menehune* of Hawaii, who were long believed to have been a people that preceded the ancestors of the present Hawaiians, were actually mythical beings without any historical reality? There is grave doubt today as to the accuracy of the celebrated Polynesian genealogies, which assume a more mythical character the farther back they go into the past. What reliance can we place in stories or myths that belong to popular literature and have only distant connexions with the religious and historical traditions transmitted by the members of the priestly caste? This folklore is a poor source of information concerning the island's past, and the rare elements of legend it contains are very fragmentary and imperfect. The natives who are still acquainted with this folk literature have no scruples about introducing new details gained from visitors with whom they have discussed their island's past. Lavachery and I gave our Easter Island friends an account of their ancestors' behaviour towards the first voyagers who landed on the island. I was greatly surprised to find later that details the Easter Islanders had learnt from us or from other travellers had slipped into the modern versions of these tales.

The importance ascribed to this legend would be justified if archaeological discoveries had revealed two distinct periods in Easter Island art or architecture, or if ethnographic analysis had compelled us to admit the presence in this culture of elements totally alien to Polynesia. In the absence of any such evidence, it seems to me fruitless to attribute an historical character to the story of the 'Big and Little Ears'. Here again, instead of starting from the precise data of archaeology or ethnography and seeking confirmation in folklore of the findings obtained by other methods, investigators have preferred to rely on a vague popular tradition in making assertions for which there is absolutely no genuine proof. It is perfectly obvious that the Easter Island monuments have been erected by one and the same population. The different types of *ahu* and the two categories of statues are normal variations within the framework of a single culture, and do not effect its homogeneity. The innumerable stone adzes collected on the island are typologically linked with specimens found in Eastern Polynesia and might very well have been made and used by Polynesians sharing a common technical heritage with their brothers on the Marquesas and Mangareva.

This is perhaps the moment to recall once more a fact we observed on Easter Island, which, though it may seem insignificant at first sight, is none the less a vitally important piece of evidence. The bases on which several of the great *ahu* statues stand have been shored up with *slabs of stone which are nothing else than the lower courses of the huts described earlier on and which were in use in the mid-nineteenth century*. In other words, the builders of the *ahu* and the sculptors of the great statues lived in huts identical with those described by La Pérouse in 1786. This simple detail by itself demolishes a good many theories concerning the great antiquity of Easter Island culture and the disappearance at some distant time of the men who carved the statues.

The *ahu* or stone mausoleums on which the great statues rose are only a local variant of the great sanctuaries or *marae* of Eastern Polynesia, whose platforms also bore the name *ahu*. Moreover, if we pass into the domain of linguistics, we find that the dialect of Easter Island is almost indistinguishable from Maori, Mangarevan and Marquesan. Furthermore, if a people speaking a non-Polynesian language had mingled with the Easter Islanders, its language could not have vanished without leaving at least a few traces. But no one has yet detected in the Easter vocabulary or toponomy any survivals of a foreign tongue.

The humorous legend of the war between the Big Ears and the Little Ears would not have aroused so much interest if many scientists had not considered the Easter Islanders racially different from other Polynesians and as showing certain points of resemblance to the Melanesians. This hypothesis, which has been vigorously disputed, has recently been revived by Imbelloni. It runs counter to the findings of Dr Harry Shapiro, our best authority on Polynesian physical anthropology, who has studied the population of Easter Island on the spot.

It is true that Easter Island skulls are 'hypsistenocephalic', that is, both high and narrow, and that in some respects they resemble Loyalty Island crania, but this, in Dr Shapiro's opinion, does not mean that Easter Islanders are Melanesians or mixed Melanesian and Australoid influences—as Imbelloni and various other craniologists have suggested. Much of the evidence rests on the connexion with Loyalty Island and from that it is generalized to 'Melanesians'. The cranial material from Loyalty Island is considered by Wagner, of whom Imbelloni approves, to be possibly an intrusion or influence from *early* Polynesians. So, if Wagner is correct, the cranial resemblances would be through Polynesian diffusion, not the other way round. Moreover, the blood group frequencies on Easter Island are typically Polynesian (low or absent for B, which is in marked contrast to the general Melanesian situation). Melanesians, apart from cranial characters, are dark skinned, with frizzy hair, and prognathic. None of these traits are typical of Easter Islanders. But even if it could be proved beyond any doubt that the Easter Islanders showed traces of intermingling with Melanesians this would not necessarily imply that they represent a local and special mixture of the two races. The admixture of Melanesian 'blood' might well date from a period prior to the arrival of the Easter Islanders' ancestors in their new country. The 'Melanesian' traits in Easter Island are not different from those found elsewhere in Polynesia, for example in the Marquesas.

The British anthropologist, Henry Balfour, has likewise supported the thesis of a Melanesian origin of Easter Island culture, basing his view on ethnographic arguments. His article has often been quoted and has exercised a certain influence on the prevalent conception of Easter Island culture. I do not wish to involve the reader in a barren ethnographic discussion, but I cannot altogether avoid it if the problem is to be examined from every side.

The connexions Balfour traces between the cultures of Easter

Island and Melanesia are as follows:

(1) Obsidian points identical with the Easter Island javelin heads have been found in the Yoda Valley, New Guinea; (2) the aquiline nose of the Easter Island wooden statuettes recalls the noses of the Papuans; (3) the deformation of the lobe of the ear among the Easter Islanders is typical of various Melanesian tribes. Similarly the protruding mouth of the great statues recalls the treatment of the lips on certain canoe-prow figures in the Solomons; (4) bird-men are common in both Easter Island and Solomon Island art; (5) the frigate bird is a motif found with equal frequency in Easter Island and the Solomons; (6) the 'hats' of red tufa worn by the statues suggest the artificially discoloured hair of the Melanesians.

These parallels are vague and a trifle inconsistent. What importance should be attached to a few obsidian points discovered in an isolated spot in New Guinea? The resemblance between the Melanesian specimens and those from Easter Island lies primarily in the identical nature of the material. There are no obsidian deposits in Polynesia except in New Zealand, Pitcairn and Easter Island. We are compelled to assume either that the Polynesian emigrants who settled in Easter Island came from the Yoda Valley in New Guinea, or that they discovered the use that could be made of obsidian on Easter Island itself, where there is a quarry of this material. In New Guinea the use of obsidian is restricted, for only the natives of the Admiralty Islands have specialized in this industry. Now, there is almost no analogy between the obsidian blades of the Admiralty Islands and those of Easter Island. It seems practically certain that the use of obsidian was a particular development of stone-working that took place on Easter Island.

No physical anthropologist would dream of establishing racial connexions on the basis of resemblances between statues carved in a conventional style. Balfour himself admits the extreme frailty of his hypothesis and recognizes that the particular shape of the nose in the Easter Island statuettes is due to the attempt to depict the face of a corpse.

Attention has quite rightly been drawn to the resemblance between the figurines of the Moriori on the New Zealand Chatham Islands and those of Easter Island. Although different in style, both sets of images represent emaciated figures with protruding ribs. Starting from the supposition that the Moriori were Polynesians interbred with Melanesians, investigators have once more inferred that the Easter Island statuettes were Melanesian in character. This deduction is fundamentally unsound, since no one has proved that the Moriori are anything but a Maori tribe. What right has anybody to describe as 'Melanesian' a type of statuette that does not exist in Melanesia? As for the likeness that Balfour sees between the mouth of the Easter Island statues and that of the Solomon Island canoe-prow figures, this is an inadequate piece of evidence on which to establish a link between the two arts.

Both the Easter Islanders and the natives of the Solomon Islands wished to portray the frigate bird with outstretched wings as realistically as possible—it is not surprising, therefore, that a certain similarity may be traced between the resulting motifs, which is quite fortuitous.

Analogies between a few features chosen at random from vast regions known for the diversity of their local cultures cannot fail to be superficial and unconvincing. In no fundamental aspect of their art, religion or social organization do Easter Island and Melanesia present common characteristics that would justify the hypothesis of a specific link between this tiny Polynesian island and the multifarious cultures of Melanesia. If we admit that Melanesia was the centre of a civilization superior to that which developed in Polynesia, it is easy to understand the desire to link it up with Easter Island; but there is nothing among the Papuans or the Melanesians properly so-called to indicate that they were the inaugurators or precursors of Easter Island culture.

Some investigators have claimed that Easter Island civilization was of a 'matriarchal' type and therefore different from the fundamentally patrilinear, partriarchal Polynesian cultures. The facts cited in support of this thesis do not stand up to examination. It is not true that the soil was cultivated exclusively by the women, nor that ownership of the fields was transmitted from mother to daughter. Inheritance passed down the male line, as elsewhere in Polynesia. The predominantly vegetable diet is not an indication of an essentially agricultural type of civilization, for this diet was imposed on the islanders by the limited resources of their habitat.

It was impossible to develop fishing to the same extent as on other islands, for reasons that have already been discussed.

If the homogeneity and distinctly Polynesian character of Easter Island culture seem to be beyond question, it still remains to establish the place of origin of the settlers who colonized the island and the date of their migration. In undertaking this investigation, it is important to bear in mind one fact that has long been recognized. Although the native cultures of Polynesia all rest on a common base, each one has nevertheless developed in its isolation peculiarities that give it an original quality of its own.

All the fundamental aspects of the Polynesian cultures recur on Easter Island. As might have been expected from its geographical position, Easter Island culture is linked with the eastern group of the Polynesian islands. None of the distinctive elements of Western Polynesia figure on Easter Island, whereas most of the techniques and traditions that characterize the Eastern Polynesians form part of the Easter Islanders' heritage.

The cultural analogies between Easter Island and the Gambiers (Mangareva), the closest of the Polynesian islands, are very remarkable. We may mention, as examples, the *ahu* or stone platforms with their mortuary vaults, the paved areas in front of the houses, the canoes with raised prows and poops, the seclusion of the chief's children, the practice of tattooing the whole body, the use of the words *ivi-atua* for 'priest' and *hurumanu* for 'commoner', and finally the existence of chanters called *rongorongo*.

Father Honoré Laval, who knew the Mangareva culture at a time when it was still intact, notes that the wooden images representing gods had 'tight-lipped, set mouths like a miser's. At other times one would have said the god was pouting.' This quotation immediately calls to mind the famous 'disdainful pout' of the great statues of Rano-raraku. Lavachery has succeeded in proving a stylistic affinity between one of the rare Mangarevan statues extant and a statue from Easter Island housed in the Musée du Cinquantenaire, Brussels. My colleague concludes from this analogy that Mangarevans might have settled on the island and were perhaps the 'Long Ears' referred to in the legend we have discussed at such length. The hypothesis of a Mangarevan origin of the inhabitants of Easter Island comes up against certain difficulties. The Easter

Islanders did not use the word *marae* for their sanctuaries, but retained the term *ahu*, whose original meaning was 'cairn of stones, stone platform'. This apparently insignificant linguistic detail proves that they had not joined together the sacred forecourt (*marae*) and the platform (*ahu*)—a development in religious architecture that occurred in Mangareva as well as in Central Polynesia (Fig. 6). Finally the Easter Islanders cannot have come from Mangareva because the inhabitants of this archipelago did not possess the chicken. On the other hand, they kept pigs, which were unknown on Easter Island.

If the Gambier Islands (Mangareva) cannot be considered as the place from which the Easter Islanders came, it seems that Maraerenga, their mythical homeland, can only have been the Marquesas. The low coral islands of the Tuamotu group are ruled out of court by the fact that the plants cultivated by the Easter Islanders all belong to high islands of volcanic origin.

The Marquesan culture, as we know it, differs in many respects from that of Easter Island; but the characteristics that distinguish it are precisely those which mark the Marquesas off from other Polynesian cultures. It would be just as unwarranted to project the aberrant aspects of this culture into the past as to regard the arts and techniques of the nineteenth-century Maoris as being those of their ancestors at the time they emigrated from Tahiti.

The *ahu* and *mea'e* of the Marquesas are not as different from the Easter Island *ahu* as they may at first sight appear. Their irregular arrangement springs from the difficulties the architects encountered when they sought to combine platform and forecourt on the steep slopes of their mountains. On the other hand the Marquesan sanctuaries, like the mausoleums of Easter Island, show the platform in which the dead were interred and the rows of statues representing the ancestors. As a matter of fact the style of the Marquesan statues is not that of the Easter Island *moai*, but they probably reflect artistic traditions that emerged after the period of the migration. It is the same with Marquesan tattooing which, like that of Easter Island, covered the whole body, but in a different style. The *tiki* or human figure with large eyes, which is one of the basic motifs of Marquesan art, was not foreign to that of Easter Island, where we found it engraved on numerous petroglyphs and

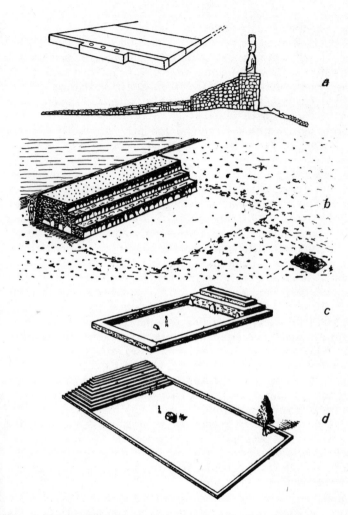

Fig. 6. Easter Island *ahu* (a) compared with religious stone structures from eastern Polynesia; (b) Mangaravean *marae*; and (c and d) Tahitian *marae*. After Emory: *Polynesian Stone Remains*, Plates IIa and IV.

where it appears on the tablets.

The association between the chants and certain objects that symbolized them may also be regarded as a parallel between the two cultures. Looked at from this angle, the knotted cords of the Marquesas correspond to Easter Island's engraved tablets.

If the Easter Islanders came from the Marquesas Islands, their migration must go back a very long way, probably to a period when Marquesan culture was still undifferentiated and similar to that of the Mangarevans and Maoris in the thirteenth century. From all this we can formulate the following hypotheses: The many analogies between Easter Island culture and the various cultures of central and marginal Polynesia cannot be interpreted as proofs of different migrations and diverse influences. These parallels can only be explained by supposing that the inhabitants of Easter Island left Central Polynesia at an early date—probably in the twelfth century—before these peoples had had time to develop disparate cultures. Tuamotuans, Mangarevans, Marquesans and Maoris must, at some point in their history, have inhabited a common fatherland and possessed a homogeneous culture. After centuries of isolation inthe various islands they discovered and occupied as a result of their migrations, they modified their cultural heritage, developing certain of its aspects and abandoning others. The numerous analogies between the Maoris and the Easter Islanders tend to prove that they left Central Polynesia at approximately the same time, that is to say, before the *ahu* and the *marae* had been combined and before Tangaroa had become the principal god in the mythology.

The Easter Islanders formed part of the waves of migration that flowed east and occupied the Marquesas, the Gambiers and the Tuamotus. After remaining on the Marquesas for a few generations, one or two tribes belonging to this ancient population broke away from it and went in search of new islands to the east. Chance brought them to Easter Island, where they settled. Navigation degenerated on Easter Island because of the shortage of timber. The scarcity of this material rendered it precious and partly explains the importance assumed by wood-carving. Wooden articles had the same value for Easter Islanders as those of jade or whale ivory in New Zealand and the Marquesas.

Every region of Polynesia has specialized in some form of art, to which it has sought to give more and more perfect expression. The Marquesans have developed farther than any other people the art of tattooing. The Maoris have devoted themselves to wood-carving, the working of jade, and intricate tattooing. If we try to explain the development of Easter Island sculpture in the light of facts generally valid for Polynesia, it appears less exceptional and less contrary to the traditions of the peoples belonging to this linguistic family. The great statues also represent a specialization of Easter Island culture, a specialization favoured by particular local conditions. That is how a group of Polynesians, undoubtedly originating from the Marquesa's, succeeded—on this tiny island, the most isolated in the world—in giving a new and original form to the culture they had inherited from their ancestors in Central Polynesia.

Selected Bibliography on Easter Island

BALFOUR, Henry: 'Some Ethnological Suggestions in regard to Easter Island or Rapanui' (in *Folklore*, London, vol. 28, 1917, pp. 356–381).

BEECHEY, Frederick William: *Narrative of a Voyage to the Pacific and Beering's Straits*. London, 1831, 2 vols.

BÓRMIDA, Marcelo: 'Algunas luces sobre la penumbrosa historia de Pascua antes de 1722.' (In *Runa*, Buenos Aires, vol. 4, 1951, pp. 5–62).

'Somatología de la Isla de Pascua' (in *Runa*, Buenos Aires, vol. 4. pp. 178–222).

BROWN, John Macmillan: *The Riddle of the Pacific*. London, T. F. Unwin, 1924.

CAMUS GUNDIAN, Daniel: 'Salubridad y morbilidad en la Isla de Pascua' (in *Runa*, Buenos Aires, vol. 4, 1951, pp. 78–88).

COOK, James: *Second Voyage towards the South Pole and round the World, performed in the 'Resolution' and 'Adventure', 1772–75*. London, 1777.

EMORY, Kenneth P.: 'Polynesian Stone Remains' (in *Papers of the Peabody Museum of American Archaeology and Ethnology*, Harvard University, vol. xx, Cambridge, Mass., 1943, pp. 9–21).

ENGLERT, P. Sebastian: *Tradiciones de la Isla de Pascua en idioma rapanui y castellano*. Padre Las Casas, impr. y edit. 'San Francisco', 1939.

La tierra de Hotu-Matu'a. Historía y lengua de la Isla de Pascua. Padre Las Casas, impr. y edit. 'San Francisco', 1948.

FORSTER, George: *A Voyage round the World in H.B.M.'s Sloop 'Resolution' during the year 1772*. London, 1777.

GEISELER, Kapitänlieutnant: *Die Oster Insel, eine Stätte prähistorischer Kultur in der Südsee*. Berlin, E. S. Mittler und Sohn, 1883.

GONZÁLEZ Y HAEDO, Felipe: *The voyage of Captain Don Felipe*

---

[1] The literature on Easter Island is very abundant. The reader will find in my *Ethnology of Easter Island* a full bibliography up to 1940. The present selected bibliography includes our most important sources on the ethnology of Easter Island and recent articles which I have utilized or discussed in chapters XII and XIV.

González in the Ship of the Line 'San Lorenzo' with the Frigate 'Santa Rosalia' in Company to Easter Island, in 1770–1801, preceded by an Extract from Mynheer Jacob Roggeveen's Official Log of his Discovery of and Visit to Easter Island in 1772, transcribed, translated and edited by Bolton Glanvill Corney . . . Cambridge, printed for the Hakluyt Society, 1908.

GÜNTHER, Klaus: 'Zur Frage der Typologie und Chronologie der grossen Steinbilder auf der Osterinsel' (in *Wissentschaftliche Zeitschrift der Friedrich-Schiller-Universität Jena*, Jahrgang, 3, 1933/54, pp. 81–107).

HEINE-GELDERN, Robert von: 'Die Osterinselschrift' (in *Anthropos*, St Gabriel-Mödling, vol. 33, 1938, pp. 815–909).

'Some Problems of Migration in the Pacific' (in *Kultur und Sprache*, published by W. Koppers in collaboration with R. Heine-Geldern and Joseph Haekel. Wien, Herold, 1952, pp. 313–362).

'Heyerdahl's Hypothesis of Polynesian Origins: a Criticism' (in *The Geographical Journal*, London, vol. 116, Nos. 4–6, 1950, pp. 183–192).

HELFRITZ, Hans: *Die Osterinsel*. Zürich, Frets und Wasmuth, 1953, 19p. 94 plates.

HEVESY, Guillaume de: 'Sur une écriture océanienne paraissant d'origine néolithique.' (in *Bulletin de la Société préhistorique française*, Paris, Nos. 7–8, 1933, pp. 29–50).

HEYERDAHL, Thor: *American Indians in the Pacific*. Stockholm, Forum A.B., 1952.

'Some Problems of Aboriginal Migration in the Pacific.' (in *Archiv für Völkerkunde*, Beiheft, zu vols. 6–7, Wien, 1952).

IMBELLONI, José: 'Las 'Tabletas Parlantes' de Pascua, monumentos de un sistema gráfico indo-oceánico' (in *Runa*, Buenos-Aires, vol. 4, 1951, pp. 89–177).

'Craneología de la Isle de Pascua' (in *Runa*, Buenos-Aires, 1951, pp. 223–281).

KOENIGSWALD, G. H. R. von: 'Uber sumatranische Schiffstücher und ihre Beziehungen zur Kunst Oceaniens' (in *Südseestudien. Gedenkschrift zur Erinnerung an Felix Speiser*. Basel, 1951, pp. 27–50).

LA PÉROUSE, Jean François de Galaup, Cte de: *Voyage de La Pérouse*

autour du monde (1785–1788). Paris, impr. de la République, an.V
(1797).

LAVACHERY, Henri: *Ile de Pâques*. Paris, B. Grasset, 1935.

Les pétroglyphes de l'Ile de Pâques. Anvers, De Sikkel, 1939.

'Sculpteurs modernes de l'Ile de Pâques' (in *Outre-Mer*, Paris,
vol. 9, Dec. 1937, pp. 325–365).

'Stèles et pierres-levées à l'Ile de Pâques' (in *Südseestudien*.
Gedenkschrift zur Erinnerung an Felix Speiser. Basel, 1951, pp.
413–422).

LAVAL, le P. Honoré: *Mangareva, l'histoire ancienne d'un peuple
polynésien*. Paris, P. Geuthner, 1938.

MÉTRAUX, Alfred: 'Ethnology of Easter Island.' (*Bernice P. Bishop
Museum*, Honolulu, *Bulletin* 160, 1940).

ROGGEVEEN, Jacob: (see GONZÁLEZ Y HAEDO.)

ROUTLEDGE, Katherine Scoresby: *The Mystery of Easter Island; the
Story of an Expedition*. London, Sifton, Praed & Co., 1919.

'Survey of the Village and Carved Rocks of Orongo, Easter
Island, by the Mana Expedition' (in *Journal of the Royal Anthro-
pological Institute*, London, vol. 50, 1920, pp. 425–451).

SAHLINS, Marshall D.: 'Esoteric Efflorescence in Easter Island' (in
American Anthropologist. Menasha, vol. 57, 1955, pp. 1045–1052).

SHAPIRO, H. L.: 'The Physical Relationships of the Easter Islanders' (in Métraux, *Ethnology of Easter Island*, Bernice P. Bishop
Museum, Bulletin 160, pp. 24–30, Honolulu, 1940).

THOMSON, William Judah: 'Te Pito te Henua; or Easter Island' (in
Smithsonian Institution. Annual Report of the National Museum for 1889,
Washington, 1891, pp. 447–552).

WAGNER, K.: 'The Craniology of the Oceanic Races' (in *Videns-
kaps-Academi i Oslo Skrifter Mat. Naturv. Klasse No. 2*, Oslo, 1937).

Several important articles written by Russian scholars on the
subject of the Easter Island tablets were received as this book went
to press. They are:

KUDRIATSEV, B. G.: 'Pie'mennoct' ostrova Pachu' (in *Sbornik
Museya antropologii i etnografii*, vol. XI, 1949, pp. 176–221).

OLDEROGGE, D. A.: 'Paralleln'ye teksty tablic ostrova Pachu' (in
Sbornik Museya antropologii i etnografii, vol. XI, 1949, pp. 222–236).

'Paralleln'ye teksty nekotoryh tabluc c ostrova Pachu' (in *Sovets-kaja Etnografija*, vol. IV, Academy of Science of USSR, Moscow and Leningrad, 1947, pp. 234–238).

BUTINOV, N. A. and KNOROZOV, Y. V.: *Preliminary Report on the Study of the Written Language of Easter Island* (a paper read in May 1956, in Leningrad, at the All-Union Conference of Ethnologists).

Index

Adolescence, 109–12
Adoption, custom of, 111
Adultery, punishment for, 117
Adzes, stone, 233
Agriculture, 64–6
Ahu (funerary platforms), 31; 119–20, 152–3, 233; origin of term, 237–8; analogies with the Marquesas, 238
Anakena cove, 92
Ancestors: chanting of their genealogies, 129–31; wooden images of, 146–50
Andes, Indians of the, 203
Ariki (term for nobility), 87, 113–14, 177
Aymara Indians, 203

Balfour, Henry, 234, 235
Bartel, Dr Th. S., 209–10
Basalt, used for carving of statues, 154
Beechey, F. W., 43–5, 79, 113
Beri, Gabriel Beri, sculptor, 149
Bernizet, M., 76
Bird-man cult, 131–40
Birth, rites observed at, 105–7
Boats. *See* Canoes
Bórmido, Marcelo, 231
Bornier, Dutroux-, French adventurer, 56–7
Brander, Mr, 56, 57
Brown, J. Macmillan, 31–2

Cannibalism, 102–4
Canoes, 70–1
Caroline Archipelago, alleged cultural analogy with Easter Is., 201
Caves. *See* Grottoes
Ceylon, alleged cultural analogy with Easter Is., 200–1
Chamisso, Adalbert von, 43

Children: rites observed for, 106–7; and sham battles, 107–8; adolscence, 109–12
Chile: annexes Easter Is., 57; deports politicians to the island, 58; and Señor Cumprido's governorship, 59
China, alleged origins of Polynesian civilization in, 198–9, 201, 205–6
Christianity, introduction of, 47–55
Civil wars, 47–8
Climate, 63
Clothing, 76, 79–80
Cook, Captain, 40, 62, 113, 151, 153, 159, 160, 179
Craniology, 33, 234
Croft, Mr, 193
Cumprido, Señor, 59
Cuna Indians, 200, 203, 205

Dancing, 178, 183–4
Davis, Edward, 29
Davis Land, 29, 39
Death and funerals, 117–20; mortuary ceremonies, 174
Demons, 122–4
Division of labour, 116
Divorce, 116–17
Dixon, 33
Domestic animals, 66–7
Dress. *See* Clothing

Easter Island: and the lost continent, 29–30; volcanic origins, 30–1; area, 31; theory of its being centre of an archipelago, 31–2; mixed blood in, 33; various names given to, 36–7; first discovery by a European, 38–9; second discovery, 40; annexed by Spain, 40; Cook's visit, 40; La

247

Pérouse's visit, 40–2; abduction of islanders by American ship *Nancy*, 42; Kotzebue's visit, 43; Beechey's visit, 43–5; visits of du Petit-Thouars and Moerenhout, 45; killing of women by whaler *Pindos*, 46; slave raiders in, 46–7; smallpox in, 47; civil wars, 47–8; introduction of Christianity, 48–56; outrages and depopulation under Dutroux-Bornier, 55–7; annexed by Chile, 57; decline, 57–8; German naval contacts in First World War, 58; under governorship of Señor Cumprido, 59; population, 59, 64; health, 60; modernization, 60; climate, 63; scarcity of fresh water, 65–6; domestic animals, and rats as food, 66–7; raw materials, and creative activities, 80–2
  See also Agriculture; Birth; Children; Death, Feasts, Fish and Fishing; Flora; Marriage; Origins of Easter Island civilization; Religion; Sex Life; Social Structure; Statues; Tablets; Tabus
Englert, Father Sebastian, 59, 229–31
Eyraud, Brother Eugène, 48–55, 71–2, 79, 121, 143, 148, 177–8, 180, 185, 190

Feasts: huts for family celebrations, 110; place in social life, 173; dialect word for, 173–4; the *paina* in honour of dead father or brother, 174; the *koro* in honour of living relatives, 174–6; the *hareauti* or profane feasts, 176–8; the *puka* and *kaunga*, 178; in celebration of visiting ships, 178–9
Feminine beauty, ideal of, 42
Figurines. *See* Sculpture
Fish and fishing, 67–70, 170
Food, 72–4
Forster, George, 171–2, 224
Frazer, Sir J. G., 140
Funerals, 117–20
Funerary platforms. *See* Ahu

Gambier Islands. *See* Mangareva
Games and Sports, 107–8
Gods. *See* Religion
González y Haedo, Felipe, 40, 62, 119, 174
Gregorio, last King of Easter Is., 34, 88, 94
Grottoes, used as dwellings, 75–6
Guilds, of craftsmen, 95–6
Günther, Klaus, 163

Hanga-roa village, 113; women of, 115
Hawaiian Islands: geological origins, 30; settled by Polynesians, 34; their stratified social structure, 168–9; the *menehune* (mythical ancestors) of, 232
Headgear, 79
Heine-Geldern, Robert von, 198–202, 204–5
Hévesy, Guillaume de, 195–7, 202, 204
Heyerdahl, Thor, on origins of Easter Is. civilization, 224–33
Hieroglyphic writing. *See* Tablets
Hopu (servants of bird-men), 135–8
Hornbostel, Professor, 200
Hotu-matu'a, King, 36, 57, 106; coverer and colonizer of Easter Is., 34, 91–2; legendary introduction of trees, 62, 88, 229; legendary division of Island among his sons, 83–4, 214; alleged to have brought Tablets to the Island, 196; alleged to be a Peruvian chief, 227, 229–30; legend of his discovery of the Island, 211–15
Human sacrifice, 128–9
Huru-manu (serfs), 96–7
Huts and dwellings, 74–6

Imbelloni, Professor José, 201, 234
Incest, punishment for, 114
Indonesia, cultural analogy with Easter Is., 200
Indus civilization, 195–6
Ivi-atua (priest), 94; (medicine men and sorcerers), 142–5

Jaussen, Monseigneur, Bishop of Tahiti, 57, 185, 193–4

Kaharoau, legendary figure, 110

Kainga, warrior, legend of, 216–18

Kakoniau, legendary figure, 110

Kamakoi, King, 47

Koenigswald, Professor G. H. R. von, 200

Koro (feast), 173–4

Koromaki (medicine men and sorcerers), 142

Kotzebue, Russian navigator, 43, 151

La Pérouse, Comte de, 40–1, 61–2, 76, 113, 151, 174, 233

Langdon, Professor, 198

Langle, M. de, 171

Language, 34, 233

Lavachery, Henri, 149, 163, 198, 232, 237,

Laval, Father Honoré, 35, 190, 237

Legends: King Hotu-matu'a's discovery of Easter Is., 211–15; War of the Long-Ears and Little-Ears, 215–16, 228, 230–3, 237; the great war of the Tu'u and Hotu-iti confederations, 216–21; the origin of tattooing, 222–3

Lemont, 179

Leprosy, 60

Loti, Pierre, 77, 165, 183

Lückner, von, German naval commander, 58

Magic, 142–5. *See also* Religion

Malinoski, B., 160

Mana (mystic or vital force), 88–91, 105, 106, 112, 116, 141

Manu-tara (sooty terns), 131

Mangareva (Gambier Islands), 32, 97; settled by Polynesians, 34, 35; forced over-eating by children in, 110–11; its stratified social structure, 168; professional chanters in, 190–1; common technical heritage with Easter Is., 233; close cultural analogies with Easter Is., 237–8

Manners, 97–8

Maoris: Polynesian origins, 34, 35; tat-

tooing amongst, 78–9, 241; their stratified social structure, 87, 168; their god Tane, 128; their canoes, 166; their feasts, 173–4; use of engraved club by orators and reciters, 207–8; wood-carving and jade work, 240–1

Marae-renga: King Hotu-matu'a's homeland, 62; identification with Galapagos Islands, 229; identification with the Marquesas, 238

Marquesas Islands: geological origins, 30; settled by Polynesians, 34; tatooing in, 78, 241; polyandry in, 115; the *meae* (mausoleums) of, 120; the god Tiki, 126; statues on, 160–1; stratified social structure, 168; professional chanters in, 190, 191; artistic script of, 199; liturgical poems and symbolism, 207–8; common technical heritage with Easter Is., 233–4; original home of Easter Islanders, 238–41

Marriage, 114–17

Masafuera Island, 42

Mata-puka, Chief, 35

Mata-to'a (warriors), 96, 101–2, 135

Mataveri, and the bird-man cult, 137

Mausoleums. *See* Ahu

Medicine-men, 117, 142–5

Melanesia, its alleged cultural analogies with Easter Is., 234–6

Moai kavakava (wooden statuettes), 146

Mortuary ceremonies, 174

Motu-nui, islet of, and the bird-man cult, 131–4, 137

Murder, rites of vengeance for, 103–4

Music, 183–4

Myths. *See* Legends

Neru (enforced idleness for children), 110

New Zealand. *See* Maoris

Nga'ara, King, 94, 189

Nordenskiöld, Erland, 200

Obsidian: abundance of, 81; development of its use, 235

Ojibway Indians, 205, 206

Origins of Easter Is. civilization: evidence of physical anthropology, 33–4; Thor Heyerdahl's theory, 224–33; craniology, and Melanesian analogies, 233–6; alleged matriarchal society, 236; fundamental Polynesian nature of, 237; analogies with Mangareva, 237–8; origins in the Marquesas, 238–41

Orongo village: centre of birdman cult, 132–4; sailing vessels depicted in houses of, 178

Palmer, English traveller, 129

Paper mulberry, 64, 69, 80–1, 165

Peru, alleged origins of Easter Is. civilization in, 224–33

Petit-Thouars, Admiral du, 45, 81, 172

Physical beauty, cult of, 110

Poetry, 181–3

Polyandry, 115

Polygamy, 115

Polynesians: migrations of, 34–7; 236–7, 240; stratified social structure, 168; charm of life in peacetime, 180; alleged origins of their civilization in China, 198–9; regional specialization in the arts, 241

  See also Mangareva; Maoris; Marquesas Islands

Pregnancy, rites observed during, 105

Priesthood, 94–5; and rites at birth, 105, 106

Puberty, 109

Punamarengo, cave at, 76

Punapau, Mount, 153

Quechua Indians, 203

Rano-kao volcano, 132, 134

Rano-raraku quarry, 154–6, 164

Rapahango, Victoria, 103, 111–12, 175, 176

Rats, as food, 66–7

Religion: disappearance of major gods, 121; survival of minor gods, familiar spirits and demons, 121–4; three

categories of supernatural beings, 125; Tangaroa, god of the sea, 125–6; Hiro, god of rain, 126, 129; Makemake, creator of the universe, 126–8, 131–7; other gods, 126; the god Haua, 127, 136; offerings to the gods, 129–30; rites to induce rainfall, 129; genealogical chants, 129–31; origin of the gods, 130–31; cult of the birdman, 131–40; Vie-Kana, birdgod, 136; the place of tabus, 140–2; and sorcery, 142–5; and ancestor images, 146–50; the great statues as images of deities, 160–1; sacred dances, 183–4

Rivet, Professor Paul, 198

Roggeveen, Admiral Jacob, first European discoverer of Easter Is., 37–9, 61–2, 151, 153, 160

Roussel, Brother Hippolyte, 54–6, 103

Routledge, Katherine Scoresby, 47, 132–3, 157–9, 167, 179, 188–9, 191, 194–5, 199

Rue (Rokunga), last birdman, 136, 139

Sahlins, Dr Marshall D., 168

Salmon, Tahitian settler on Easter Is., 229

Sculpture, wooden: vulgarity of modern products, 57; the old and the modern, 81–2; horrific images of spirits, 122; ancestor images, 146–50; resemblance to Melanesian images, 236–7

  See also Statues; Stonemasonry

Sea birds, refuges of, 133

Sex life, 112–14

Shapiro, Dr Harry, 33, 234

Smallpox, 47

Slave-raiding, 46–7

Social structure: tribal organization, 83–6, social hierarchy, 87; kings, 87–94; priesthood, 94–5; craftsmen, 95–6; warriors, 96; commoners and slaves, 97; social relations, 97–9; war, 100–4; cannibalism, 102–3; vengeance and murder, 103–4

Society Islands, 87, 120

See also Tahiti

Society of Friends of Easter Island, 59

Soil, fertility of, 74

Sooty tern, and the birdman cult, 131–7

Sorcery, 142–5

Spee, Admiral von, 58

Springs, 66

Statues: placing of, 119–20, 158–9; grandeur and mystery of, 151–3; the cylinders ('hats'), 153–4; use of basalt for, 154; the Rano-raraku quarry, 154–6; two types of, 157; workmanship, 157–8; temporary sanctity of, 159–61; fantastic theories on their origins, 161–2; typology and chronology, 161–3; volcanic tufa used for, 164, 168; tools used, 164; weight, and problem of transportation, 164–7; social and economic conditions behind their production, 167–9; sudden cessation of work on, 169–72; alleged stylistic resemblances with Andean monoliths and Cuzco buildings, 226–7; analogies with the Marquesas, 229

Stolpe, 78

Stone-masonry, 82

Surf-riding, 107

Symbolic figures, making of, 108

Tablets: discovery and collection of, 185–6; master pieces of graphic art, 186–7; rarity and value, 187–8; knowledge of a prerogative of class of chanters, 188–90, 197; question of writing on, 190–91; tabus surrounding them, 191; attempts to decipher, 191–5; alleged connexion with Indus civilization, 195–9, 201, 205; alleged connexion with China, 198–9, 201, 205; alleged connexions with Indonesia, Ceylon and Caroline Archipelago, 200–1; the author's interpretation, 201–210; alleged connexion with Peruvian script, 227–8

Tabus: against theft, 65, 141–2; imposed and removed by kings, 93–4;

dietary, 110–11; child's head, 112; corpses, 119; birdman cult, 137–83; fishing-nets, 141; penalties for violation of, 141–2; tabu symbols, 142; *ariki*, 117; Tablets, 191

Tahiti: geological origins, 30; word to denote human image, 161; the staff as symbol of liturgical poems, 207

Tahunga (priest, craftsman), 95

Talas-y-Gomez, 31

Tangata-manu (birdman), 135

Tangata-rongorongo (chanters or reciters), 188–90

Tangata-taku (medicine men and sorcerers), 142

Taropa, 114

Tatane (demons), 122

Tatooing, 76–9, 91; of children, 107; legend on origin of, 222–3; Easter Is. and Marquesan analogies, 238; its highest development found in the Marquesas, 239

Te Haha, 188–9, 191

Teao, Carlos, 143–4, 188–9, 191

Tepano, Juan, 79, 81, 87–8, 116, 136–9 149–50, 172, 179, 187–8, 211, 230–1

Thomson, W. J., 95, 130, 144, 186, 193–4, 196, 229–30

Tiki (human figures with large eyes), 238

Timber. *See* Wood

Tonga archipelago, the Trilith in, 166

Torometi, 51–4, 56, 143

Tuamotu Islands: chanting of genealogies in, 98; the *marae* (mausoleums), 120; the *ahu* (funerary platforms), 161; the staff as symbol of liturgical poems, 207; Easter Islanders alleged to originate from, 229; Polynesian origins, 240

Tufa, volcanic, used for the great statues, 164, 168

Tupu, King, 35

Turtles, 70

Tu'u-ko-ihu, Chief, myth of, 146–8

Ure, demon, 124

Vaeiko, Ure, 194
Vandesande, Captain, 166
Vengeance, for murder, 103
Viriamo, old woman, 109, 115
Volz, 33

Wagner, K., 234
War, 100–4
Water, scarcity of, 65–6
Williamson & Balfour, 57

Women: and polygamy, 115; and polyandry, 115; well treated, and influence of, 115; and domestic quarrels,
116; and division of labour, 116;
and divorce, 116–17; and adultery,
117
Wood, scarcity of, 70–2, 81, 165, 240
Writing. *See* Tablets

Zumbohm, Father, 73, 103, 185, 192